The Economics of Fantasy

THE ECONOMICS OF FANTASY

RAPE IN TWENTIETH-CENTURY LITERATURE

Sharon Stockton

The Ohio State University Press
Columbus

Library of Congress Cataloging-in-Publication Data

Stockton, Sharon.
  The economics of fantasy : rape in twentieth-century literature /
Sharon Stockton.—1st ed.
    p. cm.
  Includes bibliographical references and index.
  ISBN 0-8142-1018-X (cloth : alk. paper)—ISBN 0-8142-9094-9
(cd-rom) 1. American literature—20th century—History and criticism.
2. Rape in literature. 3. English literature—20th century—History and
criticism. 4. Power (Social sciences) in literature. 5. Masculinity in literature. 6. Violence in literature. I. Title.
  PS228.R36S76 2006
  810.9'3556—dc22

Paper (ISBN: 978-0-8142-5757-9)   2005030315

  Cover design by Jeff Smith.
  Type set in Adobe Garamond.

CONTENTS

ACKNOWLEDGMENTS

During the several years I have spent working on this book, whether or not I knew at any given time that it was this specific book on which I was, in fact, working, I have received tremendous encouragement, help, and support from a great many people.

I first want to thank Dickinson College for its generous support of me and of this project. Thanks in particular to my tireless and brilliant research assistants, Katie Ginn and Dave Emerick. Thanks also to Provost Neil Weissman and to the English Department. I am also sincerely grateful to the Mellon Foundation for the summer study grant of 2003.

In my graduate training I was lucky in advisors, namely, Linnea Alexander and Robert Markley. Thank you both for teaching and guiding me. Thank you also to Roger Chittick, the finest professor I have ever had the good fortune to encounter. Without all of you, this book would never have been written.

For my parents, Eugene and Janice Stockton, thank you for being steadfastly proud of me.

I want to express my sincere appreciation for the friends who have lent a hand or an ear during my crises and joys: Kevin Harp, Stephanie Larson, Amy Farrell and John Bloom, Sue Rose and Steve Brouwer, Judy Gill, Kelly Winters-Fazio, and Linda Chalk. A special thanks to Terry and Alistair Barber for your unwavering loyalty and support.

For my husband, Jaime Juarez, thank you for the last twenty years of love and loyalty.

Most importantly, my gratitude goes out to Eugene, Cristina, and Katherine, my best pieces of poetry.

Portions of this book have been previously published in some form. Part of chapter 2 appeared in *Texas Studies in Language and Literature* 39 (1997); part of chapter 3 appeared in *American Literature* 72 (2000); parts of chapters 4 and 6 appeared in *Weber Studies* 14 (1997); part of chapter 6 appeared in *Contemporary Literature* 36 (1995). I thank all of these journals for their permission to reprint the material.

1

INTRODUCTION

It was twenty years ago when Alice Jardine opened her powerful study of the rhetorical use of the female body within contemporary French theory with an invocation of Roland Barthes: "The 'feminine' has become," she wrote, "'a metaphor without brakes'" (34). Nor did the metastatic growth of that metaphor appear at that point in history to be showing any signs of slowing down. In fact to the contrary, *Gynesis* examines the acceleration of "the transformation of woman and the feminine into verbs at the interior of [narrative]": "To designate that process, I have suggested what I hope will be a believable neologism: gynesis—the putting into discourse of 'woman' . . . The object produced by this process is neither a person nor a thing, but a horizon, that toward which the process is tending: a *gynema*. This *gynema* is a reading effect, a woman-in-effect that is never stable and has no identity. Its appearance in a written text is perhaps noticed only by the feminist reader" (25). The "woman-in-effect" whom Alice Jardine studies signals "a certain 'crisis-in-narrative,'" an increasingly angst-ridden self-exploration on the part of the presumed masculine subject who is searching for a "'space' of some kind (over which the narrative has lost control)"; the stakes for this reconceptualization of the gynema are "survivals (of different kinds)" (25).

Luce Irigaray considers the nature of that survival, or those survivals, and writes of the preservation of the mythologized female body as the central ground for stabilizing what we have come to naturalize in the Western tradition as masculine subjectivity; in fact, ungrounded in what Jardine calls the gynema, the subject—defined generically as masculine—is unthinkable: "If there is no more 'earth' to press down/repress, to work, to represent, but also and always to desire (for one's own), no opaque matter which in theory does not know herself, then what pedestal remains for the existence of the 'subject'? If the earth turned and more especially turned upon herself, the erection of the subject might thereby be disconcerted and risk losing its elevation and penetration. For what would there be to rise up from and exercise his power over? And in? The Copernican revolution has yet to have its final effects in the male imaginary" (133). The subject of Western history—of logical and metaphysical thought, of market, industrial, and imperial capitalism—exists in thought by virtue of the feminized other. Yet the stability of that masculine subject is also chronically at risk; anxiety accompanies the obsessive return to the gynema, and canonical representations of femininity suggest the narcissistic gesture that created them. As Mary Ann Doane puts it succinctly, "The claim to investigate an otherness is a pretense, haunted by the mirror-effect by means of which the question of the woman reflects only the man's own ontological doubts" ("Film and the Masquerade" 177).

Thus, if Irigaray is correct in her claim that the "Copernican revolution" has yet to unseat Western man, it would also be true that the brakelessness and anxiety that distinguish the mythologizing of femininity suggest an inevitable instability at that presumably masculine center. And while the "new fictions . . . may, in fact, be satisfying a repressed desire in men (and women?) for what may turn out to be a very old, and, in any case, a very readable plot," they also bring into narrative existence a "gynema" that is not old at all, rather, one that shifts in accordance to the survival needs of the masculine subject in its specific historical locations (Jardine 37). So while the woman in contemporary metaphor continues to be defined through the general attribution of passivity, productivity (without agency), and penetrability—qualities that reflexively delimit the nature of man as other than—this tired narrative is at the same time subject to a certain amount of variation, suggesting a metamorphosis in the masculinity that is its function to define and preserve. Indeed still dominated by "similar memories, similar allegiances, the same father, and the same laws"—what Ellen Friedman aptly summarizes as the same "backward, oedipal glance"—twentieth-century texts nonetheless reveal a significantly changed relationship of the masculine subject to the forces of politics, history, and economic formations (148). It is this tension between the "very old, and, in any case, . . . very readable plot" on the one hand and the metamorphosis that survival demands on the other which I am interested in pursuing. More specifically, I am intrigued by the persistence and the evolution of the rape narrative in twentieth-century literature— the old story of male power and violence, female passivity and penetrability. What accounts for its persistence? And how, precisely, has the story changed over the course of the twentieth century?

What is not open to debate is the sheer number of twentieth-century literary texts the plots, imagery, and thematics of which are grounded in heterosexual rape. In the introduction to their edited book on rape and representation, Lynn A. Higgins and Brenda R. Silver note that among the "profoundly disturbing patterns" their volume examines, one that stands out "is an obsessive inscription—and an obsessive erasure—of sexual violence against women (and against those placed by society in the position of 'woman')" (2). The obsessive return to heterosexual violence suggests, as Higgins and Silver argue, that "rape and rapability are central to the very construction of gender identity" and that this (in this case aestheticized) construction shares with rape law a bias toward masculine points of view (3, 2). The masculine point of view I want to examine here—as it influences the shape of the evolving rape narrative—pertains to the situatedness of the twentieth-century white masculine subject in relation to the shifting face of capitalism. The compulsive return to the rape story, I argue, articulates—among other things—the gradual and relentless removal of Western man from the fantastical capitalist role of venturesome, industrious agency. The metamorphosis of the twentieth-century rape narrative registers a desperate attempt to preserve traditional patterns of robust, entrepreneurial masculinity in the face of economic forms that increasingly disallow illusions of individual authority.

In a psychoanalytic sense, what is at stake in the fantasy of woman is the question of masculine existence in a world haunted by absence. The enduring presence of the gynema, in other words, shines an oblique light on the gendered nature of the symbolic order of language, full accession to which founds the—inevitably, in Lacanian thought—male subject upon a void. Inducted into the symbolic through language, the subject is constituted as a function of discourse and inhabits a world similarly composed: "There is born the world of meaning of a particular language in which the world of things will come to be arranged. . . . It is the world of words that creates the world of things. . . . Man speaks, then, but it is because the symbol has made him man" (Lacan 65). In a parallel that links man with the discursive system that formulates him—with the world of words that supports itself at the level of the signified alone—the subject is "a presence made out of absence" (65). The desire that obscures that absence, that defines and motivates the subject as presence, is like that which sets into motion the movement of the signifier; in both cases desire is a function of the structure of language and not an expression of a preexisting and prelinguistic real. The "object" of desire does not precede desire but rather follows from it: "The paradox of desire is that it posits retroactively its own cause" (ižek, *Looking Awry*, 12). Through that paradoxical operation, the absence upon which man is predicated as subject of language is disavowed.

The "man" who desires is not only man in the generic sense. Jacque Lacan's figure of the lavatory doors—the "Ladies" and "Gentlemen" that represent the "two countries toward which each of their souls will strive on divergent wings"—insists that the discursive constitution of the subject depends upon the primary differential signs of gender (*Ecrits* 152). Entrance to the symbolic coincides with, as it depends upon, the composition of a subject framed by polarized sexual difference. The lack (and the desire) intrinsic to the newly constituted subject is figured as symptomatic of those "divergent wings" of gender. Thus, for Lacan, the question of being and the eventuality of subjectivity are inseparable from the establishment of heterosexual identity: "The subject is presented with the question of his existence . . . as an articulated question 'What am I there?,' concerning his sex and his contingency in being, namely, that on the one hand, he is a man or a woman, and, on the other, that he might not be, the two conjugating their mystery, and binding it in the symbols of procreation and death" (*Ecrits* 194). The uncanny aura generated through the interweaving of sex and death finds its source in the coincidence of the subject's entrance into language and sexual difference.

In the psychoanalytic tradition, the loss upon which subjectivity is founded has been figured in the traumatic discovery of the mother's lack of phallus. Heterosexual desire thus masks even as it is compelled by the horror of castration. At another level, Lacanian thought maintains that it is the phallus itself—as opposed to female genitalia—that finally signifies the lack inaugurated through entrance into the symbolic order. Castration, in this sense, as Kaja Silverman puts it, is an "unavoidable" operation, one "which every subject must experience upon entering the order of language or signification" (*Male Subjectivity* 35). "Castration" anxiety thus layers gender identity upon subject formation, both of which contingencies are established in and through a preexistent discursive order. At several levels, then, the woman as fetish promises to "[plug] the hole of symbolic castration or lack" (Silverman, *Male Subjectivity*, 22). She is, on the one hand, an ever-present reminder of the punishment that will follow from not, in a sense, punishing her—for not taking one's place in the patriarchal order that has decreed her injury. A flare in the darkness, she gestures toward a subject position of power and agency. At another level, the woman fetish covers over the basic lack upon which access to language and being, as such, depends. The retroactively constituted loss of the real, "the self's radical ex-centricity to itself"—all are disavowed in the fantasy of woman, which "translates the desire for nothing into the desire for something" (Lacan, *Ecrits*, 171; Silverman, *Male Subjectivity*, 4). Thus constituted as fantasy space, the gynema "functions as an empty surface, as a kind of screen for the projection of desires: the fascinating presence of its positive contents does nothing but fill out a certain emptiness" (i ek, *Looking Awry*, 8).

The extent to which that "certain emptiness" is filled through this "psy-

chotic projection of meaning into the real itself" (*Looking Awry* 35), however, is dubious; the obsessiveness with which the story of gender violence
is retold suggests an ongoing instability in the project of fetishistic disavowal—a certain desperate incapacity lodged within the gesture that
would establish heterosexual masculinity through the denial and outward
projection of male castration. Following Freud, Silverman makes the case
that sadism is the one perversion "most compatible with conventional heterosexuality" in a culture for which, "in utter disregard for western metaphysics, the 'true' or 'right' is heterosexual penetration" (*Male Subjectivity*
187; "Masochism," 21). Furthermore, according to Silverman, the conflation of heterosexual penetration with the "true" and the "right" has been
naturalized within Freudian psychoanalysis; she argues of Freud that he
establishes sexual violence—male aggression in particular—as normal and
perhaps even biologically necessary (*Male Subjectivity* 187, 271). As sadism
and dominance are thus legitimized as extensions of basic male sexuality,
so too does Freudian thought pronounce female masochism "an accepted—indeed a requisite—element of 'normal' female subjectivity," a gesture
that further naturalizes heterosexual violence and subordination while it
eroticizes the mechanism whereby masculine lack is disavowed (Silverman,
Male Subjectivity, 189). Heterosexual rape would thus seemingly reify the
status of man as absolute subject, foregrounding the agency of the man on
one hand and the passive objectification of the woman on the other.
Following Freud's logic, rape would serve, in fact, as a normative emblem
for heterosexuality (itself, of course, *the* normative sexuality).

It is my contention, however, that the mastery explicitly portrayed in
the spectacle of rape—and I am speaking in fact of the *spectacle* of rape, the
seductively aestheticized vision staged for Western consumption—is
almost inevitably undermined from within. The sadism to which it gives
free rein seems in the end false to the rapturous promise of absolute subjectivity, that position which would hypothetically enable the reduction of
the body of the other to object, an instrument for the satisfaction and
pleasure of the self. The representations of rape I examine here, in fact,
lend credence to Lacan's redefinition of sadism, in which "it is the 'sadist'
himself who is in the position of the object-instrument, the executor of
some radically heterogeneous will" (i ek, *Looking Awry*, 108–9). Agency
resides outside the duo of violator and victim, and the rapist is himself subject to an external gaze and a preexistent script: "The pervert does not pursue his activity for his own pleasure, but for the enjoyment of the Other—
he finds enjoyment precisely in this instrumentalization, in working for
the enjoyment of the Other" (109). As far as the representation of rape
goes, I would argue that the aestheticization finally reveals the masculine
subject to be serving rather than fulfilling the dominant and dominating

paternal function, which relationship does not cease to foreground the incommensurability of penis and phallus. Paradoxically, then, the violent intimacy of rape metamorphoses into an all-too-intimate relation with the lack that constitutes subjectivity—the lack that has been displaced onto woman and her anatomical wound. If the text opens a symbolically fertile "elision" (Silver, "Periphrasis," 116) or "psychic elsewhere" (Silverman, *Male Subjectivity*, 271) through the oblique fashion in which it narrates rape, that interpretive space threatens the deconstitution of masculinity, even as it also repeats the story of feminine passivity and rapability.

The "radically heterogenous will" to which Lacan grants agency in sadistic fantasy gestures toward the disembodied paternal function, which is destined to remain out of reach of the individual masculine subject. It is that disembodied paternal will that establishes the tableau of violent heterosexuality, into which fantasy space males and females alike are inserted in the process of identity formation. For Lacan that paternal will has its source in the Symbolic in individual moments of inauguration into a gendered discursive order. The problem here, as is oft noted of Lacanian thought, is the seemingly random and absolutely exclusive connection between sex, gender, and the symbolic order—"there is nothing inevitable, and everything quite arbitrary, about Lacan's conflation of linguistic dif- ference with sexual difference"—and the originary power granted to that connection (C. Thomas 71). One factor clearly excluded from the Lacanian paradigm is the space of the social and its role in the formation of subjectivity. It is through fantasy, after all, that we inhabit a culture, a time, and a mode of production. It is arguably *because* of a particular social and productive order that specific ideological fantasies are formulated: as Louis Althusser famously points out, in ideology "the real relation is inevitably invested in the imaginary relation, a relation that *expresses a will* (conservative, conformist, reformist or revolutionary)" (234). Gilles Deleuze and Felix Guattari go further, crediting the historical "will" with the production of the "lack" so crucial to the operation of the symbolic: "Lack (*manque*) is created, planned, and organized in and through social production" (28). Lack does not exclusively derive, in this reading, from the symbolic (or, following Freud, from anatomical difference and the Oedipal family). The subject's relation to lack, as to the fantasy that dis- avows it, is primarily social and ideological in nature and obeys the "will" of the sociosymbolic order: "Thus fantasy is never individual: it is *group fantasy* [. . . , and g]roup fantasy is plugged into and machined on the socius. . . . *There is only desire and the social, and nothing else*" (30, 62, 29).

Social fantasy, in turn, is for Deleuze and Guattari generated specifical- ly by the "capitalist machine [. . . ,] in all its violence" (33). The subject's relation to that machine is lived through the ideologies of gender and sexuality (as well as race, ethnicity, and class), and the lived experience of both is scripted and rendered coherent through social fantasy in ways that naturalize and eroticize the conditions necessary for capitalism in its specific historical forms. Mechanisms like fetishism and sadism, for example, not only establish and position a gendered subject within the discursive order but mediate the role of individual subjects within the dominant mode of production. By the same token, as is my case here, the specific forms of violence historically associated with capitalism are echoed—and legitimized—within and through the long and kaleidoscopic history of the heterosexual rape story. Promising absolute subjectivity (and passivity), instrumentalizing the bodies involved, and finally undermining the masculine power and presence initially assured, the aestheticized rape tableau focuses one's attention on sex and power, obscuring the extent to which it also prepares and maintains the ground for a predatory and increasingly abstract mode of production. In what follows, then, I will be conceptualizing masculine subjectivity and rape fantasy in ways that take into account the determinative roles of subject formation, the symbolic order, and mode of production. I will rely on R. W. Connell's argument that "the entrepreneurial culture and workplaces of commercial capitalism institutionalized a form of masculinity, creating and legitimating new forms of gendered work and power" (247). There is much to be gained in linking the violent forms of subjectivity to the erotic and aestheticized images of capitalism; if nothing else, such an examination foregrounds the contingent nature of both. It is an intrinsically valuable exercise, similarly, to study the ease with which seemingly individual fantasies of lack, desire, and sexual dominance can be treated, as Jana Evans Braziel puts it, as "fragments functioning in social machines" (872).

In general terms, critical and theoretical analyses of the interconnections between gender and production in Western thought have concentrated on femininity and the extent to which the feminine has been represented as a function of reproductive capacity as it is managed under patriarchy—defined as passive materiality receptive to the father's will and pattern. So for Jean-Joseph Goux: "While the male is associated with the transmission of a pattern, a model, the female braves the contradiction of a material reproduction and is merged with what is *other* in relation to constant ideal form: that is, with amorphous, transitory, inessential material . . . chaos, disorder, and the abnormal but also the sensory, the concrete, the nondeductible are identified with the woman (whatever the mythical or ideological version), and . . . permanence, order, organization, and law are on the male side" (222–23). This model has adapted easily to the ideological formations of early, industrial, and imperial capitalism, and both Irigaray and Goux have studied the close fit. Goux draws a parallel between the child produced on the material, effaced body of the mother and the surplus value produced on the material, effaced body of the worker: "The value produced (children, goods) is a lost positivity, a 'surplus' that becomes estranged from the producer. The relation between mother and offspring, under the father's control, is like that between worker and product under capitalist domination. There is an *inversion of fertilities.* As Marx writes, 'This is the relationship of the worker to his own activity as something alien and not belonging to him, activity as suffering (passivity), strength as powerlessness, *creation as emasculation*'"(233). The emasculation implicit in the alienation of labor under patriarchal capitalism is inverted in this ideological formation of gender to return value to the father. Masculinity is thus identified with ownership of the means of production and is closely connected to capital itself. Irigaray similarly remarks upon the parallel between mother and the alienated worker under capitalism—neither will be able to find a connection with the finished product. She also notes the proximity of the father to capital itself as a result of this alienation: "Woman is nothing but the receptacle that passively receives his *product.*" She is the "Matrix—womb, earth, factory, bank—to which the seed capital is entrusted so that it may germinate, produce, grow fruitful, without woman being able to lay claim to either capital or interest since she has only submitted 'passively' to reproduction. Herself held in receivership as a certified means of (re)production" (18). The gynema, then, is that space that allows masculinity to think of itself as not alienated, not effaced by the crushing wheels of capitalism. She is the bank that, although open to the one, will not be penetrable by any other; she will thus protect and increase the essence of his worth. And she will give physical form to that mysterious entity, capital, which the directive for circulation and the tendency toward accumulation within the hands of a very few keep otherwise hidden—like wind, visible only in its effects.

The disquiet that accompanies the reproductive, banking model for femininity is, unsurprisingly, associated with the fear that the value hidden within the material body of woman might not truly be marked with the name of the father, or might well be vulnerable to theft. Under early forms of capitalism, in cultures still managed by patrilineal descent, the father's "function with regard to the origin of reproduction—is hence asserted as less than evident, as open to doubt. An indecision to be attenuated both by man's 'active' role in intercourse and by the fact that he will mark the product of copulation with *his own name*" (Irigaray 23). Consider, for example, the violent anxiety that marks the question of chastity within Jacobean drama. Thomas Middleton and William Rowley's *The Changeling* in typical fashion establishes the moral horror of the unchaste woman as the central fulcrum of the dramatic plot, in this case a plot that involves a fatherless son achieving a father-in-law along with a place at the top of the social hierarchy. The source of the horror Beatrice-Joanna evokes is distilled in her illegitimate tampering with the secret tests hidden away in her husband's library: "'How to know whether a woman be with child or no' . . . 'How to know whether a woman be a maid or not'" (4.1.26). These tests for virginity, chastity, and pregnancy are designed so that external signs (sleeping, "incontinently gaping," "sudden sneezing," and "violent laughing" [4.1.49–50]) will appear as accurate and transparent signifiers of internal status. But because Beatrice-Joanna can penetrate the secret chamber and disrupt this secret language of the patriarchy, she threatens the very social fabric of the play (as she also does through her adulterous affair). Her "moral degeneration" is remarked not only by her dramatic fellows but by over 400 years of critical response (Crupi quoting T. S. Eliot 142).[1]

By the same token, in a culture that depends upon the female vessel for the transmission of wealth from father to son, or father to son-in-law—or in a culture that symbolically defines the female body as source for the generation and propagation of capital—the aestheticization of rape can come to articulate, whether in celebration or fear, the ability of the man of powerful agency to erupt into the sealed transaction between father and son/son-in-law, to insert himself by virtue of violence into an otherwise frozen class system. In other words, the rapability that is so much a part of feminine representation articulates not only closure but openness and potential mobility. If the woman under patrilineal descent is indeed symbolically a "hinge . . . [s]et between—at least—two, or two half, men [, . . .] bending according to their exchanges," she is also the access point for a third man—the entrepreneur, the up-and-coming member of the rising middle class, reinvigorating the system with new energy and the imperative to keep wealth circulating (Irigaray 22). Thus, a work like George Pettie's *A Petite Pallace of Pettie His Pleasure* returns constantly (and ambivalently) to the potential openness of the female body: the presumed audience of "gentle Gentlewoman" is beseeched by turns to consider adultery and to remain chaste, to be the active suitors in affairs of the heart and to be the passive recipients.[2] It is upon the fantasy of this unstable and unnerving access point—this signifier of upward mobility—that the ideology of capitalism stands or falls. At the same time, the fantastical rapist hero of early capitalism also manages to embody Marx's principle of "value in motion," "the circulation of capital restlessly and perpetually seeking new ways to garner profits" (Harvey 107).

The questions I take up here have to do with what happens to the gynema under a system of advanced capitalism. What changes does the rape narrative undergo when only the barest ideological remnants of patrilineal descent remain intact? What becomes of the rapist hero in the literary imagination when capitalism moves into its twentieth- and twenty-first century incarnations? Certainly the rape victim continues to be defined by her penetrability; there is a small enough swerve from the "rapability" that Catharine MacKinnon has argued has come to delimit the boundaries of "woman": "To be rap*able*, a position which is social, not biological, defines what a woman *is*" (651). The material conditions of female existence remain obscured by the aestheticization of rape, a mechanism Laura Tanner has compared to "Marx's unveiling of the way in which the laborer's suffering body is rendered invisible by the machinery of capitalism" (8). Metaphor continues to render the female victim passive, still identified with materiality and chaos. The woman continues to be, as Tanner points out, "the object rather than the subject of violence, a human being stripped of agency and mercilessly attached to a physical form that cannot be dissolved at will" (3). On the other hand, as the European/American gentry system splits and gives way to new hegemonic forms, in turn displaced by advanced or late capitalism, the woman's body no longer has the absolute prerequisite for chastity, nor is the purity of her reproductions centrally at issue. In fact rarely is the raped woman productive—*of a child or a pregnancy, of a material product*—in twentieth-century literary fantasy. In fact, to the contrary, except within the rhetoric closely allied to the ideology of fascism, the female body is obliterated through rape, shown, in shades of horror, to be empty and perhaps even absent.

Thus, in significant ways figurations of rape increasingly reveal the distance between twentieth-century masculinity and productive power, and between masculine agency and the ownership of capital. Further, the proliferation of raped female bodies seems more and more to articulate the effaced status of man himself under a self-organizing form of capitalism that appears to function without recourse to human agency—certainly without dependence on entrepreneurial initiative. Representations of rape thus mark, among other things, what Connell terms the emergence of "an array of subordinated and marginalized masculinities" (249). The reasons for these changes are admittedly complex, and the evolution is not linear, but it makes sense to accept the three general causal factors that Connell identifies: "challenges to the gender order by women, the logic of the gendered accumulation process in industrial capitalism, and the power relations of empire" (249). These material changes central to the fabric of capitalism have served to weave a tangled pattern of gender violence in literature. Even in a feminist era, writers return to the rape story with a tenacity seemingly born of sadomasochistic compulsion: those aestheticized images preserve the dream of violent agency while repeating the contemporary message of masculine failure and loss. If, then, what Sharon Marcus terms the "grammar" of rape does indeed "[induce] men who follow the rules set out for them to recognize their gendered selves in images and narratives of aggression in which they are agents of violence," that semiotics of self-recognition also acts in the twentieth century to contradict itself, relentlessly pronouncing the "absolute impotence of the wage earner as well as the . . . dependence of the industrial capitalist" in that "fathomless abyss where profit and surplus value are engendered"—the "semiautonomous organization" of capital (Marcus 393; Deleuze and Guattari 238–39, 142).

If the history of European/American masculinity has been neither coherent nor linear—even as it does follow a general trajectory in literature that I hope to trace—neither can the masculine subject of any particular historical era be understood to be singular. As Connell puts it, "dominant, subordinated and marginalized masculinities are in constant interaction, changing the conditions for each others' existence and transforming themselves as they do" (254). Thus, as white masculinity cannot be thought of as homogenous, neither can it be thought of, demographics aside, as necessarily or wholly dominant; although it is true that "elite" white men do in fact "control more resources and exercise more power" than others and more than elite white men of thirty years ago, the profound economic and social changes that have accompanied the evolution of global, corporate capitalism—Newton lists "corporate downsizing, the reduction of well-paid unionized jobs, the fall in men's wages, the growing necessity of dual-income families, cuts in worker safety nets, the further racialization of poverty, and the growing division between the rich and the middle-class and poor"—have radically revised the meaning of white, heterosexual manhood (176). Michael Kimmel and Michael Kaufman make the easily persuasive case that "[m]any middle-class, white, middle-aged heterosexual men—among the most privileged groups in the history of the world—do not experience themselves as powerful. Ironically, although these men are everywhere in power, that aggregate power of that group does not translate into an individual sense of feeling empowered. In fact, this group feels quite powerless" (262). The white, European/American masculinity under consideration here has always, not just over the past forty years, been relational and contingent, and has always been haunted by powerlessness. In spite of, and quite possibly because of, this contingency and instability, however, white masculinity has managed generally to maintain a highly aestheticized and politicized image—if not always a felt sense—of unity. It has retained its position as natural, normative, and ideally human.

Many would maintain that the fantastical homogeneity of white masculinity has been established in large part through its portrayed relationship to racial and ethnic otherness, a point of view that many of the texts examined here will explicitly support (e.g., Ezra Pound's *Cantos* and

Thomas Pynchon's *Gravity's Rainbow*). Just as it would be shortsighted to understand the connection between masculinity and violence to be purely personal or discursive, it would also leave too much uncovered to treat the culture of capitalism apart from its global and imperial rootedness, for, as Connell has noted, "European/American masculinities were deeply implicated in the world-wide violence through which European/American culture became dominant" (245). More famously, Homi Bhabha has called into question the originary status of the white European/American man—the hypothetical subject of capitalism—by arguing that his existence as such has been and continues to be dependent on the silent presence of the nonwhite other, who haunts the field just beyond peripheral vision: "the image of post-Enlightenment man [is] tethered to, *not* confronted by, his dark reflection, the shadow of colonized man, that splits his presence, distorts his outline, breaches his boundaries, repeats his action at a distance, disturbs and divides the very time of his being" (44). The agency the violently phallic narrative promises is thus undermined not only by the woman, who confronts the masculine subject with the lack he has disavowed through and by entry into the socio-symbolic; it is also troubled by the dark other whose role it is to play the looking-glass role of masculine nonsubject, masculine being without agency, violent body without prerogative. In Thomas Pynchon's *Gravity's Rainbow,* for example, the breakdown of Slothrop's penile quest is marked by hallucinations of being raped by black men, of having to escape by crawling down through toilet and sewers, reentering primal abjection; similarly, Blicero's sexual sadism and the firing of the rocket are shadowed by the mythical African Herero and their campaign of self-extermination. The evolving genre of rape narrative I treat here, then, is precisely a white masculinist one. Its function is to define, maintain, and legitimize the systems of relation and differentiation upon which global capitalism depends.[3]

It seeks to do so, moreover, in a language that would deny the political stakes involved or even their placement in history. Unlike the type of rape story told within texts like, for example, *The Women of Brewster Place* or *Native Son,* the category of narrative I study rarely attempts an explicitly political commentary on rape and/or race. Few of the texts I study focus the audience's attention on the psychological or physical reality of the victim or the impact of rape on her life. And few consider—at least centrally—the negative social and economic conditions that might tragically and/or horrifically incline individuals toward violence, sexual or otherwise. Rather, the literature here, a mere sampling of a vast humanist tradition, focuses almost exclusively on the spectacle of rape as a poignant occasion for sympathetic rumination on the status of (white) man in the face of (capitalist) existence. It is a genre given to contemplation, pathos, and an aura of secular transcendence. It seemingly concerns itself with every-thing that would be opposed to politics, history, or economics.

In order to highlight the specific artificiality and political nature of the genre, consider in more detail the counterexamples above. Some contem-porary writing by women, in particular by women of color, has overturned the mainstream form of the rape narrative by locating point of view with-in the mind of the rape victim. This is a resistant genre studied most notably by Laura Tanner, who argues, specifically here of *The Women of Brewster Place,* that this new form of the narrative "attaches the reader to the victim's tortured body, subverting the scopophilic gaze of the reader by turning it inward to focus on the victim's pain. By denying the reader the freedom to observe the victim of violence from behind the wall of aesthet-ic convention, Naylor disrupts the connection between violator and view-er. . . . The power of the reader's imagination is not unleashed in a tumult of speculative violences but is channeled within the confines of the victim's body" (x). This focus on the material body and experience of the rape vic-tim undercuts the vision of woman as passive receptacle, troubles the image of pure agency distilled by the figure of rapist, and discourages spec-ulation on the transcendent meaning of it all (Y. B. Yeats's speaker wonders of Leda, "Did she put on his knowledge with his power / Before the indif-ferent beak could let her drop?"). Instead, one is confronted by a particu-larized image of the ways that constructions of race and gender intersect in the material bodies of women. In the final chapter, I discuss other forms of narrative resistance developed by women writers.

Twentieth-century literature written by African American men also returns repeatedly to the theme and image of rape, and in ways also qual-itatively different from the tradition I am tracing. Texts by James Baldwin, Chester Himes, Eldridge Cleaver, George Wylie Henderson, Ishmael Reed, and, of course, James Wright foreground instances or metaphors of rape in order to explore issues of racial politics and black masculinity. A note of caution: In these texts, as in the ones I examine, the woman, white or black, is generally objectified and defined by her passivity. The difference is that in this group of works, there is a tendency for connections between public and private, sex and violence, and gender and race to be made relentlessly explicit, and there is no missing the political underpinnings of the rape story. In other words, the spectacle of rape—and it is spectacular-ized—is located firmly within its socioeconomic and historical context. Its explicit metaphoricity—or, as Eileen Julien puts it, of rape in some African texts, its metonymic content—tends to apply not so much opaquely to a transcendent state of man but transparently to a specifically historical sub-ject, and that subject is always in part a function of race as it has been con-structed under Western patriarchal capitalism.

A discussion of rape in African American texts, no matter how brief, must necessarily engage the ongoing and ever deepening critical discourse surrounding the vexed issue of black masculinity and the ways it has been and continues to be associated with sexual violence and/or castration. There is to contend with the historical fact of slavery, a condition of being that would run counter to any Western definition of manhood. Frederick Douglass claimed that "A man without force is without the essential dignity of humanity," thus articulating the extent to which slavery prevented black men from experiencing a sense of manhood (as well as the extent to which ideal manhood involves force) (in Gilroy 63). At the same time, the myth of the black rapist that accompanied and followed slavery posited an animalistic hypermasculinity, to be "corrected" through castration and lynching. "Rape" is in this case necessarily associated with castration—at the level of fantasy and at the level of material experience. On a white man, thus (problematically) suggestive of the phallus, male genitalia have become for the black man "the depriving mark of a forced animality rather than a sign of masculine control and self-control," as well as a part of the body and marker of masculinity rendered vulnerable to violent, and in fact sexual, destruction (M. Ross 319). Gender, then, in this case, cannot possibly be understood outside of the context of race and class, a fact manifestly clear to a writer like Richard Wright, for whom black male identity entailed the anomalous situation of being on the one hand fully cognizant of the idealized portrait of masculinity painted by an oppressive white patriarchal culture and on the other confronted by the subordinate social and economic position that guaranteed black men continued animalization and emasculation. Gilroy argues that the contradiction resulted in a "doubledness, what Richard Wright calls the dreadful objectivity which follows from being both inside and outside the West" (30). In *Native Son*, Bigger Thomas is caught in that double bind, quite aware of the idealized and specifically white image of masculinity, and yet constantly at risk of figurative or even literal castration. The result is escalating violence toward women, first the murder of Mary Dalton—the scene itself heavy with the suggestion of sexual violence—then the rape and murder of Bessie Mears.

There can be no doubt that Wright self-consciously figures gender violence within the novel—material, imagined, or figurative—as a function of an oppressive and violent race-class system. The point is made so explicitly as to border on didacticism, as in the following, in which scene Bigger realizes that he will be accused of raping Mary Dalton before killing her, even though he has not, because that is the only script available to a black man: "He committed rape every time he looked into a white face. He was a long, taut piece of rubber which a thousand white hands had stretched to the snapping point, and when he snapped it was rape. But it was rape when he cried out in hate deep in his heart as he felt the strain of living day by day. That, too, was rape" (214). Not only is the novel heavily seeded with this type of self-conscious reference to the political nature of rape and of "rape," but Wright includes a foreword that further clarifies the connection:

> Any Negro who has lived in the North or the South knows that times without number he has heard of some Negro boy being picked up on the streets and carted off to jail and charged with "rape." This thing happens so often that to my mind it had become a representative symbol of the Negro's uncertain position in America. Never for a second was I in doubt as to what kind of social reality or dramatic situation I'd put Bigger in, what kind of test-tube life I'd set up to evoke his deepest reactions. Life had made the plot over and over again, to the extent that I knew it by heart. (xxviii)

The novel is thus an explicit challenge, a self-conscious refusal to participate in white patriarchy's rape story. Rape here is no occasion for a meeting with the transcendent. Rather, through this refashioned rape narrative, "Wright dramatizes the parasitic nature of the class system" and draws attention to "the wealthy Daltons' participation in the systematic exploitation and destruction of Bigger Thomas and his family" (Guttman, "What Bigger Killed For," 170). The rebellious struggle the novel stages is a political one between white masculine oppressor and oppressed black male. The female body serves as the token over which the battle is waged, and "both Mary and Bessie—[the] two female bodies—are violently blotted out in [that] struggle between white and black men" (177). One embodies white capital, the other the obliteration of the black woman and the irrelevance of her suffering in the face of that valuable whiteness, and so it is not surprising both are "blotted out" by the overarching race-class structure and its attendant ideology—just as Bigger himself is "blotted out" in "fulfilling the role that the [rape] myth demands of him" (170, 179).

What *Native Son* and texts like it share with the white narrative tradition I treat here, of course, is that it is onto the wounded bodies of women that the problematics of masculine identity are projected. Another shared feature is that it is the raped *white* woman who comes to stand in for the abstract forces against which manhood conceptually formulates itself. The rape of the woman of color is hardly more than the occasion for the expression of excess masculine emotion. Bessie herself, for example, "is literally frozen out of the story," as Guttman aptly puts it: "With Mary, Bigger's actions are predetermined by the knowledge that what he does is one part of a very public play of forces. He feels 'strange, possessed, or as if he were acting upon a stage in front of a crowd of people.' With Bessie, however, Bigger feels no one is watching. He is free to commit rape because he knows, subconsciously at least, that those in power don't care what he does to her" ("What Bigger Killed For" 184). In fact, in a radical denial of historical veracity, given the fact, for example, that the "sexual access of white men to black women was a cornerstone of patriarchal power in the South," the rape of women of color is not often represented or even referred to in literature written by men, particularly white men (J. Hall 332). When it is, it is not invested with the symbolic heft garnered by representations of raped white women. Thus we witness a strange continuance of the logic that supported castration culture as Guttman describes it: "While the white woman was cast as the desirable and inaccessible symbol of white power and culture, the black woman occupied the place of her opposite, the easily accessible symbol of the uncivilized, animalistic, black masses" (171). It has been noted that white feminism, particularly during the 1970s when the emphasis was often on constructing a unifying image of "woman," has similarly sometimes overlooked the specific and historically driven nature of sexual violence against women of color. As with the unmarked universal man, the universal woman tends to be white, European/American, and middle- or upper-class. As Sujata Moorti puts it in *Color of Rape,* "the majority of feminist rape theories were formulated around the universal subject of Enlightenment, this time though she was female" (66).

The genre of rape story studied here presumes a white masculine subject and a white feminine object. This fantastical structure has only a tenuous relationship to local knowledge and has little to do with what a rape victim—any rape victim—might actually have experienced. Nor, I hope, does the predominance of rape fantasy suggest that all men—or all white men, or all people steeped in the idealizations of Western storytelling—imagine rape to be just the far end of the normative heterosexual continuum, although obviously one is given pause, particularly given the national numbers for stranger and acquaintance rape alike. Rather, I want to make the case that the aestheticized rape narrative is a significant part of Western fantasy, and that a study of that fantastical narrative reveals particular things about the way white masculinity represents itself. Like Laura E. Tanner (*Intimate Violence*) and Lynn A. Higgins and Brenda R. Silver (*Rape and Representation*), I am interested in what the story excludes, what it must elide in order to function, as I am interested in how certain retellings and revisions of the story seek to correct or at least draw attention to those exclusions. But more centrally, I am interested in what the story enables, what it generates. As does Sabine Sielke, I want to focus on "refigurations of rape as well as on rape as refiguration [, thus acknowledging] that texts do not simply reflect but rather stage and dramatize the historical contradictions by which they are overdetermined" (5). Like Sharon Marcus, I want to understand not only the language of rape, but "rape as a language," one that mediates the relationship of the subject to history. The "rape script," as Marcus puts it, takes its form from a "*gendered grammar of violence*," and that grammar positions ("predicates") white men as legitimate subjects; black men as subjects of illegitimate violence; (white) women as subjects by virtue of being (valuable and legitimate) objects of violence (392). Most specifically, for my purposes, the rape script fantasizes a believably powerful subject position in the face of historical, material evidence that would trouble it; it daydreams a potent relationship of white, mainstream men (or men identified with the white mainstream) to late capitalism. It does this by casting a "tremulous female body" opposite, in the position of "immobilized cavity" (Marcus 400).

It might seem incongruous that the choice here has been to focus upon constructions of masculinity rather than femininity in a study of rape narrative. Further, the explicit concentration on the *representation* of rape might suggest the perpetuation of a tradition that has at many levels depended upon the silencing of women. Marcus's "linguistic" approach to rape has been critiqued for related reasons; Mardorossian accuses her of "downplay[ing] the 'materiality of gender' and ignor[ing the fact] that social inscriptions—that is, our physical situatedness in time and space, in history and culture—do not simply evaporate because we are made aware of them" (755). One must acknowledge the danger of "reproduc[ing] the cycle . . .—that is, erasing women as the routine targets of rape in order to metaphorize . . . violence" (M. Ross 314). At the same time, it bears saying, again, with Sielke, that "rape narratives relate to real rape incidents in highly mediated ways only. They are first and foremost interpretations, readings of rape that, as they seem to make sense of socially deviant behavior, oftentimes limit our understanding of sexual violence while producing norms of sexuality in the process. As they have evolved in historically specific contexts, these narratives moreover interrelate with, produce, and subsequently reproduce a cultural symbology that employs sexual deviance for the formation of cultural identities" (2–3). The feminist project of unveiling the mechanisms of patriarchy is worth the risks it entails. It is of crucial importance for a new generation of scholars to identify the ways in which masculinity has reconstituted itself in the face of the feminist challenges of the late twentieth century, because although such a collective project might seem vulnerable to its own practice of treating rape as (just) representation, it "at least enables us to expose [the] blindness at the heart of influential Euro-American psychoanalytic, gender, sexuality, and cultural theories" (M. Ross 312). If it is true that the social script does not "evaporate because we

are made aware of" it, it is at least to be hoped that "we can locally interfere with it": "By defining rape as a scripted performance, we enable a gap
between script and actress which can allow us to rewrite the script, perhaps
by refusing to take it seriously and treating it as a farce, perhaps by resist-
ing the physical passivity which it directs us to adopt" (Marcus 392).

Equally useful is the exploration of the ways the rape script supports
and is supported by specific forms of capitalism. These linkages help to
destabilize in very concrete ways the common-sense notion that gender as
we know it is inevitable, as well as the often-held but dangerous proposi-
tion that rape is somehow a natural consequence of anatomy. It is unfor-
tunate that early studies of rape sometimes moved in this general direction; Susan Brownmiller's 1975 manifesto can be taken as representative:
"[I]n terms of human anatomy the possibility of forcible intercourse
incontrovertibly exists. This single factor may have been sufficient to have
caused the creation of a male ideology of rape. When men discovered that
they could rape, they proceeded to do it" (14). Certainly a body-centered
approach can have in its favor the acknowledgment of women's lived realities, before this time written out of the legal, medical, and criminal theorizing of rape. But a model like Brownmiller's also conflates rape, gender,
and anatomy in ways as incontrovertible as the link the rape story establishes between sexual violence and transcendent meaning. Catharine
MacKinnon's work on rape, similarly, has come under scrutiny in recent
years for defining women as "inherently rapable," "objects" whose worth
is determined by virtue of their patriarchally conceived "purity" (Marcus
387, Rooney 94). Situating the rape narrative within its enabling socioeconomic context, on the other hand, denies the inevitability of forcible
intercourse as the natural consequence of human anatomy. Plotting violent sexual fantasy on the grid of economic concerns, moreover, locates
masculine agency in relation to an explicitly contingent material system of
power, value, and order. It is in this way that the violent intimacy of the
rape story finally discloses the increased desperation with which the body
has been made to carry ideology under systems of advanced capitalism.

The turn of the twentieth century witnessed several marked changes in the
economic forms of Europe and the United States, including the evolution
toward finance capitalism, rationalized corporate control, and a new politics of labor management. In chapter 2, I set out to show that representations of the divinely raped female body enabled some "high" modernist
artists and writers to conscript and eroticize entrepreneurial fantasies of
invasion and empire to the service of the new ideologies of controlled cap-

italism and a managed working class. The aestheticized female body thus becomes in much high modernist literature a stand-in for material chaos generally and class, labor, and gender displacement and democratization particularly. The violent invasion of this body by some transcendent and/or abstract force, furthermore, articulates the attraction that writers like Eliot and Yeats felt toward totalitarianism. For all three writers, further, the rape is often a central metaphor for the hierarchic infusion of value even as the role of the implicitly or actually masculine protagonist and/or speaker wavers and gains strength in relation to the event. Thus masculinized and individualized "productivity" comes to exist side by side with feminine and anarchic subordination to homogenous and abstracted power. The repression of man that might otherwise be implicit in the vision of divine domination is more or less neatly avoided, even in the face of capitalism's rape story excising from its own narrative the agency of the (human) rapist.

Chapter 3 investigates the parallel constructions of the rape victim in the Fordist model of labor and production and the ideological superstructure of fascism. Both models emphasize hierarchy, concentration, and control, and both ultimately move beyond turn-of-the-century rhetoric by validating themselves in the figure of the great man, whether the fascist leader or the heroic engineer. The idealized role of the leader in some ways resolves the split between the capitalist rhetoric of entrepreneurial agency and the twentieth-century reality of controlled capitalism. Writers like Ayn Rand and Ezra Pound yoke "factive" leadership to technological mastery and validate that conjunction through the image of the raped woman. As in Eliot, Yeats, and E. M. Forster, the raped female body suggests abstract value, but her presence speaks much more forcefully to the power of the factive personality to mobilize the dissociated elements of production into a model of humming efficiency that expresses his highly individualized will. The raped women in *The Fountainhead* and *The Cantos* ultimately speak not of divinity in all of its transcendent incomprehensibility but of the force of great human personality to reenergize production, thus to control the crisis possibilities endemic to capitalism. The victims speak not of their own effacement before the absolute—although certainly they are effaced—but of their now-increased (re)productive capabilities. Thus female (re)production is not only conscripted to the symbolic and actual service of the virile hero but is crucial in ideologically legitimating the force necessary for the unification and mobilization of economic and technological enterprise.

Not all mid-century figurations of white masculinity could participate fully in the triumphant rape story told by Pound, or Rand, or even Eliot or Yeats, however; nor could man always be so easily identified with the rising productivity of capitalism, with the tremendous concentration of state and military power in the West, or with the explosive productivity and new industrialization that accompanied and followed the world wars. In fact, I argue in chapter 4, such factors as increasing automation resulted in a mid-century reconstruction of masculinity often marked by nostalgia, or even grief. In a sense, it was technological production itself—the engine that powers capitalism—that was silently (and sometimes not so silently) coming to be understood as the force that would displace the white man. At the same time, consumable technology establishes the phallus as explicitly artificial and transferable, its power up for grabs and available to anyone with enough money to buy it. In this context, the rape narrative proposes a story of accessibility and inaccessibility in which the prerogative for violence against women has been stolen in a gesture of mechanical piracy. Rape is thus redefined as technological abduction—without human or divine antagonist. In *Tarr*, published in 1918, Wyndham Lewis crafts a machine to supplant man and usurp his prerogative for gender violence. If Lewis meets machined emasculation with bitter resignation, many of his contemporaries greet the same nightmare of technological castration with rage, and the proliferations of the machine—first embodied as phallic accompaniment, later as woman—become subject to increasingly brutal displays of violence. In the work of D. H. Lawrence, for example, rage against the machine is explicitly played out against the body of woman. What the brutalized female body finally expresses, however, is a lament, as in the case of William Faulkner, for the lost white gentleman of the past.

The anxiety articulated in the work of writers like Faulkner and Lawrence begins to investigate a masculinity explored more fully in chapter 5: one defined not in relation to production but in relation to consumption. As is often noted, after the Second World War, first-world economies turned more fully toward postindustrial structures on one hand and toward commodity production and consumerism on the other. The commitment ideologically crucial in an earlier form of capitalism to the notion of the individual who sells his labor to the market shifts more completely to a faith in the individual who freely consumes in a gesture of personal expression. The consumerist quest for what purports to be an expression of the true self is mapped onto the objectified female body (as it is onto the commodity item). A novel like Vladimir Nabokov's *Lolita*, then, is structured by Humbert Humbert's frustration over Lolita's increasing removal and obscurity, an affective response doubled by the reader. The text is itself draped in veils that do not ultimately reveal anything other than the violent desire of the subject. Like the novel of the postmodern striptease generally, *Lolita* speaks to commodity fetishism under late capitalism and to the ways in which consumer culture relies heavily on the victimized female body to create the illusion of an abstract universal essence behind the material commodity. D. M. Thomas's *The White Hotel* is similarly structured to bring the reader up against the blank wall of a feminine materiality which resists fetishism and the work of interpretation.

By most accounts, 1973 marked the decisive end of the postwar "boom" and initiated a new economy that would have a powerful impact on what would come to be called the postmodern subject. Chapter 6 examines masculinity as it is developed in postmodern fiction. David Savran argues that what he terms "reflexive sadomasochism" has become "the linchpin . . . to a new American white masculinity" (190). Produced in response to such factors as feminism, civil rights, gay rights, the loss of the Vietnam War, and, most importantly, "the end of the post–World War II economic boom and a resultant and steady decline in the income of white working- and lower-middle-class men," Savran's "reflexive sadomasochism" gave voice to "a new masculinity . . . that was no longer contingent either upon the production of enemies *out there* or upon nakedly imperialistic forays abroad" (191, 194). The rape narrative is not at all lost in this revised account of white masculinity. In the postmodern text, however, the prerogative for rape is often forcefully dissociated from masculine agency, and it is precisely the trauma of this dissociation that focuses the portrayal of masculinity. No longer promising subjectivity, the raped and disappearing female body shows man his relationship to the techno-economy of late capitalism, and that relationship is revealed to be one that finally nullifies him as subject, spreads that hypothetical subjectivity across the information "space" that constitutes him. In the end the new white man is an exhausted information worker, consigned to a cubicle, detached from any understanding of the larger project of which he is (apparently) a part, producing under compulsion (in the clearly ideological name of pleasure) what does not have the palpable materiality of a "product." Ultimately, the rape dreams of an older time turn traitorously, masochistically, against the soft, vulnerable body of man himself.

Thus John Barth's *Giles Goat-Boy* stages in 1966 the kind of masculine anxiety that accompanied the growth of the techno-economy and its colonization of information flow. The masculine protagonist in the novel is secondary, "produced as a residuum alongside the machine," doomed to a farcical reliving of the quest narrative; like the subject of late capitalism as described by Deleuze and Guattari, the hero "is not at the center, which is occupied by the machine, but on the periphery, with no fixed identity, forever decentered, *defined* by the states through which it passes" (20). It is the machine which rapes. Cyberpunk also stages the return of the masculine rapist hero only to consign him to the margins of an informational world. It is *Gravity's Rainbow*, however, that most relentlessly dwells on the

vulnerability of the new man. In spite of its domination by violent phallic imagery, what it stages is the disappearance of the feminine—the
enabling feminine "other" whose rapability used to promise masculine
agency—and the spectacular growth of male masochism. The machine, it
turns out, has appropriated the traditionally masculine prerogative for sexual violence, and the true sexual event is between the lethal technological
phallus and the vulnerable, rapable masculine body. It is a further disempowerment of the masculine body that even the sexual response to the violence of the rocket—a response replicated throughout the text in various
scenes of sadomasochism—is a conditioned response; it reflects no desire
originating in a subject per se, but is rather a subject-effect constructed
through technology and transnational corporate power. The masculine
subject is absorbed into the "Their" system—the "They" who manufacture the war as they manufacture gendered and sexual response—for the
radical reorganization of spatial bases required for the endless circulation
of capital.

Chapter 7, on the other hand, examines the ways the rape narrative is
also employed within postmodern fiction to resuscitate the white male
subject. There are texts that suggest—precisely through heterosexual violence—a regrouping, or a reemergence of the father amidst post–cold war
consumer glut, finance capitalism, and waste management. Ironically, the
white masculinity reestablished in this type of postmodern rape narrative
is defined in sharp contrast to sexual violence, is actually dependent on the
repeated and emphatic casting out of the desire to rape. One is tempted
to claim that the essence of the shift is the emergence of compassion, an
installation of the kindness so explicitly and self-consciously absent from
Pynchon's texts. There is an overarching grief in the texts of Don DeLillo
and John Irving, the two writers I will take up here—grief for a lost masculinity, and grief for the raped girl or woman. That grief, however, as
(massively) sympathetically rendered as it is, is predicated on the presence
of a victim for whom to feel grief. Like the accumulated and recycled
waste of late capitalism, the rapist is thus preserved as he is scapegoated,
and he remains to haunt the borders and underground of the text; his violence necessarily continues to operate, denounced and yet crucial for masculine (anti)definition. At the same time, the rape victim herself is heavily fetishized, becomes a holy martyr in what would otherwise be an abject
universe.

Don DeLillo's *Underworld,* itself a reworking of *Gravity's Rainbow,*
achieves narrative epiphany in the saintly, post-death apparition of
Esmeralda Lopez, the twelve-year-old raped and murdered in the wastelands of the Bronx. Esmeralda is the ultimate throwaway commodity—
she gains value in being thrown, literally, from a building and, figurative-

ly, into the Internet; her rape is the underbelly of consumerist fetishism in an age of waste crisis, and her holy return redeems the postmodern wasteland. Similarly, John Irving's protagonists achieve mature masculinity when they acknowledge that a rape victim is "holy" (*Hotel New Hampshire* 441). The sexually victimized female body is thus defined both as vulnerable to the touch of displaced masculine violence and yet untouchable to the average man. Rape becomes the occasion to reflect on the "redemptive qualit[y]" of the flows and re-circulations of late capitalism, the miraculous fact that the compromised masculine self has been rendered invisible but has not been obliterated (*Underworld* 809). In a significant way, abstract value is thus ideologically produced in a way that nullifies and condemns the laborer (the rapist) while building up the consumer/investor—s/he who watches and witnesses and grieves. This masculine regret and disavowal, in the midst of claiming ownership, is a part of a new vision of subjectivity, a vision explicitly celebrated in the novel as "real" finally, outside the fantastical illusions of late capitalism.

The final chapter examines the struggle over the last thirty years to reclaim the rape narrative for feminist purposes. Toni Morrison, Margaret Atwood, A. M. Homes, Kathy Acker, Angela Carter, Christa Wolfe, Jeanette Winterson, Julia Alvarez—to name just a few—rework the sadomasochistic narrative in ways that call into question the ways the presumed feminine subject has been traditionally represented. I note above that Sharon Marcus argues that a politically efficacious approach to the study of rape begins with the explicit examination of "rape as a language": "[A] way to refuse to recognize rape as the real fact of our lives is to treat it as a *linguistic* fact: to ask how the violence of rape is enabled by narratives, complexes and institutions which derive their strength not from outright, immutable, unbeatable force but rather from their power to structure our lives as imposing cultural scripts. To understand rape in this way is to understand it as subject to change" (387, 389). To understand that the physical event of sexual violence is everywhere framed by the semiotic leads to the ability "to imagine women as neither already raped nor inherently rapable" (387). The writers I take up in the concluding chapter work in tandem with Marcus in struggling to disentangle representations of women from "an identity politics which defines women by our violability" (387). Some do so by staging in self-conscious terms the enduring construction of women as rapable-by-definition. Others interfere with the rape story by focusing on what Janice Haaken describes as the "inevitable disjuncture between rape as a metaphor and rape as a concrete act of violence" (784). Laura Tanner has shown that some contemporary writers reconstruct the rape narrative by "pushing the reader into a position of discomforting proximity to the victim's vulnerable body[, . . .] collaps[ing] the distance between a disembodied reader and a victim defined by embodiment" (10), and Higgins and Silver have insisted on the necessity of "taking rape literally," "restoring rape to the literal, to the body: restoring, that is, the violence—the physical, sexual violation" (4). My concluding chapter examines a range of resistant narrative forms that include the above.

The struggle of contemporary women writers to reclaim the rape narrative calls to mind the advice we routinely give young women and men in the college orientation process. Certainly at my institution, we are careful to organize mandatory workshops during which we exhort students, among other things, not to perpetuate the "rape myths" that support a culture in which one out of four college women has been the victim of rape or attempted rape since age fourteen (Goodman et al.) and in which 91 percent of victims are female (Haws). The obvious rape myths are those which generally condemn the "victim," to the extent that one believes there to be one, for her attire, behavior, or demeanor. Other legitimate variations include the impossibility of "rape" committed by husband or boyfriend. I would argue that the rape myth is more pervasive yet. It is a form manifestly diverse in its permutations, and like any ideological mold, it changes gracefully in response to the particular features of history and economics that benefit from it.

What the mythic variation relies upon is the extent to which in Western culture the "feminine" is, again to invoke both Alice Jardine and Roland Barthes, "a metaphor without brakes." Endlessly shape-shifting, the rapable female body persists in highbrow literature as the precondition for the masculine subject of capitalism, the agent to whom all imperial prerogative is granted. In the grotesque repetitions to which capitalism lends itself, the raped woman continues to function as the "'earth' to press down/repress, to work, to represent, but also and always to desire (for one's own)" (Irigaray 133). Without the presence of this ideological object, "which in theory does not know herself," then upon what foundation does one think the masculine subject? "If the earth turned and more especially turned upon herself, the erection of the subject might thereby be disconcerted and risk losing its elevation and penetration. For what would there be to rise up from and exercise his power over? And in?" (133). The subject of Western history—of logical and metaphysical thought, of market, industrial, and imperial capitalism—exists in supreme metaphysical thought by virtue of the violable feminized other, rendered visible in every banal figuration and event of our lived experience. Where, thus, to move? To invoke again the language of rape prevention at my institution:

> [Question]: How do we all contribute to the problem?
> [Answer]: Remaining silent. *Silence is a form of passive support. Men who harm women sexually will always view our silence as a form of approval. Women who have been assaulted will view our silence as a lack of support.* (Chalk and Checkett)

2

HIGH MODERNISM AND THE RAPE OF GOD

Calvin Bedient argues that representations of rape in such modernist texts as "Leda and the Swan," *A Passage to India,* and *The Waste Land* articulate a twentieth-century sense of "God as force, not as idea." The appropriate religious "mode" is "terror before the divine": "In lieu of received religious opinion, many modernists were seeking, at about the same time, the *one reality* of religious terror: inexplicable ontological power. There arose the fiction of the sacred blow—the assumption that the divine could not manifest itself to man [*sic*] except through a violence of passage, a rude impact" (204). The modernist god leaves the recipients of his attention "staggering, disoriented, terrified, *killed*" (204), as well as depersonalized and "redeemed" through the spectacular vision of impersonal and horrible power. The pose of modernist subjectivity, by extension, is submission before such a transcendent ontological force. What Bedient fails to mention, or apparently to find worthy of note, is that it is the *woman's* body (Leda, Adela Quested, Philomela) which thus legitimates violence as divinity—whether for narrator, speaker, writer, or reader. It would seem, then, that the image of feminine violation and submission is silently countered by the more or less unarticulated presence of masculine force and aggression. The raped female body thus allows a shifting masculinist point of view; identification can vacillate between the rape victim, brought under control and silenced by abstract and totalized power, and the rapist, the abstraction of individualist agency, initiative, and sovereignty.

The stakes in this gambit have to do with subjectivity and with value—with preserving the ideology of the individual while at the same time reconceptualizing the authoritarian imposition of order.[1] I would like to make the case, then, that the popularity of the image is related to specific changes within the machinery of capitalism witnessed by the early twentieth century. Most centrally, this period saw the evolution of Western economies toward finance capitalism, a development Lenin describes in *Imperialism: The Highest Stage of Capitalism:* "The Concentration of pro-

26

duction; the monopoly arising therefrom; the merging or coalescence of banking with industry—this is the history of the rise of finance capital and what gives the term 'finance capital' its content" (unpaginated). As Lenin's title suggests, the concentration of capital and the unification of industry and bank capital develop in tandem with the rise of imperialism, a co-development that marked the late nineteenth and early twentieth centuries. Rudolf Hilferding draws the connection this way:

> The policy of finance capital has three objectives:
> (1) to establish the largest possible economic territory;
> (2 to close this territory to foreign competition by a wall of protective tariffs, and consequently
> (3) to reserve it as an area of exploitation for the national monopolistic combinations. (326)

The burgeoning body of imperial, finance capitalism in the early twentieth century served in turn to validate the forms of national and/or corporate centralized control that would seem in theory opposed to the free market that the ideology of capitalism so celebrates. Rationalized corporate control was hardly new, of course, as David Harvey points out, particularly in the nineteenth-century organization of the railroads. Nonetheless, around the turn of the century controlled capitalism became the dominant economic form, and the model perfected by the railroads "spread, particularly after the wave of mergers, trust and cartel formation at the end of the century, to many industrial sectors (one-third of U.S. manufacturing assets were subject to merger in the years 1898–1902 alone)" (Harvey 125).

As if mirroring the centralized and centralizing forces of early twentieth century economics, the period is remembered as well for "[a] new politics of labour control and management": "The separation between management, conception, control, and execution (and all that this meant in terms of hierarchical social relations and de-skilling within the labour process) was also already well under way in many industries" (Harvey 126, 125). F. W. Taylor's *The Principles of Scientific Management* was published in 1911, and Henry Ford's automated car-assembly line began operation in Dearborn, Michigan, in 1914. For all the automation and control of human labor that both of these developments suggest, however, this was also a time of increased working-class organization. Michel Beaud makes the case assertively: "The . . . underlying movement which marked this period was the rise of the working classes. Indeed, this was the most fundamental movement, for it indicated the passage of a phase in which capitalism was able to develop by utilizing a labor force that was uprooted, dependent, subjugated, and crushed. The new phase was one in which the capitalist bourgeoisie had to contend with a working class which was increasingly conscious of its own position, which organized itself, and which finally imposed a new balance of forces" (144). The desire to manage the expanding labor force, in other words, seemed to be (almost) matched by a rising and discontented working class, bringing nightmares to the new ideological dreams of controlled capitalism. And thus imperial domination of the native other was echoed in the domestic European and American homeland by the felt need to dominate the rising tide of working-class rebellion. In the popular middle-class imagination, chaos reigned.

Images of the divinely raped female body enabled some "high" modernist artists and writers to conscript and eroticize entrepreneurial fantasies of invasion and empire to the service of the new ideologies of controlled capitalism and a managed working class. As metaphor, the figure validates the use of force on any system that evidences little tendency to hold value. The aestheticized female body thus becomes in much high modernist literature a stand-in for material chaos generally and class, labor, and gender displacement and democratization particularly. The violent invasion of this body by some transcendent and/or abstract force, furthermore, articulates the attraction that writers like T. S. Eliot, W. B. Yeats, and E. M. Forster felt toward totalitarianism. For all three writers, the rape is often a central metaphor for the hierarchic infusion of value even as the role of the implicitly or actually (presumably white, presumably non-working-class) masculine protagonist and/or speaker wavers and gains strength in relation to the event. Thus masculinized and individualized "productivity" comes to exist side by side with feminine and anarchic subordination to homogenous and abstracted power. The repression of man that might otherwise be implicit in the vision of divine domination is more or less neatly avoided, even in the face of capitalism's rape story excising from its own narrative the agency of the human rapist.

Eliot in particular feared and was disgusted by what he perceived to be the anarchy of increased democratization, and throughout his work the image of the raped woman articulates these feelings. The image withstands Eliot's first marriage and divorce, his conversion to Anglo-Catholicism, two world wars, and all the other personal and historic changes of the early twentieth century. The two major texts examined here, *The Waste Land* (1922) and *Murder in the Cathedral* (1935), return obsessively to the theme of feminine submission, the "awful daring of a moment's surrender" that might suggest a redemptive ordering of the "immense panorama of futility and anarchy" that was Eliot's overly democratized and secularized modern wasteland (*Collected Poems*, 68; "*Ulysses*" 480). It is generally agreed that the "moment's surrender" is represented for Eliot in sexual terms, as Anne Wright has pointed out. Jewel Spears Brooker has argued, somewhat similarly, that Eliot's "experience of fragmentation and his long-ing for the Absolute," although religious in nature, are often expressed as desire for "sexual transcendence" (14). Generally speaking, however, sexual transcendence for Eliot implies heterosexual subordination and violence. Rape is the ideal image to suggest the "daring" of Eliot's desired "full surrender to God" in that it allows masculine agency to be thought at the same time that the implicitly male reader/poet is enabled safely to associate with the subdued and effaced victim (Blamires 184).[2] The female body stands in for the meaningless material proliferation that must be crushed into meaning—or which invites even as it presumes through its mere existence the intercession of absolute force.

Eliot is thus both attracted to the woman figured as a rapable window of transcendent possibility and repulsed by what he sees as an excess of the personal, the material, and the chaotic in her "rank" body; the symbolic female body allows the transmission of value while the actual body eludes the trustworthiness of such a "language."[3] The speaker/poet/reader's relationship to the raping absolute, on the other hand, is always understated, always muted, and always and increasingly (if quietly) celebratory; realistically presented male characters, on the other hand, are generally sterile.[4] Because of this approving removal, what Eliot constructs through his many and interlocking images of rape is a voyeuristic fantasy in which the subject position vacillates between association with the force that rapes and the victim who is raped. A certain alienated solitude is thus confirmed at the same time that anarchy is checked: masculinized and individualized "productivity" exists side by side with feminine and anarchic subordination to homogenous and abstracted power.

In *The Waste Land*, it is the symbolic function of the woman's body to be permeable—to be a channel for undefined external force. Sexual violence, as opposed to male sterility, is far from "unnatural" in Eliot's work, as Philip Sicker would claim (422). The female body is represented as more or less degraded—more or less repulsive—depending on whether or not its materiality tends toward dissolution and effacement in its "rapability," as Catharine MacKinnon terms it, that condition/"position which is social, not biological, [and which] defines what woman *is*" (651). In general, actual female bodies of the twentieth century are limited to material proliferation and noise; this delineation accounts for "the various women in the poem who fail the quester," as Timothy Materer puts it (2). No doubt this same construction of femininity is associated with Eliot's thematic fascination with murdered women (Johnson 20). Susan Roberson argues that all women of Eliot's early period negatively indicate the "flesh" that he could not infuse with "spirit"; it would seem, however, that the raped bodies of history, literature, and myth do suggest something more—a more perfect horror and effacement (477). The mythicized and/or mythic female escapes her material constitution as "rank" and anarchically productive; her body as material sign is subdued to the invisible force of abstract value.

In *The Waste Land*, a useful contrast, for example, can be made between the woman typist and the Thames daughters of "The Fire Sermon"—all of whom generally represent the "archetype" of "the sexually violated yet sterile female" (Sicker 420). Sex, for the typist, is a degraded violation, meaninglessly bankrupt. She is "assault[ed]" in the midst of her drying underclothes by an all-too-personalized individual, the "carbuncular" clerk, himself constructed as a repulsive image of social mobility "on whom assurance sits / As a silk hat on a Bradford millionaire." The event, similarly, connotes nothing but its depraved materiality and is to be drowned out with the automated sound of the gramophone: "Her brain allows one half-formed thought to pass: / 'Well now that's done: and I'm glad it's over'" (*Collected Poems* 62). The solitude of the isolated woman, opiating herself on the mass-produced "art" of the mechanical age, clearly stands in for what Eliot constructs as the condition of humanity generally in the early twentieth century. It is important to note that in this scene, Eliot places the reader and narrator (Tiresias?) of the poem beside the woman and not the man, as Brooker and Bentley point out (56). In fact, Eliot excised earlier portions of "The Fire Sermon" that follow the progress of the clerk as he departs the scene:

> —Bestows one final patronizing kiss,
> And gropes his way, finding the stairs unlit;
> And at the corner where the stable is,
> Delays only to urinate, and spit.
> (*Waste Land Facsimile* 47)

The excision heightens the extent to which the point of view remains with her who is violated and not with the violator; the reader, then (by virtue of reading—by virtue of entering Eliot's wasteland), must not only side but remain with the victim.[5] This is not to say that point of view *is* the woman's; Tiresias remains voyeuristically apart from those he watches, enabling a flirtatious association with rape: Eliot thus "theatricalizes," as Christoph Irmscher puts it, "the peculiar tension between the two positions of looking (the voyeuristic seeing-without-being-seen) and of being looked at" (590). It is hard to see in this mobility of the voyeuristic gaze the "collapse of gender distinctions" that Purnima Bose—and Eliot himself—argue Tiresias represents; rape fantasies in *The Waste Land* speak more to Eliot's need for a palatable vision of submission than to his desire for androgyny.

The position assigned to the male reader is similar to that of Yeats's "Leda and the Swan," in which point of view does not soar with the swan but remains below, watching the raped woman.[6] Only three years before the publication of "Leda and the Swan" Yeats had, in fact, written another poem ("Nineteen Hundred and Nineteen" [1921]) in which the swan, explicitly used as metaphor for the individual soul, does focus the reader's view point:

> Some moralist or mythological poet
> Compares the solitary soul to a swan;
> I am satisfied with that,
> Satisfied if a troubled mirror show it,
> Before that brief gleam of its life be gone,
> An image of its state;
> The wings half spread for flight,
> The breast thrust out in pride
> Whether to play, or to ride
> Those winds that clamour of approaching night.
> (*Selected Poems* 115)

In "Leda" Yeats relinquishes the image of riding the wind to focus instead on the spectacle of the object of such powerful attention—not feeling her pain but watching, questioning her resistance, wondering—enviously?—about the precise nature of the gift that has fallen upon her unasked: "Did she put on his knowledge with his power / Before the indifferent beak could let her drop?" Hardly an "indictment of rape itself" (Nitsch and Parry 10), the poem, as Johnsen eloquently shows, was successively rewritten by Yeats to emphasize the awesome violence of the attack and the helplessness of Leda. Even as Yeats tentatively associates the speaker/reader with the female victim, then, the fact of the rape silently reinforces another *uninterrogated* point of view—that of the Yeatsian sense of "achieved masculinity" that is "marked" by "violence" (Vlasoplos 118). In *The Waste Land,* the point of view is similarly focused on the victim, but in the case of the typist there is no wonder or envy; this violated female has "put on" neither power nor knowledge.

The scene is followed by another scene of violation, however—that of the Thames sisters—in which more is promised. Again, point of view follows the victim, but this time that victimization offers the merest suggestion of the power and knowledge for which the speaker of "Leda and the Swan" yearns. First, the violation/rape of the Thames sisters is elevated above that of the modern woman by virtue of its literary and historical context—Edmund Spenser's *Prothalamion,* Robert Herrick's "His Tears to

Thamasis," the figures of Elizabeth and Leicester, and a letter of De Quadra to Philip of Spain. The event itself is further elevated above materiality in that it is not directly narrated but rather mourned from some future moment. In addition, the rapist/violator is abstracted through his complete excision from the narrative (we are not even sure if there is one or more, given that there is more than one woman and thus perhaps more than one sexual event). The most significant difference between the Thames sisters and the typist, however, is that the Thames sisters as a community mourn their violation and loss of the past. They speak their own rape and loss in a manner that subordinates any specific, material event to an abstract lament for modernist decay generally:

> 'Highbury bore me. Richmond and Kew
> Undid me. By Richmond I raised my knees
> Supine on the floor of a narrow canoe.'
> 'My feet are at Moorgate, and my heart
> Under my feet. After the event
> He wept. He promised "a new start."
> I made no comment.[7] What should I resent?'
> 'On Margate Sands.
> I can connect
> Nothing with nothing.[8]
> The broken fingernails of dirty hands.
> My people humble people who expect
> Nothing.'
> (*Collected Poems* 64)

As Yeats desired of Leda—to put on his knowledge with his power—this modernist voice of mourning "recognizes" and articulates the rhetorical function of her own body: she acknowledges herself as metaphor, echoing in her own violation the condition of humanity within the twentieth century as a whole. "Undone" and erased by the sexual violation—Richard Kane points that only parts of her body are visible to us (11)—the speaker recognizes that she no longer possesses a distinct "self" in need of expression: "I made no comment. What should I resent?" (*Collected Poems* 64). Self-effacement in the name of knowledge follows effacement in the name of power.

This "recognition" on the part of the raped woman of an essential emptiness through which the horror of absence might somehow express itself (thus in effect becoming a very present ontological force) marks what is in this poem, as well as in the voice of the chorus in *Murder in the Cathedral,* a point at which one might begin to think that the bodies of early-twentieth-century life might be organized in such a way as to produce value. Consciousness becomes a matter of a collective sense of mankind's helpless and depraved state in a society whose cultural fabric is in tatters: "My people humble people who expect / Nothing . . . I can connect / Nothing with nothing." It is this *recognition* of bankruptcy and the uselessness of signs ("I made no comment") that sets the Thames daughters apart from the typist of the preceding violation and that leads directly to—and is explicitly connected with—the revelation of St. Augustine that closes "The Fire Sermon": "Burning burning burning burning / O Lord Thou pluckest me out / O Lord Thou pluckest / burning" (11.308–11).[9] The violated woman, like the soul cleansed in purgatory and then taken back into the bosom of God, becomes a vessel for the expression of transcendent meaning—as force and as horror. Hers is a face wiped clean of illusions about democracy, individuality, and material accumulation; it is a face brought low before the Absolute. If anything can in *The Waste Land*, it is her body that becomes a "receptacle" for the engendering of value— that becomes, in fact, through the transubstantive spectacle of willing submission to hierarchy and power, a new form of specie: she is the money form whose value can be imposed from outside and above, the product that has accumulated value at the cost of human repression, and she is the word form whose meaning is similarly an expression of some greater power. She is, then, the nodal point of St. Augustine's vision that enables interpenetration between the City of God and the City of Man (Hay 49).

That the Thames sisters speak their effacement, then, is not to say that it is human (female) speech and/or agency that leads to the vision of purgatory. On the contrary, nonliterary speech (particularly female speech) is the heaviest form of material noise that *The Waste Land* offers; female speech is clearly fixed, as Tate argues, "in a subordinate hierarchical relationship to the other discourses in the poem, which together represent the complementary terms 'male/written/literary'" (163).[10] Speaking women (who do not speak their own effacement) constitute the largest body of evidence in the poem that Eliot's wasteland refers to a valueless, ugly twentieth-century world of overly democratized labor. Unlike the victims of rape and violation, these women are presented without sympathy; the reader is rarely invited to associate. Their speech is "chatter"—excessive noise without significance, mirroring the disorganized and uncontrolled people who have inexplicably come to set the moral climate of Western civilization— and who at the same time threaten the era's economic security. Lil, for example, whom Eileen Wiznitzer argues is the "repressed thematic center" of *The Waste Land*, does nothing but talk—about her anarchic material productivity and her physical decay. There is no evidence that her productivity makes of her a fertility symbol, as many try to argue; on the contrary, her labor produces what Eliot calls elsewhere the "filthy, sturdy, unkillable infants of the very poor" (*Collected Shorter Poems* 93). David Trotter is correct to claim that Lil represents Eliot's fear of "the 'defective element' in the population [that] was multiplying too rapidly," engendering "urban apocalypse" (152) and economic catastrophe. Lil's too-productive body speaks to the disastrous condition of surplus production, a condition to be closely associated with capitalism's vulnerability to crisis.[11]

The woman with "nerves" in "A Game of Chess" is equally garrulous, and her physical sterility only highlights the emptiness of her productions.[12] Her vociferousness contrasts with the male speaker/narrator's language, which is not only terser and to the point but registers the depths of horror of their situation, of their century:

> 'My nerves are bad to-night. Yes, bad. Stay with me.
> 'Speak to me. Why do you never speak. Speak.
> 'What are you thinking of? What thinking? What?
> 'I never know what you are thinking. Think.'
> I think we are in rat's alley
> Where the dead men lost their bones.
> (*Collected Poems* 57)

Embedded within this "dialogue" is a fragment of a scene from *Hamlet* in which Hamlet's speech and vision similarly contrast with Gertrude's: "'Do / 'You know nothing? Do you see nothing? do you remember / 'Nothing?'" (1.121–23). In this scene, Hamlet and Gertrude discuss, or talk around, the presence of Old Hamlet's ghost, and here it is the male speaker who interrogates the female:

> Hamlet: Do you see nothing there?
> Gertrude: Nothing at all; yet all that is I see.
> Hamlet: Nor did you nothing hear?
> Gertrude: No, nothing but ourselves (3.4.132–35)

The "nothing" of Hamlet's and Gertrude's dialogue is clearly not actually "nothing": Hamlet's "nothing" refers to his father's ghost, whose presence is confirmed by the audience; it is Gertrude's vision that is therefore in question and not Hamlet's ability to see an immaterial "something" within the emptiness of "nothing." In this case, then, once again, it is the male whose speech registers greater scope; Gertrude's voice articulates only the obvious material layer of things and as such puts the woman herself in the position of adding to the already problematic surplus of human talk, reason, and emotion. In fact it is this surplus of the feminine—the meaningless excess that is Gertrude—that flaws *Hamlet* as a play in Eliot's view: "it is just *because* [Gertrude's] character is so negative and insignificant that she arouses in Hamlet the feeling which he is incapable of representing. . . . [H]is disgust envelops and exceeds her" (*Selected Essays* 125). The play's lack of "objective correlative" is a result of excess (depraved) sexuality on Gertrude's part[13] and excess emotion on Hamlet's part when he cannot grapple with the fact of her body, her sexuality, and her speech.

An early draft of *The Waste Land* includes Fresca, who provides the most damning judgment in the poem—perhaps in Eliot's work generally—on the materially productive woman. The Fresca section, at best "marred by an unpleasant misogyny" (Svarny 189), is modeled on Alexander Pope's *The Rape of the Lock* and mocks, in this case, a female poet "baptised in a soapy sea / of Symonds–Walter Pater–Vernon Lee" (*Waste Land Facsimile* 41). In some "other time or place" Fresca might have been "A meek and lowly weeping Magdalene; / More sinned against than sinning, bruised and marred," but in her present place, surrounded by her own proliferating verbiage (seventeen lines of chattering letter, "clever books," "scribble[d] verse," etc.), she has been reduced to secondary visions of effacement, "dreams of love and pleasant rapes" and the "pathetic tale of Richardson" (39). The source of the humor, then, is twofold: her attempt at aesthetic productivity on one hand and her association with "pleasant" and/or acceptably bourgeois rape on the other. Although Tiresias (as well as the reader) can silently "vibrate between two lives," between subject and object of rape or of art, for example, the positions are mutually exclusive when examined closely. Fresca is "by fate misbred"—"the inevitable product of an unnatural age of transvestite costumes, masks, disguises" (Gilbert 79)—and becomes in the poem a grotesque image of female fertility: she is represented in the act of defecation, and what her "labour" brings forth represents the "good old hearty female stench" that defines her (*Waste Land Facsimile* 39). The reek of her production, of her "mother wit," cannot be "disguise[d]," even by perfumes "confected by the cunning French" (41, 39).

These material excesses of the female body (chatter, sexuality, children, feces) are ideally emptied out, or silenced, by rape; in this way the unruly female body is forced to speak only the music of the transcendent. Many have commented on the multiple allusions to Philomel in *The Waste Land* (and in much else of Eliot's work); her presence speaks to this desire for silencing. Briefly,[14] Philomel—Milton's spelling of Philomela, the nightingale in "Il Penseroso"—is the figure in Greek myth who is raped by her sister Procne's husband (Tereus) and whose tongue is then cut out by the rapist to prevent her telling the story.[15] Bypassing speech, Philomela weaves the story of her violation into a tapestry, and in revenge for the rape, she and Procne kill Itys, Tereus's (and Procne's) son, and serve him to the father in a meal, which he consumes. The gods then transform the sisters into birds—Philomela into a nightingale, Procne into a swallow—in order that they can escape Tereus's wrath.

Thus eroticized, bloody, violated, speechless and yet possessed of unspeakable knowledge, it is this female body—and not the body of the woman who is physically fertile, who breeds the "swarming life" of London—that offers redemption to the wasteland, ideological value to an otherwise disorganized, useless populace (*Waste Land Facsimile* 43). Her feminine excesses (her tongue, her [sister's] children) have been cut away—to the point where she becomes something other than a woman. In fact, it is "the *change* of Philomel" (my emphasis) that is represented, the metamorphosis orchestrated by the god, the transformation of the material body "by the barbarous king / So rudely forced" to the more ethereal nightingale of "inviolable voice" (*Collected Poems* 56). Through a "violent appropriation" of her own "power to speak" (Joplin 41), Philomel is made into the "inviolable"—if incomprehensible—sign of a transcendent other; her horror and mutilation enable this other to speak, or, more accurately, to suggest itself in the inhuman music of birdsong. All clean lines and empty interior, she forces, in turn, the message of this new body onto man, feeding him the murdered embodiment of (his) material (re)production: "Twit twit twit / Jug jug jug jug jug jug / So rudely forced" (*Collected Poems* 61). The final appearance of Hieronymo reinforces the references to Philomel and Procne as well. The reference is to the scene in Thomas Kyd's *Spanish Tragedy* in which Hieronymo, after his garbled play of many languages, bites out his own tongue and spits it at his torturers, thus refusing to speak. The scene is, like Philomel, a bloody sign of human speech and the impossibility of reasonable and useful human agency; only through violent curtailment is the human element with its entire material surplus subordinated to the meaningful and valuable.[16]

The raped woman in this way eroticizes submission for the modern reader/voyeur at the same time that rape is rescripted as graceful subordination to an external force "never to be revealed to humankind" (North, "Eliot," 179). In the case of Philomel, for example, we gradually get the impression that she is "forced" less by Tereus than by the god himself; he is the one who effects her metamorphosis. A mortal man cannot violate in the mythic sense. "Sweeney," then, is not the rapist "among the nightingales" who "[sing] within the bloody wood / When Agamemnon [cries] aloud"; Sweeney is only the debased figure ironically distanced from the reader and speaker who chants that "Any man has to, needs to, wants to / Once in a lifetime, do a girl in" ("Sweeney Among the Nightingales," "Fragment of an Agon"). A clearly masculinized space is thus opened for violent agency, but this terrain remains opaque, and whoever inhabits it—Sweeney? God?—is undefined. *The Waste Land* waits, a heap of broken images, rapable in its disorder like its series of women in the vulnerable moment of or just before penetration. The subject position can well be imagined, then, to have the active potential to shore fragments while yet confronting the commandment to submit to external control.[17] The female (i.e., rapable) body provides this symbolic option, becoming thereby a vision of "salvation." This is not to argue that Christian dogma informed Eliot's earlier thinking so much as to suggest that his later conversion to Christianity meshed easily with the tropes of his early work that enabled him to establish (male) agency in the face of some unnamed other. The humility of the "masses," the effacement of the individual in the face of ontological force, the redemption through the debasement of the material (female body)—all of these were concerns of Eliot's before his conversion to Anglo-Catholicism. In his mythic rapes, Eliot can believe in the violent reinfusion of pure and unobstructed value into what he seemed to see as capitalism gone mad in useless, pointless material proliferation.

In *Murder in the Cathedral,* written after, of course, Eliot's religious conversion, the raped woman endures as a dominant, even controlling, image and has become more clearly developed as the blank body through which God will speak. In this religious play, the wasteland is at last redeemed. Society, figured as a collective woman, the chorus, is symbolically assaulted and raped by the god, its fragmentation infiltrated by irresistible and impersonal power; in this way an integrated and hierarchically arranged society is established. The role of the (male) protagonist in this redemption, however, has become more central: instead of merely watching, vacillating as does Tiresias between the prescribed gender positions of rapist and rape victim, the male subject now subsumes the role of priest and has at his command the transubstantiation of bread (the female body) into divine essence. Thomas Becket, priest/protagonist of *Murder in the Cathedral,* serves a function not unlike that of Eliot's great poet, the "shred of platinum" who catalyzes the transmission (or transubstantiation) of the absolute into language, thus constructing an art form that approaches the liturgy and a liturgical form that is art (*Selected Essays* 7). Still subordinate to the transcendent (in this case, the Christian God the Father), the subject position now includes the ability to direct the hierarchal flow of external information, power, and value. Becket is poet, priest, and banker—faceless agent of exchange for the transcendent (whether that "transcendent" be conceived as meaning, God, or value). The word, the wafer, and the female body are the forms in which he traffics.

Murder in the Cathedral opens on the (all-female) chorus, which remains on stage for almost the entire play, relentlessly bringing to mind the shattered and segmented society which it represents and which is a backdrop for and cause of the central action (the murder of Thomas). Although the members of the chorus speak from a collective "we" point of view, "individual wom[e]n disappear[ing] into an amorphous" group, they see themselves as essentially alienated, not unlike the Thames sisters (Roberson 479):

> We have suffered various oppression,
> But mostly we are left to our own devices,
> And we are content if we are left alone. (12)

Not only do the women feel a severance from each other, but from their leaders as well. A great gulf separates the powerful and the not-so-powerful, allowing for "oppression" and "extortion" (43). The economy is equally disassociated, equally anarchic, production and exchange having no interdependence:

> We try to keep our households in order;
> The merchant, shy and cautious, tries to compile a
>   little fortune,
> And the labourer bends to his piece of earth, earth-colour,
>   his own colour,
> Preferring to pass unobserved. (12)

The merchant hoards, the laborer suffers, no product results, and no value accumulates to keep the system circulating.

This social and economic fragmentation grounds the sense of horror that dominates *Murder in the Cathedral;* as in *The Waste Land,* the "fear in a handful of dust" haunts the isolated individuals who are ready for redemption (*Collected Poems* 54): "We have all had our private terrors, / Our particular shadows, our secret fears" (20). One by one the people seem to be dissolving, meeting some horrible and unknown end that speaks of violation and torture: "Several girls have disappeared / Unaccountably, and some not able to" (20). The community, or, more accurately, conglomeration of individuals, is dominated by this impending sense of doom. The women of the chorus claim that theirs "is no continuing city" (18), a description that resonates with the "unreal city" of *The Waste Land* in which the dead masses flow over London Bridge, "And each man fixed his eyes before his feet" (*Collected Poems* 55). The members of the chorus lack a sense of continuum; any flow consists of a random movement of disconnected particles.

Similarly, at a more abstract level, the chorus's lines register a certain metaphysical desolation as well. Experience itself has been split, at least into dualities; a mythically whole past, it is implied, has been lost to "A heap of broken images" (*Collected Poems* 53). The women are possessed with "A fear like birth and death, when we see birth and death alone, / In a void apart" (20). Significantly, it is the experience of the productive female body (giving birth) that has entered the void, becoming meaningless through disconnection from the experience of death. Human (female) productivity is not—as it is not in *The Waste Land*—a source or symbol of fertility and life. Like Lil and Fresca, productive women speak more to the specter of decay, the "humble and tarnished frame of existence" that is theirs: "O late late late, late is the time, late too late, and rotten the year" (20, 18). Existence as totality and continuity has run its course, and the chorus asks only to be left "to perish in quiet" (19). The women feel at home only in an atmosphere of death or dying, in "decaying October" (13), "sombre November" (11), and "dismal December" (17), seasons that reflect the status of the community generally:

> Since golden October declined into sombre November
> And the apples were gathered and stored, and the land
>   became brown sharp points of death in a waste of
>   water and mud. (11)

The dominant anapestic rhythm of this section is broken by the spondees; attention is drawn to the "brown sharp points of death," long-stressed syllables with waiting gaps between. The prosody reflects the women: they are broken, effaced, open, and waiting.

Into this sociopolitical wasteland of fragmentation, horror, and despair comes Thomas Becket. At first the chorus and the reader/audience mistakenly believe that he will be the fisher king, will redeem and heal the land and this society. He is presented, in fact, as another Christ. The women ask whether "the Son of Man [shall] be born again in the litter of scorn" (13), and they call upon Thomas to "save us, save us" (44). The greeting with which they meet Thomas is a clear parallel to the people's welcoming of Jesus into Jerusalem:

> He comes in pride and sorrow, affirming all his claims,
> Assured, beyond doubt, of the devotion of the people,
> Who receive him with scenes of frenzied enthusiasm,
> Lining the road and throwing down their capes,
> Strewing the way with leaves and late flowers of the season. (15–16)

The chorus is convinced that Thomas, like Christ, will ultimately "[lay] down his life for the sheep," will be sacrificed for the health of the entire flock. The women thus place themselves in Tiresias's position; they believe that their role in the eternal design requires only that they witness the archbishop's martyrdom. They paint themselves at a sovereign remove from the sacrificial action:

> . . . .Some presage of an act
> Which our eyes are compelled to witness, has forced
>   our feet
> Towards the cathedral. We are forced to bear witness.
> [. . .]
> For us, the poor, there is no action,
> But only to wait and to witness. (11, 13)

The women of the chorus present themselves as being like the circle of women around Christ's crucified body, removed from the central drama.

In *Murder in the Cathedral,* however, it is not precisely the body of Christ (or the saint—Becket) that comes to stand as the symbol of mediation between God and man. After successfully confronting the tempters who try to turn him away from the narrow road of heroic purity and endeavor, Thomas turns (to the chorus? the tempters and priests? the audience?) and relinquishes the role of redeeming savior:

> But for every evil, every sacrilege,
> Crime, wrong, oppression and the axe's edge,
> Indifference, exploitation, you, and you,
> And you, must all be punished. So must you.
> I shall no longer act or suffer, to the sword's end. (46)

In the archbishop's next appearance he is administering the Christmas mass, presiding over the transubstantiation of the bread. His voice, having lost individuality in repeating the mass, has entered into the solemn power of (male) tradition. From this point to his death, he experiences no noticeable internal conflict. He meets death unflinchingly, dissolving without protest into the murder that is represented as homoerotic ecstasy. Thomas dies in a "consummation" (23, 70) with God as absolute power. It is not the knights, ultimately, or King Henry, who is completely removed from the scene, but the "good Angel, whom God appoints / To be my guardian" who "hover[s] over the swords' points" (46), driving them through his body. In this "joyful consummation" (70), previously sensed boundaries are dissolved and Thomas enters into the canon of saints (as great poetry jostles its way into the canon of great literature in "Tradition and the Individual Talent").

Nonetheless, the audience is clearly invited to associate with the women of the chorus and not with Thomas; Richard Badenhausen argues that Eliot himself felt that it was the chorus that represented his own position the most clearly. It is certainly the case that, from this early point in the play, dramatic attention turns to and remains with the chorus and its meeting with God. The reader is thus united with the rootless, democratized mass that, paradoxically, speaks for the poet even as it is crushed by some Other power.[18] Unlike Thomas, the women neither experience their "consummation" as "joyful" nor articulate the sense that they are entering into the absolute. Instead, the "gaps" of their social alienation are violently invaded by the embodiment of their own horror before God, and they are subdued, effaced, and homogenized through the experience. In this way, their alienation and fragmentation are "healed," washed in the blood of (their own) sacrifice. The first sign we have of the change of the role of the chorus from witness to victim is located in the scene of Thomas's confrontation with the Fourth Tempter, at the same time that the archbishop's role as savior is abandoned. Here, the women articulate their growing sense of religious despair:

> God is leaving us, God is leaving us, more pang, more
>> pain than birth or death.
> Sweet and cloying through the dark air
> Falls the stifling scent of despair. (44)

Desire for God's return is associated with the (physical) pain of childbearing, which is in turn associated, once again, with death. The source of the pain, the source of the desire, is the womb; the womb, at the same time, is associated with death. If the desired God returns, surely he will subdue this source of pain, desire, and material death. In fact he does return—and as promised in *The Waste Land,* what he brings is "fear in a handful of dust" (*Collected Poems* 54). The women's own horror surrealistically gathers itself into a visible form that infiltrates this decaying society/collective woman through all its fractures and gaps, all the holes, cracks, and orifices of the architecture and the body:

> . . . but now
> a new terror has soiled us, which none can avert,
> . . . flowing . . .
> Under doors and down chimneys, flowing in at the ear
>> and the mouth and the eye. (43–44)

The women's fear is hardly represented as "illusory" here, as Michael Goldman argues it is; it seems rather to have achieved a relatively high ontological status (45). Originating in social fragmentation and isolation, the terror is externalized as an attribute of the divine that finds its passage-way back into the community through the very gaps that have created it.[19]

The penetrative power of this externalized terror increases in the sec-ond act as Thomas's death comes nearer:

> Still the horror, but more horror
> Than when tearing in the belly. (71)

Just as their own fear is externalized and figured in the force that will vio-lently penetrate them, their reproductive processes ("tearing in the belly") are similarly externalized as a description of rape or abortion ("tearing in the belly"). They become, in effect, alienated from their own "labor." As in *The Waste Land*, what women produce is the sign of what must be violated, sub-dued, and effaced—here, in the name of the Father. In the "death-bringer" passage the women even more clearly state that they are undergoing a rape:

> Nothing is possible but the shamed swoon
> Of those consenting to the last humiliation.
> I have consented, Lord Archbishop, have consented.
> Am torn away, subdued, violated. (68)

They realize that they will be forced to act, but that that act will be limit-ed to submitting to this "final ecstasy of waste and shame" (68). Thus they fulfill their half of what Kurt Tetzeli Von Rosador argues is the "paradox-ical" nature of "the Christian history of salvation" played out in *Murder in the Cathedral:* the "simultaneity of willing and consenting, of action and suffering" (522). They call out their subordination to Thomas, the admin-istrator of this mass/transubstantiation/violation.

The rape is presented as a violent cleansing, an emptying out (thus the "tearing" that connotes both rape and abortion). The women as women are effaced completely, united with the material earth:

> . . . I have tasted
> The living lobster, the crab, the oyster, the whelk and
>   the prawn; and they live and spawn in my bowels. (67)

This union with materiality is ultimately a "foul" one; it presents to the women the vision of their essential depravity and valuelessness. It also makes the women realize—as do the Thames sisters—the extent to which their violation is ultimately only the revelation of the depraved condition that defines humanity. In this wasteland,

. . . there are no objects, no tones,
No colours, no forms to distract, to divert the soul
From seeing itself, foully united forever, nothing with nothing.
[. . .]
We are soiled by a filth that we cannot clean, united to supernatural
 vermin,
It is not we alone, it is not the house, it is not the city that is defiled,
But the world that is wholly foul. (72, 77–78)

The irony here is that the chorus has at this point lost its sense of fragmentation; it conceives of itself as without boundaries and divisions—a picture of homogeneity in the face of obliteration:

The agents of hell disappear, the human, they shrink
 and dissolve
Into dust on the wind, forgotten, unmemorable; only
 is here
The white flat face of Death, God's silent servant. (70)

In the horror of this "foul" integration, the women continue to call for God's intercession: "Help me, Lord, in my last fear" (72). As Thomas has told them, however, there will be no intercession; all must be "punished." He warns the women, in fact, that this horror will become more intense, that a deeper penetration is forthcoming, one that has its source less in their own reflexive terror and more in God himself as an external and highly masculinized force:

Peace, and be at peace with your thoughts and visions.
These things had to come to you and you to accept them.
. . . This is one moment,
But know that another
Shall pierce you with a sudden painful joy
When the figure of God's purpose is made complete. (69)

As Yeats's speaker hopes of Leda, the women of the chorus will put on knowledge as they "put on" the god's power. They become, again like Leda, "the mere pivot of Zeus's [God's] power to make his own history"—a history that refutes their own culture (Johnsen 83–84):

Have I not known, not known
What was coming to be? It was here . . .
[. . .]

> In our veins our bowels our skulls
> As well as in the plottings of potentates
> As well as in the consultations of powers.
> What is woven on the loom of fate
> What is woven in the councils of princes
> Is woven also in our veins, our brains. (68)

As in the Philomela myth, the raped and mutilated women are associated with weaving—weaving a "true" story that is significant not so much for its content but for the horrible fact that it is unspeakable—and ultimately incomprehensible as it mutates (by the power of the god) into the song of the nightingale.[20] In *Murder in the Cathedral,* however, the women are denied the *act* of weaving; it is they who are woven into fate's incomprehensible story.

Throughout the last sections of the play—during that other moment that "shall pierce you with a sudden painful joy"—the wasteland begins to bleed. The women themselves are thus "washed in the blood"—although there is no crucified god here, only their own bodies to provide the healing substance. In terms of image, the blood actually emerges from the land itself:

> . . . I wander in a land
> of barren boughs: if I break them, they bleed; I
> wander in a land of dry stones: if I touch them
> they bleed. (77)

All material objects—including the female body—serve as chalices, holding within them the blood that in Christian mythology is endowed with the power to transmute all substances to the same (divine) essence:

> Can I look again at the day and its common things,
> and see them all smeared with blood, through a
> curtain of falling blood? (77)

Pure value flows unobstructed through this effaced world; no anarchy, no desire, no difference blocks its transmission. Material proliferation is smoothed over, subdued to a single, externally based essence.

Only at this point, "enriched" with blood, can the wasteland be said to be fertile; from the bloody land "springs that which forever renews the earth" (87). The debased fertility of their bodily productivity has been transformed—as is Philomel—through a divine act described no more precisely than a "tearing in the belly." Imagistically, then, it is more the blood that is associated with violent penetration that provides the image of redemption than that which is associated with childbearing. In their final speech the women of the chorus acknowledge this newly fertile ground and their involvement with its renewal:

> . . . we acknowledge
> That the sin of the world is upon our heads; that the
>   blood of the martyrs and the agony of the saints
> Is upon our heads. (88)

The audience is presented with female shame, guilt, and sacrifice as the Eucharistic offering; in this bread the pure (if incomprehensible) essence of God is given to man. The violated and effaced female body thus comes to resemble what Gilles Deleuze and Felix Guattari refer to as the necessary nodal point in advanced capitalist systems which (mindlessly) control the flow of surplus value; Thomas presides over the hollowing out of this nodal point, this joint in transmission (226), this vessel for God's word.

The broken female body, by extension, provides figurative proof of the transmission of ineffable value. In "La Figlia che Piange," written years before *Murder in the Cathedral*, Eliot is already suggesting this symbolism. In the poem, a voyeuristic speaker, not unlike Tiresias, watches a man leave a woman and finds in the image the sign of the classic soul and body split:

> So I would have had him leave,
> So I would have had her stand and grieve,
> So he would have left
> As the soul leaves the body torn and bruised,
> As the mind deserts the body it has used.
> (*Collected Poems* 26)

Like the wasteland itself, in Eliot's work the broken female body always suggests the silent presence of its "opposite," and whether that immaterial opposite be figured as value, meaning, soul, God, or sheer ontological force, it is always masculinized, and it is always implicitly violent. The matter/mater that the woman's body has generally represented in Western history, particularly under capitalism, is thus given a particular twist in the high modernist period. Still the embodiment of materiality, the modernist female image is not so much nature to be understood, virgin territory to be explored, conquered, and/or settled, or an open market for amassing wealth; she is rather the anarchy that must be crushed by power, the democratization that must be subdued to social hierarchy, the proliferations of capitalism that must submit to (state? monopoly?) control, and—

most obviously—the epistemological fragmentation that must be infused with transcendent meaning.

The raped (or rapable) female body thus provides Eliot with the symbolic ground on which he can struggle with the very real economic and sociopolitical forces that problematize masculine Euro-American identity even as that always present image of submission quietly reestablishes "the [male] individual [as] the conceptual limit of Eliot's . . . discourse" (Venuti 178). This gambit to return ineffable value to a democratized and anarchic twentieth century is not a unique one, however; it merely brings to fruition a prevalent modernist tendency to locate in the raped female body the suggestion of transcendence. E. M. Forster was another modernist who undertook a remarkably similar project, using the raped female body to articulate modernist concerns about empire and race in addition to those about democratization and the instabilities of capitalism. As in Eliot's work, in Forster's *A Passage to India,* Adela's vague experience works to transform rape into an immaterial event imposed not by the force of the (in this case raced) man but by the unnamably abstract. Brenda Silver examines the ways in which the text recoils from an explicit naming or narrating of the incident—it interprets itself quickly away from a consideration of the material base of Adela Quested's experience. It is of crucial significance that Forster rewrote the "rape" scene, in fact, to make the event into a "non-event"; in an earlier draft of *A Passage to India,* Aziz does actually assault Adela.[21] That the "rape" does not happen in the published version—that it is presented instead as either the hallucination of a sexually repressed female or the encounter of that female with some horrible and abstract truth that she misinterprets—removes the (non)event from the realm of the material to that of the symbolic *and* unspeakable; Fred D. Crawford has traced the similarities between the sound of the caves and "what the thunder said" (Eliot, *Collected Poems,* 66) In fact the word "rape" is never used, as Silver points out. What is thus disguised—above and beyond the reality of rape—is a very Western disgust with the body, with bodily contact between whites and nonwhites, and with the more general notion of imperial breakdown. What is brought to the center is not only the possibility of abstract masculinized force but also the suggestion of transcendent meaning—even the horrible "meaning" of nothingness—in the wasteland of material blankness. The rapable female body is the terrain on which all of this is played out; she enables a book about imperialism and rape to become a book about horror in the face of the undying worm.

The rapable female body thus offered certain varieties of modernist ideology a way of transmuting the material of history—war, monetary depression, vast, automated production—into the sign of a transcendent

other: If sadism demands a story, it also suggests a protagonist. One cannot help but think, then, not only of the fascism Eliot (unconvincingly)
denied as a cure for the decaying and seemingly valueless world of
post–World War I Europe but also of the role the female body played in
validating fascism generally. Certainly Ezra Pound turned again and again
in his *Cantos* to the image of the raped woman as backdrop for the "factive
personality"; there are literally hundreds of references in the work as a
whole to violated females of myth and history. Before writing his celebration of Hitler, Wyndham Lewis wrote *Tarr*, which has a rape as its central
event; the Blast and Futurist movements clearly celebrated masculine penetrative violence. For the European avant-garde, as Naomi Segal has established, "the heroic phallus is an instrument not of love, but of rape" (237).
In short, the narrative rapability of the metaphoric female body served as
a plank upon which some modernists attempted to cross the abyss of the
early twentieth century with their gods, their gold, and their sovereignty
intact: "For Modern Man does seem to be crossing some kind of Great
Void. There is a Track to be followed and he has been told that the map to
the Oasis is inscribed on her Body . . . is Track to accompany him in his
quest? if yes, in what way? and if no, where is it that she would like to go
instead? What will she ultimately make of this unexpected twist in the
patriarchal story?" (Jardine 64).

3

ENGINEERING FASCISM
AYN RAND, EZRA POUND, AND
THE VIRILE HERO

History generally credits the United States with ideological removal from the fascist thought that swept across Europe after World War I. Instead, "Taylorism" or "Fordism" serve as slogans for our collective memory of the zeitgeist of the American 1920s and 1930s: as Europe dreamed of force, autocracy, and genocide, the United States lived an almost collectivist ethic of efficient production, scientific management, and affordable technology. While Germany and Italy worshiped at the altar of the charismatic leader, the United States worked, led to the front of the world economic order by the technological application of visionary science. Mark Antliff has shown, however, that in reality the two worlds were not necessarily so distinctive: many European fascists actually celebrated the "collaborative spirit" of Fordism as an exemplary model of industrial production that would promote a strong and adequately rewarded working class through increased production, lowered costs of goods, and simultaneously increased wages (156). Similarly, one might connect the American "cult of the engineer" with the hero cults of Europe. Cecelia Tichi and Lisa Steinman have established that in the United States modernist desire was directed at the figure of the engineer and/or inventor—the master of matter (mater), chaos, and dissolution. The American engineer—whether physical or social—could be imagined the still point of the turning world, the falconer whose voice could still be heard; the politics of these representations argue for an explicitly reactionary response to what was perceived as the disorder of modern society.

In Europe, the epic vision of the fascist leader promised a similar redemption. While it is true, as Zeev Sternhell argues, that "few contemporary political concepts are so fluid and so ill defined" as fascism, theorists of fascist ideology, culture, and rhetoric have long accepted the central and spectacular role of the leader in the fascist body politic (2). Russell

Berman, for example, makes the case that although fascism is "hostil[e] to particular identity," it simultaneously celebrates the "incarnation of the will in the body of the leader" (109). In fact, it is precisely the idealized role of the leader that gives every appearance of having resolved the split Jeffrey Schnapp has identified in fascist "ideology" between "corporate conformity" and "heroic individualism"; hero worship is one of the many ways that fascism gives itself over to "aesthetic overproduction . . . to compensate for, fill in, and cover up its forever unstable ideological core." It is in this way that the hero worship endemic to fascism "makes of paradox a productive principle" (3), investing the idealized "new man" with all the "vital" symbolic heft of technological dynamism (Mosse 94–95). Nothing short of the total naturalized reengineering of the nation-state rests in the hands of the leader. His use of violence, further, is not only the "vehicle of . . . regeneration; it [is] the authentic source of creative energy in a fascist order" (Schnapp 5). His productive violence is a stand-in for "barbaric vitality," "a new creative spirituality" (Gentile 30). It is in this way that "virility," as Barbara Spackman argues, becomes the master term of fascist ideology, to the extent, in fact, that "Fascist rhetoric *is* a rhetoric of virility" (my emphasis, 5).

Representations of the raped female body show how high modernist thought eased into the aesthetics of fascism through the celebration of the virile hero.[1] Writers like Ayn Rand and Ezra Pound moved away from a vision of the raping god toward representations of secular, heroic rape. (The move from divine to secular mirrors the fascist maneuver of appropriating the symbolic power and hierarchy of Christianity by secularizing it.)[2] Both Rand and Pound yoke "factive" leadership to technological mastery and validate that conjunction through the image of the raped woman. As in T. S. Eliot, the raped female body suggests abstract value, but her presence speaks much more forcefully to the power of the factive personality to mobilize the dissociated elements of production into a model of humming efficiency that expresses his highly individualized will. In addition, Pound in particular deals in highly sexually realized and productive women—women who represent the unrestrained proliferations of twentieth-century capitalism. Unlike Eliot, who also deals in productive women, Pound does not place the proliferating female body in traditional opposition to "meaning," however; if she is still the matter/mater/matrix upon which abstract value is manufactured, her physical productions are rarely evidence of material decay or depravity. This difference speaks in part to the fact that Pound's meaning economy, like that of fascism, is not a particularly mimetic one: it does not depend upon a transcendent body of value that must break forcefully into the material realm. No less hierarchical than Eliot's, then, Pound's vision of the relationship between power and value rests upon the subordination of bodies, things, and meaning systems to masculinized power. The result is a flattening of reality to a single plane on which human (masculine) potency replaces the possibility of a transcendent realm. Like the pocket toy cut by Gaudier-Brzeska, which, as "a sacred object," is "elusively anthropomorphic and ichthymorphic, with no god but its own vigor" (Kenner, *The Pound Era,* 53), the mimetic image loses a great deal of ground.

Similarly, under fascism proper, the invaded female body no longer suggests transcendent intervention but signifies instead deified state control over the means of production and reproduction. Under fascism—in both its German and Italian varieties—the state owned the female body; it was figured (in itself and in its representations) as a natural resource. Because this was the case, that body was conscripted to the "cult of motherhood," which was in turn in the service of the leader—whether his programs were defined specifically as purification (in the case of German eugenics) or energized (re)production (in the case of Italian campaigns encouraging increased birthrates).[3] In the same way, the raped women in *The Fountainhead* and *The Cantos* ultimately speak not of divinity in all of its transcendent incomprehensibility but of the force of (great) human personality to reenergize production, thus to control the crisis possibilities endemic to capitalism. The victims speak not of their own effacement before the absolute—although certainly they are effaced—but of their now increased (re)productive capabilities. Thus female (re)production is not only conscripted to the symbolic and actual service of the virile hero but is crucial in ideologically legitimating the force necessary for the unification and mobilization of economic and technological enterprise. This conjunction of virile leader, technological enterprise, and raped feminized figure is made glaringly obvious in the work of the Italian futurists. Filippo Tommaso Marinetti's misogynist technophilia, for example, is graphically imaged in this encouragement to war written in 1909:

> My airplane runs on its wheels, skates along, and then up again in flight! [. . .]
>   Continue the massacre! . . . Watch me! I seize the stick and glide smoothly down. . . . See the furious coitus of war, gigantic vulva stirred by the friction of courage, shapeless vulva that spreads to offer itself to the terrific spasm of final victory! . . . I raise my sights to a hundred meters! . . . Ready! . . . Fire! (87, 42, 53–54)

The "shapeless" wasteland of matter—read explicitly here as mater—will be given form through the violent penetration by the sovereign masculine cyborg.

Although defending herself throughout her life against charges of fascism, Ayn Rand is a writer who demonstrates clearly how high modernism edged toward fascist thought via the reification of personality—and how rape served as a central trope in this development. Rand is capitalism's celebrant extraordinaire whose project is always to represent the subordination of the proliferations of capitalism (including the democratized masses) to the great personality/entrepreneur/architect. Capitalism is thus validated by being pictured as containing within its machinery not only recurrent crises of accumulation and stagnation but the "heroes" whose factivity is based in the opportunity to mobilize this chaotic matter into coherent expression. What is expressed in this gesture remains opaque: is it the absolute, the vigor of the organizer, or the very act of organization itself? It is a function of the violence of gender constructions and the centrality of those images to Western thought that rape helps to negotiate these questions. Rand's *The Fountainhead,* written in the 1930s and published in 1943, stages an explicit connection between rape, capitalism, and production written in this period.

The novel's rapist and protagonist, Howard Roark, is a brilliant young architect who resists without wavering the mediocre and derivative art of his time. In the climax of the novel, he blows up a building that he has designed and whose facade has been tinkered with by others. He stands trial as a result and is acquitted after personally presenting to the jury a long and stirring speech about American individuality and his own right to expression. Thus, on one hand—particularly in the beginning of the novel—Roark's heroic status is a function of the unique interiority of his own vision and the "competence" of that vision to correspond reflexively to external reality; his productivity is actually "productive utility"—the ability to make visible the juncture between interior and exterior truth (Baker 95). This emphasis gradually fades from the text, however, and Roark comes to reify production for its own sake; "production becomes the value," as Andrew Hewitt argues of fascist modernism generally (138). "Truth" in Rand becomes not the realization of correspondence between inner and outer (even if abstract) reality but rather an endless "push for achievement" realized in the person of the architect (Uyl and Rasmussen 174).

Cecelia Tichi's *Shifting Gears* has established that in modern (American) popular culture and literature, the engineer embodied the highly individualized (and masculine) force that promised to organize and redeem the deplorable conditions of waste and inefficiency imagined to plague productive systems. My own understanding of Tichi's thesis assumes that the structures envisioned and built by great engineers (of which category the architect is a subgroup) did not in and of themselves offer redemption to a disorderly world; rather, those structures were perceived to be expressions

of human energy, and they reified not the return of permanent and structured value but rather the power of the factive spirit and the mythical force
of controlled production. It seems to me that this is how the "cult of the
engineer" validated Fordist changes in material production and human-
ized the philosophy of Frederick Winslow Taylor (1856–1915), mechanical engineer and author of the extremely authoritarian "cult of efficiency,"
which promised to maximize production.

True to the Taylorist vision of efficiency, a significant part of the productivity of Roark the architect is the subordination (or self-subordina-
tion) of crews of men to the great man's will and vision. As Roark submits
during his apprenticeship to the greater experience of Henry Cameron, so
does he expect the same submission of his men to his architectural projects. The inherent "right of the ego" is thus balanced by men's individual
recognitions of their "proper function":

> "No work is ever done collectively, by a majority decision. Every
> creative job is achieved under the guidance of a single individual
> thought. An architect requires a great many men to erect his build-
> ing. But he does not ask them to vote on his design. They work
> together by free agreement and each is free in his proper function.
> An architect uses steel, glass, concrete, produced by others. But the
> materials remain just so much steel, glass and concrete until he
> touches them. What he does with them is his individual product
> and his individual property. This is the only pattern for co-opera-
> tion among men." (682)

Rand rightly defends herself that her belief in egotism does not inspire
anarchy.[4] Only a few have the innate capacity for Roark's type of achievement (the talent to approximate an external truth that is always receding
from view and importance), and all other men do well to recognize the
brilliance of the leader and their own functions in relation to him.

In her essays, Rand makes explicitly clear that by subordination to a
great man she does not imply force or violence on the part of that leader.
"Force and mind," she claims, "are opposites; morality ends where a gun
begins" ("This Is John Galt Speaking" 134). This type of collectivism is at
the heart of capitalism, for Rand; it registers the spirit of contractual agree-
ment. Nonetheless, it is difficult to overlook the suggestions of violence
and of violent force in Rand's fiction, particularly in *The Fountainhead*. At
one level, Rand and her heroes clearly celebrate the force of man over
nature, as in this scene where Roark contemplates the natural scenery
before him: "These rocks, he thought, are here for me; waiting for the
drill, the dynamite and my voice; waiting to be split, ripped, pounded,

reborn; waiting for the shape my hands will give them" (16). At a more troubling level, Roark is also a rapist—at least of the woman whom he loves, and the act of rape defines and delimits his person, outlining the features of his power that might not otherwise be apparent:

> [Dominique] fought like an animal. But she made no sound. She did not call for help. She heard the echoes of her blows in a gasp of his breath, and she knew that it was a gasp of pleasure. She reached for the lamp on the dressing table. He knocked the lamp out of her hand. The crystal burst to pieces in the darkness. He had thrown her down on the bed and she felt the blood beating in her throat, in her eyes, the hatred, the helpless terror in her blood. She felt the hatred and his hands; his hands moving over her body, the hands that broke granite. She fought in a last convulsion. Then the sudden pain shot up, through her body, to her throat, and she screamed. Then she lay still. (216–17)[5]

Walter Benjamin and Barbara Spackman, among others, have shown how the masses are represented as "raped" by the fascist ruler in ways remarkably similar to the way Dominique Francon is raped by the visionary architect. In both cases, nature, women, workmen, the body politic—all are subordinated to the expressive will of the leader. Equally significant in this particular scene is the extent to which Dominique Francon is satisfied by this episode; at this point in the book she begins to see an escape from her stultifying cynicism. This is also the point where she first breaks out of her sexual frigidity, having found a social contract within which she feels she can honestly function. Dominique is "freed" by the rape, now that she has been forcibly incorporated into the productive vision of the architect. As Erin G. Carlston argues of fascist ideology generally, the hero's sexuality is shown here to overcome the superficiality of bourgeois culture (38).

In some ways, Dominique fulfills the mimetic role of Eliot's divinely raped woman: her body signifies human access to a vision of truth that transcends the materiality of a productive system gone over to stagnation and frigidity. At the same time, for both writers, rape scenes naturalize social and economic hierarchy. Rand, however, is willing to define the rapist as supremely and quintessentially human—if idiosyncratically great—and Eliot (like W. B. Yeats) never goes so far. At a very basic level, Dominique Francon's rape is a signature, an inscription that makes visible the inner presence and power of the productive male. Rape is thus defined as an act of self expression, and the hidden treasure ultimately revealed is not a message from God but proof of the power of man to maintain some semblance of control over value systems generally.

Through rape, the dream moves from the visionary to realization in stone, in society, and in flesh. The vision moves in benevolent violence, resolutely, a harsh gift to the masses, as we see in the following similarly constructed vision of the dream and the people: "Italy, gentlemen, wants peace, wants tranquility, wants industrious calm. This tranquility, this industrious calm, we'll give it to her with love, if possible, and with force, if necessary" (qtd. in Spackman 141).

Mussolini's rhetoric makes relatively explicit the natural outcome of this vision of a dream transferred. Zeev Sternhell and Emilio Gentile have established the extent to which fascism generally aestheticizes violence as an ethical value in and of itself. In the work I examine here, violence is in fact a part of the glory of the dream of the visionary social or physical engineer, proof of its authenticity and not merely a means to an end. In similar fashion the *process* of production comes to overshadow in importance the concrete object that is produced. In *The Cantos* of Ezra Pound, the heroes are granted by virtue of the depth of their dreams and the extent of their personal dynamism the right—even the duty—to compel the state and the public to participate in their own personalized act of endless production. Rape articulates this power to mobilize the dissociated or blocked elements of production into a model of humming efficiency. The leader, as Carlston puts it, restores "integrity, health, and authenticity" through his "ecstatic, erotic fusion with the physically well disciplined masses" (38).

"The virgin [who] receiveth message" (XLV, 229), for example, one of the hundreds of references to rape in *The Cantos,* does not consent to a final (Eliotic) humiliation, but rather sings of the "God in my belly." She sings her now productive self, and the lyrics express the moment of (re)energized production. Excluded from her song is the content of the God's "message." Thus, Pound silences discussion not only of the actual birth of the divine child—the delivery of finished product—but also the inhuman Word of which the virgin is the recipient. It is this latter—the knowledge of the swan, the unspeakable language of God—that Eliot and Yeats stress in their own images of divine rape. No narrative voice asks enviously/longingly of the "knowledge" the raped woman may have "put on" with "his power"; instead, Pound's poetic voice establishes that "all that she knew was a spirit bright / A movement that moved in cloth of gold into her chamber . . . light over light" (XCI, 613). "[T]he bride awaiting the god's touch" (V, 17) is receptive to and proof of the shining movement of the engineer or architect, a man who can be said to exist only by virtue of his spiraling energy, which incorporates everything it touches into its own ephemeral and non-mimetic order. There is no hidden realm of unspeakable knowledge in this vortex; all is phallic light, immediately visible and present—if spinning out of focus. This moving phallic light, furthermore, is creative—is "Iamblichus' light" of Canto V (17).

Pound's images of divine rape thus speak to a form of production that does not express a preexistent body of abstract value; the god is an architect, like Roark, and the raped woman proves his existence as surely as a bridge, for example, provides the evidence of human mastery over gravity. The reader, like Cadmus, must figuratively pursue Europa's rapist throughout the early Cantos, but Zeus is forever just out of reach, evident only in Europa's body as it forever whirls out of sight (II, 9; IV, 13). Value is produced amidst what is represented as a shower of masculine vigor—which accounts for one of Pound's favorite images of rape, Danae, "the god's bride, . . . waiting the golden rain" (IV, 16). The golden light/value of the god's manifestation obliterates all hidden spaces and private accumulations, just as the rape of Tyro by Poseidon is accomplished in "a tin flash in the sun-dazzle," under "cover" only of "glare azure of water" (II, 6). Carroll F. Terrell points out that the color azure symbolizes for Pound "the continuum in which the gods exist"—"collective memory" (17). What Tyro's raped body represents, then, locked in the "twisted arms of the sea-god," is an ideal space much different from that imagined by Eliot; here is nothing unspeakable or hidden away, and the god himself is transparent, his "Lithe sinews [made] of water" (II, 6). Similarly, the continual references to gold (golden light, "sun-tawny sand stretch") in the context of these rapes refute the notion of a gold standard, an idea Pound thoroughly distrusted throughout his life as a fetishization of money sign at the expense of the transparence and mobility of value. The "golden" light of the power source does not denote a physical referent that might or might not correspond in turn to stable abstract value; it signifies what Jean-Michel Rabate has established was Pound's firm and unshakeable belief—that economic and aesthetic value are born in movement and in continuum.

The shower of gold that frames Pound's images of divine rape is informed by his vision of economics. In this vision, the flow of capital is governed by entropy, a gap forever arising between wages and purchasing power. This gap can only be closed by the return of value to the people in the form of state credit (the azure light, the golden shower). Richard Sieburth explains that in C. H. Douglas's Social Credit economics, of which scheme Pound was much enamored, the state distributes a mixture of subsidies to industry and dividends to the populace in order to "'bridge' the 'gap,' fill in the widening 'gulf,' and restore to circulation the purchasing power that was somehow 'sucked up, or absorbed or caused to disappear' by the black magic of Usury" (159).[6] In actuality, then, Pound's poetry attempts to sidestep the central and irreducible risk of capitalism, a phantom that Walter Benn Michaels has shown haunts literature of the period generally; as Leon Surette points out, Pound is attracted to an economic plan that promises to resolve this perennial problem of capitalism "without any significant alteration of prevailing political and social structures" (444). Symbolically, however, Pound imagines that the plan is a radical one; that in the scheme the circulation of capital becomes a function of the intervention or "penetration," violently imposed if need be, of the factive personality. Zeus's golden rain and Poseidon's transparent force thus translate to any leader who will reorganize production on the basis of a rigid hierarchy that will enable energy to be reinjected at necessary intervals so as to keep the process of production moving at a steady and controlled state. It is the responsibility of the great leader to assign monetary value, thus feeding back into all cultural systems—including the economy—the value that is lost from it in exchange. As "the fuzzy bloke sez" in Canto XLVI, "any government worth a damn can pay dividends . . . instead of collectin' taxes" (231). Pound's loyalty to Mussolini—about whom, as Fredric Jameson points out, Pound felt "manifest hero worship"—is based in the belief that he is the human equivalent of this government "worth a damn," the raping god, able to inseminate the modes of production with new value, thus saving the people from the darkness of private accumulation and usury (*Fables of Aggression* 120).

The enemy such a rapist/ruler must confront, then, is usury. Much like the usurious "second-handers" in Rand's fiction, usury is itself in *The Cantos* "a malevolent form of retention, an 'obstruction'" that blocks the circulation of capital (Sieburth 148). Symbolically, usury is dependent for its representation on images of (in Pound's view) dysfunctional sexuality. For example, usury is the force that obstructs production and reproduction:

> Usury kills the child in the womb
> And breaks short the young man's courting
> Usury brings age into youth; it lies between the bride
> and the bridegroom
> Usury is against Nature's increase. (LI, 250)

Robert Casillo points out that the symbolic action of usury is thus that of castration, cutting short the phallic source of hierarchical power: the consequence of the usurer/Jew is the "'curtailment' and 'maiming' of the sexual instinct" (246). Alongside the usurer and Jew—as the Hell Cantos (XIV and XV) make clear—is the homosexual, whom Pound classified as the embodiment of obscenity in his refusal to participate in the sexual economy of phallic production and in his deliberate turn to the "anal gift," as Rabate puts it (221). Metaphorically, all forms of "usury" cheat the common man by obstructing the natural dissemination of the father. This is the crime of which Rand accuses her "second handers"; they shield the populace from the wealth of Roark's architecture. Like Rand, Pound struggles desperately against this force that seems to be "leveling" everything to one homogeneous state. His rage is palpable: the sin-specific punishment of all of these "monopolists" is condemnation to the productive decay of a place of excrement and "living pus, full of vermin, / dead maggots begetting live maggots" (XIV, 63). In Canto XV the "guide" explains to the narrator that "this sort breeds by scission, / This is the fourmillionth tumour" (65). Usury's corruption of a sexualized economy results in the obstruction of circulation and an eternity of fetid and hollow repetitions.

In Pound's historical survey, humanity reaches a dark age whenever a ruler ascends who cannot break past the (hymeneal) monopolists in order to reenergize production. Chinese history is marked by recurrent periods of darkness because its great leaders "never got rid of the eunuchs," the unmanned rulers who "disliked the academy" and oppressed the people with taxes (LIX, 281). Similarly, Italian history is brought down by the recurrence of visionless leaders, those law-abiding and "affable" men who "brought seduction in place of / Rape into government" (XXIV, 112). The heterosexual rapist is thus constructed as an image of transparent and righteous force; the malevolent ruler is not only constrained by the dead law but is a creature of darkness and secrecy (seduction), a man of private accumulations. The reigns of great rulers, such as Henry II and Sigismondo Malatesta, are marked by rape.[7] This is so much the case, in fact, that rape becomes a marker of the "factive personality," the man whose "phallic heart is from heaven / a clear spring of rightness, . . . bright gleaming" (XCIX, 697).

It is significant that in this symbolic economy, extramarital rape takes precedence over the procreative sexuality of lawful marriage, which the latter, as a form of private "ownership," becomes implicitly associated with monopolist accumulation. Canto V—the canto of the "bride awaiting the god's touch" and of "Iamblichus' light"—makes this hierarchy explicit. Pound contrasts the story of Gausbertz de Puegsibot (Poicebot) with that of Pieire de Maensac in order to celebrate the raping troubadour at the expense of the cuckolded husband. Pieire de Maensac, as Terrell points out, was a wandering troubadour, a landless aristocrat, who in Pound's confused version of the story seduces the wife of Bernart de Tierci and/or abducts (and rapes) Gausbertz de Poicebot's wife (19). On the other hand, Gausbertz de Puegsibot (Poicebot), roaming in search of sexual adventures, believing his wife to be safely at home with the rest of his possessions, is enlightened when she offers herself to him in a brothel, matching his betrayal with her own: "And for this grief he ceased to sing and to compose" (Terrell 18). Terrell is correct to interpret this juxtaposition as a highlighting of "the opposing attitudes of the two troubadours to sex and property: the possessive Gausbertz de Poicebot . . . loses all, including his creative powers, whereas Pierre de M., careless of property, gains all and also keeps the woman he abducted. . . . The theme of possessiveness versus the free unencumbered poetic spirit is thus exemplified" (19). Poicebot, believing foolishly in the laws of property, is symbolically castrated: he is not only cuckolded, his property/wife raped by a more phallic man, but he also loses the generative power of poetry. The object of his owning, at the same time, loses its/her worth; his wife is "let . . . go to the dogs" by her rapist. The wandering rapist, on the other hand, embodies the force that ensures "freedom," "poetry," and "spirit"; the circulation of value is maintained through his periodic violent penetration of the female flesh which—like nature itself, like the proliferations of market capitalism—is always available in plenty. Sordello, referenced throughout the Cantos, is another troubadour greatly admired by Pound. Like Pierre de Maensac, Sordello is said to have fallen in love with and then to have abducted and raped a woman, Cunizza da Romano, the wife of Count Ricciardo de San Bonifazzio (Terrell 5).

In contrast to the repeating image of the raping troubadour, Pound stages the specter of the Trojan War, fought in his view not over the rape of a woman but over her ownership. The light and life to be appropriated in Helen's rape is lost in her retention; there is no music, no spirit of poetry, in her extended captivity. Helen herself, typically enough, is held responsible for her own degradation, and the voice of Odysseus condemns her, a destroyer of ships and destroyer of cities. The oppressiveness of hoarding is deflected back onto the object of that owning; Helen becomes "evil" with "the face of a god," a walking "curse" against mankind (II, 6). The old men warn, but are unheeded, that she should be allowed to "go back to the ships"; the young persist in keeping her beyond the moment of the rape. She is associated with Eleanor of Aquitaine, the forcibly cloistered wife of Henry II, who "spoiled in a British climate," in an English dungeon, figuratively for Pound losing value ("spoiling") through oppressive ownership. The spoilage of an "owned" woman projects back to the owner, "stifling his creative potential," as Eugene Paul Nassar puts it (49). The "ownership" that might produce offspring, then, is disparaged, as is the product itself. The emphasis, as in the case of divine rape, is on the ephemeral act itself and on the abstract value infused through the energy and violence of that event. Pound freezes this moment of injection, cuts it away from what might have come before, what might follow.

It is significant that Pound contrasts Helen to Isotta degli Atti, "Who hath not Helen for peer" (VIII, 30), the mistress and later third wife of Sigismondo Malatesta. Isotta is not explicitly raped, but she is the consort of a rapist, and her sexuality is conscripted to his symbolic service in ways that help to explain Helen/Eleanor's "spoilage." Of Pound's heroes—and there are many, including Confucius, Thomas Jefferson, and Benito Mussolini—Sigismondo Malatesta is the one whose productive economy most explicitly makes rape coincide with the infusion of abstract value. An obscure prince of fifteenth-century Italy as well as architect, patron of the arts, and mercenary, Malatesta fulfills Pound's vision for fascism, "the organization of the energy that is the people toward a visionary goal of beauty and order" (Sicari 165); this will to order and/or to beauty realizes the metaphor of the vortex as sheer productive control—an image that, as pointed out above, does not claim referentiality or accumulation as virtues, only power and focus. Historically, Malatesta embodies the "new man" whom Pound saw in Il Duce.[8] For Pound, Malatesta's Renaissance mirrors the Italian corporate state in that it "hinged on the will and benefice of its one patron and defender" just as "the new cultural and political order of fascism was inseparable from the force of Mussolini's own personality" (Sherry 156).

Malatesta is also the Poundian hero most explicitly rooted in the rhetoric of constructive enterprise. He exists in *The Cantos* as an expression of the heroic engineer who through will, decision, and organization keeps a system optimally productive while preserving hierarchy, distinction, and energy. The bulk of the Malatesta Cantos relates the difficulties involved in the design and construction of the Tempio Malatestiano, a temple built to house the remains of Sigismondo and Isotta degli Atti. Built around and within an existing Gothic church dedicated to San Francesco, the Tempio is structurally more of a conglomeration of detail and different styles than a unified creation. As such, it mirrors the architectural productions actually commissioned by Mussolini, which "projected a decision to mix and combine, rather than exclude" (Stone 205–238, 206). In Marla Stone's argument the mixed architectural forms of Italian fascism generally can be read as "hegemonic pluralism—the acceptance, appropriation, and mobilization of a variety of aesthetic languages" in the attempt to formulate a specifically fascist voice (206).

It is telling, then, that the Tempio, like *The Cantos* themselves, is an incomplete and cluttered bricolage of memory and voice, as Pound was quite aware.[9] As such, it draws attention not to the finished product, but to the (violent) action of production—collection and arrangement—and to the will to order of the man in charge. Thus, although the Tempio Malatestiano is "a jumble and a junk shop," Pound can claim on the frontispiece of *Guide to Kulchur* that "There is no other single man's effort equally registered"; if the Tempio is "a failure," it "nevertheless registers a concept" (Pound, *Guide to Kulchur,* frontispiece). Michael North finds in this tension between the failure of the Tempio—and, equivalently, of *The Cantos*—and Pound's celebration of the form of clear demarcation (which refers, in effect, to the correspondence between expression and external object of Rand's competence) an unintended contradiction and a sad misjudgment on Pound's part of his knowledge of narrative technique, architecture, and sculpture. I would argue that this tension registers less a contradiction than a reformulation of "clear demarcation" to signify not the static coincidence between word and thing but the sheer organizing force of the powerful personality. The finished product becomes, in fact, less and less of an issue throughout *The Cantos,* and "the dynamic flux and chaos of events" that define that product serve to highlight neither the referential power of art nor the impossibility of closed narrative (the latter is Froula's argument; *To Write Paradise* 158); the dynamic "junk shop" emphasizes rather the energy of human production. Malatesta, as Robert von Hallberg argues, is Pound's response to other modernists and futurists who would deemphasize the crucial role the individual personality plays vis-à-vis meaning and order (62–63). The Renaissance is the model for the heroic "acute and violent effort" that Pound calls for in the twentieth century in order to set in motion a vortex of abstract production freed from the imperative to "signify" a stable "truth."

Lawrence Rainey points out that Pound explicitly hoped in *The Cantos* to discern a parallel between himself, Mussolini, and the perhaps unlikely Italian prince, between his own and Mussolini's "vague hopes for a new cultural era and the construction of the church in Rimini, between the magnum opus he wished to write and the unfinished [fragmented, nonrepresentational] monument of Rimini" (19).[10] Daniel Bornstein shows the blatant identification Pound felt with Malatesta in an early draft of *The Cantos:*

> Chien de metier,
>   hopelessness of writing an epic,
> chien de metier,
>   hopelessness of building a temple
> in Romagna, in a land teeming with cattle thieves. (qtd. in Moody
> 88)

The product will never be completed; closure will not be attained. Nonetheless, the attempt itself is inherently worthwhile for Pound, as the process of expression is perhaps all that can be hoped for.

As the "second-handers" set out with unflinching tenacity to destroy

Roark for his individuality and desire to express that interiority, so do the "usurers" and middleman—the mediocre masses who freeze progress and production—determined to destroy Malatesta and to see that his Tempio is not built. These middlemen are representatives for Pound of a society governed by the dead letter instead of the living personality—just as the "second-handers" are governed by dead rather than "living" architectural forms. The large portion of the Malatesta Cantos given over to the church's condemnation of Sigismondo shows Pound's fascination with the hero outside the law and outside the norms of society, shocking in his disrespect for and violation of the moral code. Sigismondo cannot be contained by law; he operates only under the imperative to produce. His "crimes," listed at length by the pope and included in *The Cantos,* all have to do with broken social contracts: he is, among other things, a "perjurer," "killer of old men," "adulterer," and "betrayer" (X, 44). His punishment, beyond excommunication, is to have his effigy burnt; he refuses to be present at his trial. Thus Sigismondo's trace or simulacrum, all of him that can be contained, is destroyed in an act clearly meant by Pound to be humorous. The powerlessness of the pope's word and the ironically desired exclusion from the Word is what is at issue in Pound's representation of the excommunication; Sigismondo is left not only unharmed but validated in his continuing refusal to honor societal contracts or to allow external "meaning" to take precedence over active production.

The glory of the Tempio, then, is that its production realizes Sigismondo's dream but its physical structure is formed of lies, energy, and social opposition. Like *The Cantos* themselves and *The Waste Land,* the Tempio is formed out of stolen bits and pieces of others' completed projects, signifying, then, more the action of collection and ordering than of lawful and comprehensive "creation." Pound is careful to point out that the Tempio's marble is supplied from another—looted—church, the great basilica of Saint Apollinare in Classe, Ravenna, which Terrell claims is "the most important Byzantine church in Italy, dating back to 534" (44). Like Roark, Malatesta has no respect for the architectural dead, and he openly strips the basilica of its marble decorations (porphyry, serpentine) in order to continue the work on his own Tempio. For Pound, however, the marble is not stolen—thus the use of the quotation marks whenever the word is applied to Sigismondo. His language is "stolen" (36): this emphasizes the productive quality of Sigismondo's lawlessness, a quality that destroys the very meaning of the words meant to condemn him. The outraged citizens of Ravenna receive only laughter and tokens in repayment, "200 ducats / Corn-salve for the damage done in that scurry" (IX, 36). Recompense is, for Sigismondo and for Pound, a matter for laughter, an impossibility and an irrelevant desire. The equivalence of money and marble is not an issue, and thus the condemnations of thievery are equally misplaced, a source of humor, always contained in real or implicit quotation marks.

The one type of contract that Sigismondo will not break is that which binds him to his workers. Like Roark, Sigismondo will share his vision and his dynamism with those who submit to the personal totality of that vision and who are willing to serve as component parts of its expression. The Malatesta Cantos are full of snippets of letters to or from Sigismondo that collectively establish a vertical network of communication: he emerges as the architectural and/or engineering mastermind who hands down his vision and power through these hierarchical lines to his painters and sculptors:

> . . . tell the *Maestro de pentore*
> That there can be no question of
> His painting the walls for the moment,
> As the mortar is not yet dry
> And it wd. be work chucked away. (VIII)

Significantly, Malatesta not only oversees artistic creation, ensuring efficient production of architecture, painting, and sculpture; he also serves as the primary consumer of the product, which is thus freed from the imperative to enter the public marketplace—a stricture which Howard Roark struggles with continually. Neither the worker nor the work of art will be thrust into a free market where their value will be a function of repetition, conglomeration, or democratic socialism (Brenkman 119). The beauty and/or value of the aesthetic work is dependent only on the extent to which it remains true to the one who originates and consumes it. The fantasy, for Pound, is real. Malatesta's involvement in the Tempio is an explicit defense of the system of patronage devised by the Mussolini government in which a wide range of artistic endeavors were supported and consumed (and thus controlled) by the Italian state.

The individual worker is folded completely into this circle of production, tucked comfortably between architect and patron. At the same time, totalitarian and paternal power are legitimated through Sigismondo's (Mussolini's) insistence that he is responsible not only for the final worth of the architecture produced but also for the economic and social security of the workers who will construct his Tempio:

> And in order that he may enter my service
> And also because you write me that he needs cash,
> I want to arrange with him to give him so much per year
> And to assure him that he will get the sum agreed on.

You may say that I will deposit security
For him wherever he likes.
And let me have a clear answer,
For I mean to give him good treatment
So that he may come to live the rest
Of his life in my lands. (VIII, 29)

The engineer/patron returns to art, both its personal and its class character, and he offers to the people an explicit and stable social hierarchy
(Berman 55). He breaks the boundary between public and private, making the political the encompassing sphere of the individual, as Mabel
Berezin argues of Italian fascism generally. Thus, although the nonheroic
subject is denied autonomy and individualist politics in Pound's ideal
political system, s/he is given a voice nonetheless with which to express the
self that is now circularly constituted by the state or the ruler. S/he is given
the opportunity to participate in the art that the ruler directs and consumes. Modern dictatorship, as it is rhetorically constructed by Pound,
thus redeems itself and provides "salvation" to its mediocritized populace
by replacing the politics of the liberal bourgeois era with a nonsocialist collectivist aesthetic—by "giving the masses," as Walter Benjamin describes
fascism, "not their right, but instead a chance to express themselves" (242).
In many ways aesthetics replaces or stands in for politics throughout the
overtly political Cantos, registering Benjamin's claim that fascism in the
early twentieth century offers art to replace autonomy. The ruler gives the
masses the possibility for participating in the production of art; he provides
the pattern and then in turn wills the different efforts into one expressive
representation of the transcendent value that only he can "see."

    That Sigismondo Malatesta is a rapist (as well as a murderer, thief, adul-
terer, etc.) serves to underscore the extent to which he is gloriously outside
the mundane social code that would stifle personal and phallic energy.
Sigismondo, again, cannot be contained by law; he operates only under the
imperative to produce. His rapes of the women on his land (or elsewhere)
are thus represented on a par with his patronage of the arts and his super-
vision of the construction of the Tempio. For example, the story of "the
girl," the "young pullet" who has been paid the attentions of Sigismondo
but who is "[keeping] her end up," runs up against details about the
Tempio's progress: "First: Ten slabs best red, seven by 15, by one third, /
Eight ditto, good red, 15 by three by one," etc. (IX, 38). Rape and production are represented as different aspects of the same force, both accomplished in defiance of the law; the stones for the Tempio are stolen, and
Malatesta's sexual encounters (whether conceived as rape or not) are generally outside of marriage (although he is also married several times and is

accused by history of murdering existing wives in order to marry new ones).

In this way, rape and production become intertwined in a text that further mythologizes both to such an extent that Sigismondo symbolically comes to supplant the productive capabilities of nature "herself"; his is the "prong" that "entered these hills," "entered more deeply the mountain," and it is his "light" that has "entered the cave," "gone down into the cave," and it is on his body that grass grows (XLVII, 238). A significant part of Sigismondo's appeal for Pound is the exploitability of his associations with pagan fertility ritual. Rainey points out that the consecration of the chapel of "San Sigismondo" took place on May 1, 1452, a date that to Pound seemed "especially resonant" because he associated, as did Eliot, pagan fertility ritual with artistic creation. Production for its own sake is thus associated with the life-giving energy of the Eleusinian mysteries developed in the previous Cantos. Demeter, as Kay Davis points out, is embodied in the Tempio's deification of Isotta degli Atti, "Divae Ixotta" (104), Sigismondo's third wife and "mother" not only to her own legitimate and illegitimate offspring but also to Sigismondo's other children (legitimate or otherwise) and the girls and women whom he sleeps with and/or rapes as well. Both her sexuality and her maternity are uncontainable—one might say a function of the Poundian symbolic economy that does not rely upon dependable referentiality: femininity is released from the dualistic construction of chastity or whoredom that it bears in either aristocratic or bourgeois patriarchal ideology. In a system of reified production, femininity can be relegated instead to the symbolic territory of lawless and unrestrained procreation (production); "the mistress," as Walter Benn Michaels points out of Theodore Dreiser's fiction, "is also (by nature's illogic of excess) a figure for infinite productivity" (75). Michael North goes so far as to claim that "in fact, the Tempio might be thought of as essentially identical to Isotta, bearing as it does her initial intertwined with Sigismondo's as its chief device and containing a number of arcane references to her in its decorations" (374). Her divinely productive presence could thus be said to give the timeless meaning of the riot of spring to a structure that by its very "jumbled" quality suggests not the value of the commodity but the energy of production.

Ultimately, however, in Pound's work and in the ideology of fascism, (the control of) production is finally a male prerogative; as Andrew Hewitt puts it, "(re-)production [becomes] an essentially masculine activity which by some biological freak has fallen to the lot of women" (151). Significantly, recent evidence now concludes that the intertwined S's and I's in the Tempio actually signified not the interwoven souls of Sigismondo and Isotta but rather the first two letters of Sigismondo's name in an archaic manner of initialing. Silent Isotta, the one member of Sigismondo's community never to be given voice in *The Cantos,* is finally more absent than present, and her death is oddly a part of her productivity. North points out that, at least as far as Pound's interpretation is concerned, Sigismondo "had work begun on Isotta's sarcophagus before any other feature of the building" (374). It is Isotta's death as much as her sexuality and maternity that provides the central "meaning" of her existence and of her deified presence in the Tempio and *The Cantos.* Although blooming with mythic fecundity, she refers ultimately to a factory for mechanized production, grinding out objects endlessly. Thus although "beautiful to look at," Isotta's "worth" lies in her conventionally feminine silence and the sarcophagus that provides the "reason" for the Tempio's construction, or, more accurately, for the collective productive effort that expresses Sigismondo's dynamism but which results, if one thinks in terms of a finished product, in only a "junk shop" and a jumble of meaningless detail. Her epitaph reveals that her value lies in her centrality to the group as institutionalized state: "she was liked by the people (and the honor of Italy)" (IX, 41). She is the mindlessly and voicelessly productive body that offers the leader of the state the opportunity to guide production in a meaningful and valuable way. It is *his* personality and identity that is outlined.

It is not Demeter at all, then, to whom Isotta is likened: I would argue that it is Demeter's daughter, Persephone, who provides the model for "divae Ixotta." Proserpine/Persephone is as central a figure in the Eleusinian mysteries as is her mother because it is she who returns each spring from the underworld, bringing life to the earth. She is thus both a goddess of fertility and of death. The myth tells that she was consigned to this dual existence when she was abducted and raped by Dis, god of the underworld. After her abduction, she unknowingly confirmed her status as queen of the dead by consuming six pomegranate seeds; she would thus forever remain below for six months of every year and yet be allowed to live above ground with her mother for six months. While Persephone is in the land of the dead, Demeter grieves and the earth is barren; when she returns, Demeter rejoices and fertility abounds. In a very crucial sense, then, Dis controls Demeter's fertility/productivity. His yearly rape of Persephone places a limit on what would otherwise be a scene of blindly unlimited production. His rape is paradoxically both an insemination and the blockage of fertility. It is this aspect of the Eleusinian mysteries to which Pound returns throughout *The Cantos* (except once or twice in the Pisan Cantos, which are in many ways quite different from the rest, as is discussed later). "Proserpine" is called "Dis's bride," then, heralded in the same sentence with "Pluto the strong" (I, 4; CVI, 752); her moment of glory is when "Dis caught her up" (XXI, 100); her "bower" and "threshold" is "in hell" (XLVII, 236; XCIII,

631), where she oversees oblivion, and not above ground, where she over-sees life. Likewise, Demeter is represented in mourning, her hair "thin" (LXXIV, 431), her only production the pomegranate (LXXIV, 490); Italian women wear "black shawls" in her memory (XCVIII, 684, 685; CII, 728; CVI, 752). Isotta, similarly, is always underwritten by her own death, and it is not her fertile body but her sarcophagus—like Demeter's black shawls, referencing death—that is aestheticized in the body of *The Cantos*.

On the other hand, Sigismondo Malatesta, like Dis, is about produc-tivity and about the force that curtails fertility at the same time; in either case, the object produced is bracketed from significance, consumed by the producer (in the case of the Tempio, by the patron who is also the archi-tect). The overproduction that Rabate shows was so problematic for Pound is controlled in the cry of the swallow and nightingale: "Ityn! Ityn!," the name of the son eaten by the rapist/father, is given new mean-ing—becomes the sign of the father's bloody control over the mother's proliferations (IV, 13).[11] Nowhere is value lost in this economy—and the sovereignty of masculine personality is retained as well. Nowhere is this point made more clearly than in Sigismondo's rape/murder of the German woman (IX, 36), an event that underlines the oddly nonproductive pro-ductivity of the Poundian factive personality. Pound deliberately chose to represent Sigismondo's involvement in "the row about the German-Burgundian female" (IX, 36), the pilgrim who is killed, mutilated, and then raped on her way to Rome in the jubilee year. Pound struggles with the placement of this incident in letters and drafts of the Malatesta Cantos, finally resolving it as a "row." His difficulty with the event, as John Steven Childs puts it, is "with accurately portraying the textual inac-curacy" (150), with showing how Sigismondo should heroically "escape" from the law and morality of the land. Pound's rhetoric aims to establish that the *order* of the atrocities will never be known, that words cannot cap-ture Malatesta—that his value cannot be held in his finished project, that truth does not live in a sign, that production is its own forceful end, and that rape is not fathering but murdering. The event bears witness to the fact that Sigismondo will always cheat the attempt to snare him in words and in judgment of his action; "phallic and poetic energies," as Philip Kuberski puts it of Pound's agenda generally, are here "metaphoric[ally] combined" (110). The muse of history cannot resolve an act whose over-whelming and dynamic savagery defies the law and all form of social con-tract: "Authorities differ as to whether Sigismondo Malatesta raped a ger-man girl in Verona, with such vigor that she "passed on," or whether it was an Italian in Pesaro, and the pope says he killed her first and raped her afterwards: . . . in fact all the *minor* points that might aid one in forming an historic rather than a fanciful idea of his character seem "shrouded in mystery" or rather lies" (qtd. in Terrell 45). Woven into the Malatesta Cantos is this masculine "vigor" that realizes itself in the violence, death, and broken contracts that define the "productive" or "reproductive" act. The vortex thus established by the "factive personality" is set in opposition to the ability to know and to assert; it withdraws from stasis, conclusion, and coherence, and thus "history" cannot contain Sigismondo. "Unconjurable documents," as Hugh Kenner puts it, close the mist around "the Malatesta debacle" (*The Poetry of Ezra Pound* 202).

Sigismondo's dealings in female death speak to Pound's association of the woman's body with the money sign. As he moved into his fully fascist period, Pound came to believe that the Douglasite notion of social credit (in which plan the state would essentially inject and reinject the money sign with value) could work only with the addition of the phenomenon of "stamp scrip," paper money that decayed in value for each month it was held—just as the product is also subject to decay (the Tempio itself was damaged in World War II). The point of the plan was to keep money circulating, a part of the flow of production, and to reinforce the null value of the product itself. Symbolically, Pound desired insemination without fertilization. Malatesta's rape/murder—as well as his role vis-à-vis death generally—foretells this plan for dying scrip. The death that surrounds him and that seems to exemplify his role (he is, after all, by profession a killer—a hired mercenary) speaks to the fact that his productions do not signify any objective idea or external truth; they have value by virtue of— paradoxically—his personality and their intoxified and nonreferential productivity. His great architectural masterwork is a sepulchre, "the final resting place of Sigismondo, Isotta, and the humanists of Rimini's court" (D'Epiro xviii), and he rapes a dead woman—or kills her by raping her, or after raping her. This conjunction of rape and death is actually a recurrent motif in *The Cantos*. In Canto V, the death of a slave girl seems to be confused with the abduction of a nymphet by the same name (Erotion) (Terrell 21). Similarly, Daphne appears throughout the work, always frozen in the moment of her attempted flight from Apollo, killed in *The Cantos* not into a laurel but, ironically, into coral, an attribute of Aphrodite, who rises from the sea.[12] References to Persephone abound.

In sum, the product, if there is one, is dead, perhaps eaten by the father who creates it in violence. The mater/matter is dead; if anything, more dead matter is begotten on her corpse. She is the "disappearing body" that Karen Pinkus has shown dominated Italian advertising during Mussolini's reign. The father, however, is alive and virile, never washed under the proliferations of energized productivity—always rising above even his own "aesthetic overproduction" of masculinist imagery (Schnapp 3). This tendency perpetually to humanize (i.e., to masculinize) the proliferations of the machine is what sets Pound's fascist modernism apart from that of the Italian futurists.[13] The Odysseus-like narrator prays to Proserpine in the first canto for salvation from the "impotent dead," which seek to hold him from his journey. Sacrifice is made to this end—the "scarlet flower" of virgin blood is "cast on the blanch-white stone" (IV, 15). The prayers shift throughout *The Cantos* from this goddess of the dead to Aphrodite, goddess of love and fertility, but in fact the two goddesses merge. The first canto closes with a (mistranslated) reference to Aphrodite's abduction by Hermes in which Pound's "Odysseus" offers her "the golden bough of Argicida," the token that Proserpine required of Aeneas before allowing him to enter the underworld (Terrell 3). The goddess of fertility thus becomes the goddess who is annually raped—by death—each fall. The Mater is energized and then murdered, almost simultaneously, in a gesture that preserves one clean moment in which one might believe in capitalism's favorite myth: that the sovereign individual needs to operate only under the imperative to produce; that all else will follow or will resolve itself. As in Mussolini's cultural campaign, the sovereign masculine leader is presented paradoxically as rising above (and thus enabled by) not only the unstable overproductions of capitalism but the overproductions of his own aestheticizing machine as well.

Rhetorically, rape enables Pound to divest himself of the burden of transcendence and the problematic instabilities of capitalism (e.g., overproduction) while preserving the "reality" of abstract value and the legitimacy of factive personality. Not coincidentally, sociopolitical oppression and the traditional violence of gender roles are preserved and aestheticized at the same time. It is not until the Pisan Cantos, written during Pound's incarceration in Italy following World War II, that this rhetoric falters. When Louis Till is hanged "for murder and rape with trimmings" in Canto LXXIV, for example, the narrative comments ironically that Till, "thought he was Zeus ram or another one" (430). The divine potential of masculinity has somehow been foreclosed, and the narrative must go on to ask, in the same canto, "where are Alcmene and Tyro," both victims of divine rape, and where is "the Charybdis of action," and what is to be done in a world in which "femina, femina, . . . wd / not be dragged into paradise by the hair" (431). All that appears left for the "man on whom the sun has gone down" is to pray for the presence of the vanished women, to listen in the wind for "the voices, Tiro, Alcmene / with you is Europa" (443). The man regains some strength from the renewed space opened by these voices, and he dreams again of history, of "the time of Ixotta," of a past in which "madonnas [were] still in the tradition" (448). These are small comforts, however, and these Cantos do not re-achieve the aggressivity of the earlier ones. Mussolini's project has failed; the Tempio is perhaps destroyed: "Divae Ixottae (and as to her effigy that was in Pisa?)" (LXXVI, 459). The voice becomes one of pleading, and the female divinities to whom it prays are ones of unconquerable power in their proliferations and productions: Dione, Thetis, Maya, Aphrodite, Athena. In this context, Pound wonders whether "Mr. Eliot may have / missed something, after all, in composing his vignette [about Grishkin]" (LXXVII, 466). Pound refers here to T. S. Eliot's "Whispers of Immortality," in which Russian ballet dancer Grishkin appears as the embodiment of *material* excess and depravity:

The humility of this stance—this recognition of failed rhetoric—is most significantly apparent in the invocations to Cassandra, which appear in Cantos LXXVII and LXXVIII and which usher in the later dominant image of the "lovely" and inviolable Lynx:

> Cassandra, your eyes are like tigers,
>   with no word written in them
> You also have I carried to nowhere
>   to an ill house and there is
> no end to the journey. (LXXVIII, 477)

Cassandra, of course, is in Greek myth a daughter of King Priam of Troy who is given the gift of prophecy by Apollo but is punished for rejecting his sexual advances by having her truthful prophesies never believed. During the sack of Troy she is dragged from Apollo's temple and raped by Ajax; she then becomes a possession of Agamemnon's and is murdered with him by his wife, Clytemnestra, upon returning home. If Cassandra is one more reference to rape (and murder), however, she also rewrites the script followed up to this point. As an image that Pound has "carried to nowhere" throughout his long poem, Cassandra will not die silently but will speak truth—incomprehensibly—at the end; she will not speak of the true identity of her rapist, as in the myth of Philomel, but of his death. Cassandra is figured, with her tiger eyes, as relatively autonomous in her own potential aggressiveness—as relatively aggressive in her incomprehensible depth. She denies the triumphal phallic light of *The Cantos* generally, refusing the masculine imprint ("no word written in them") as well as the violent penetration and reenergizing:

> Cassandra your eyes are like tigers'
> no light reaches through them (LXXVII, 482)

She is a threatening hole of incomprehensible proportions upon which value cannot be arbitrarily imposed; she is the abyss in which the factive personality dissolves, called upon during the time when the personality of Pound himself, according to Kenner, "was dissolving into recollections" (*The Pound Era* 72), unable to find a coherent inscription of itself: "Nor could you enter her eyes by probing" (CVI, 754). The loss of rape as a viable poetic option reverberates out to the central issue of white, masculine identity, which in turn articulates the increasing difficulty of imagining human management of the proliferations of late capitalism. "We thought we could control . . . ," Pound writes in Canto CII (729); the ellipses speak his disappointment and fear:

> Black shawls still worn for Demeter
> in Venice,
> in my time,
> my young time. (CII, 728)

In ways, then, the (loss of the) raped or "rapable" woman's body comes to figure masculine loss generally: loss of identity, loss of sovereignty, loss of "meaning," loss of the illusion of control over a frenetically proliferating/decaying modern world. Pound's response to Persephone's permanent disappearance is sorrowful collapse, grief for a lost "love" and a lost "self":

> M'amour, m'amour
> what do I love and
> where are you?
> That I lost my center
> fighting the world.
> The dreams clash
> and are shattered—
> and that I tried to make a paradiso
> terrestre. (notes for CXVII et seq., 802)

The death of Italian and German fascism questioned the extent to which the "great man" and his "cult of personality" could cover over the massive chasm between a dualistic world of transcendent potential and a postmodern world of fractal multiplication. Pound mourns the end of this possibility. This is perhaps to his credit. More commonly, even after World War II, feminized resistance to the establishment of a "paradiso terrestre" is greeted with rage, and the proliferations of capitalist production—embodied as a woman—become subject to increasingly brutal and increasingly human displays of violence.

4

MOURNING THE FATHER, DISPLACED BY TECHNOLOGY

WYNDHAM LEWIS, D. H. LAWRENCE, AND WILLIAM FAULKNER

Ezra Pound's defeated sadness following the fall of Italian fascism is not a lone lament. Many of his contemporaries developed the same tone, even those who remained staunchly liberal throughout this period and had nothing to mourn with the fall of fascism per se. They too—even when associated with the side that won the war(s)—shared in the sense of loss that more and more accompanies representations of white masculinity. Ernest Hemingway, for example, is generally known as the author of hypermasculine representation and self-representation who nonetheless and paradoxically portrays that masculinity in the anxious midst of its dissolution: Jake Barnes is in large part the man he is because of—and not in spite of—his sadness over the lost penis; Robert Jordan dies to protect the woman who has already been raped by the fascists, her braids already sheared away in mute articulation of Robert's own castration anxieties.[1] At perhaps the opposite end of the scale, notably masculine Stanley Kowalski rapes Blanche DuBois in a gesture that resonates with petty cruelty and pathos. Mid-century thus witnessed the development of a wide-ranging vision of white masculinity that could not participate fully in the triumphant rape pictured by Pound, or Ayn Rand, or even T. S. Eliot or W. B. Yeats—nor could it finally identify wholly with the rising productivity of capitalism, with the tremendous concentration of state and military power in the West, with the explosive productivity and new industrialization that accompanied and followed the world wars. Michel Beaud points out that the industrial growth rate during the ten-year period from 1938 to 1948 "equaled the highest growth rates attained since the middle of the nineteenth century," and that it was on top of this "already high base" that an even stronger, "exceptional phase of growth began" (217). Yet the

portrayal of white masculinity during this period—presumably reflective
of that segment of the world population most likely to benefit from these
burgeoning changes—is often marked by nostalgia, or even grief, for lost
or endangered manhood.

The weakening faculty for identifying white middle-class masculinity
with the growth of industrial capitalism can perhaps be attributed to the
extent to which that growth was accomplished not so much through labor
power, as Beaud points out, but through labor productivity, meaning that
"the rise in productivity was obtained by using [a variety of dehumaniz-
ing] means for pumping out surplus labor," including increased automation, the phasing out of the small entrepreneur and shop, the extension of
Taylorism, Fordism, and wage systems, and the utilization of continuous
and intensified labor (219–20). In part, then, it was technological production itself—the engine that powers capitalism—that was silently (and
sometimes not so silently) understood to be displacing the white man. F.
Gavin Davenport has demonstrated that James Agee's *A Death in the
Family* is dominated by an intense but indirectly stated ambivalence
toward technology and technological production: the father teaches the
son of the autonomy, power, and joy to be felt in the presence of the
machine, and yet the same man is killed when a mechanical failure in his
Model T's steering mechanism causes him to lose control of his "Tin
Lizzy." The son is bereft, cheated of the sovereign inheritance that had
been promised to him in such childhood visions as the "quiet deep joy"
the neighborhood men used to take in the use of the mechanical nozzle, a
scene that suggests to the narrator the "urination of huge children stood
loosely military against an invisible wall, and gentle happy and peaceful"
(5). The angst felt by the son is thus constructed in phallic terms: the
machine and the father have promised autonomy and identity, sovereign
control over a harmonious mechanical/natural world, and that promise
has been brutally retracted; the father's life has been cut short by "Lizzy,"
leaving a wounded son to grapple with the absence. The novel thus speaks
to the vulnerability of masculine identification with the forces of industrial capitalism. On the one hand, as Cecelia Tichi and Lisa Steinman have
established, modernist desire is directed at the figure of the engineer
and/or inventor—the master of matter (mater), chaos, and dissolution.
On the other hand, modernism is haunted by the fear that the master's
creation will not only become more powerful and autonomous than he,
but will actually supplant him, demonstrating its (his) sovereignty through
the rape and murder of his bride. The technological product begins to glit-
ter in its own autonomy, a monstrously androgynous figure, promising the
masculine subject that it will either rival him as a man or kill him as a
woman.

In celebration or in fear, rape articulates this ambivalent relationship of the masculine subject to the forces of technology.[2] As is previously discussed, for example, Pound's sacred techne is realized in the "factive" and raping personality of such characters as Sigismondo Malatesta, and for Ayn Rand, the rapist/architect forces into meaningful expression the concrete, steel, and frigid female bodies that surround him. Filippo Tommaso Marinetti's misogynist technophilia is well known; his commitment to "the life of a motor" is expressed generally in terms of "scorn for women," graphically imaged in this encouragement to war written in 1909: "My airplane runs on its wheels, skates along, and then up again in flight! [. . .] Continue the massacre! . . . Watch me! I seize the stick and glide smoothly down. . . . See the furious coitus of war, gigantic vulva stirred by the friction of courage, shapeless vulva that spreads to offer itself to the terrific spasm of final victory! . . . I raise my sights to a hundred meters! . . . Ready! . . . Fire!" (87, 42, 53–54). The "shapeless" wasteland of matter—read explicitly here as mater—will be given form through the violent penetration by the sovereign masculine cyborg. The underside of this modernist rhetoric of mastery, however—even Marinetti's bombast—suggests that a vulnerability hangs about that powerful seat astride the flying machine— surely one might be shot down, lose control, or plunge too deeply into an earth that might be less soft and pliable than it appears to be from a distance. This trepidation is as modern as is the sense of confident and phallic mastery over or in union with technology and technological production, and this fear is articulated in terms of gender violence. Vorticism, the largely British movement too often conflated with Marinetti's Futurism, evidences in spite of its shrill virility an anxiety in the presence of the machine, an anxiety that is addressed with further misogyny. D. H. Lawrence is another writer said to be under the influence of Futurism (if in spite of himself), yet his male characters are explicitly threatened by technological production—represented as nothing short of cuckolded and/or castrated by the machine; the Lawrentian response is rage at the unrapable "Magna Mater" who burns man with her industrial light. At the same time, however, the literature I take up in this chapter evidences a deep and mournful sympathy that begins to weave its way into the rape story, although the male protagonists and narrators themselves—all literally or figuratively castrated—weep not so much in solidarity with the female rape victims who litter their world but rather out of a sense of impotence. Thus, the sadness that pervades Faulkner's *Sanctuary* and the (non)narration of Temple Drake's rape finally works to mourn the passing of the Southern white gentleman.

The vortex of *Blast* suggests very early on in the twentieth century a pronounced unease with the Futuristic phallus-machine. As William Wees and Naomi Segal have both argued, Vorticism as a semi-coherent movement took a small step away from the hard, thrusting piston of the Futurists—an image which the Vorticists retained but which they both did and did not perceive anthropomorphically. Wyndham Lewis's vortex machine was, for one thing, a static presence not given to the rush of time (this, paradoxically, in spite of the fact that a "vortex" is always by definition in motion). Equally paradoxically, the Vorticist image established the coexistence of sharp point and concave (feminine?) surface leading to unfathomable depths, depths that would seem to exceed the external phallic outlines. It is not surprising, then, given this unstable shape, that the vortex machine faded in and out of synonymity with humanity—in and out of identification with masculinity, in other words—and I would like to make the case that this is nowhere more clear than in the fiction of Wyndham Lewis. In his novel *Tarr*, published in 1918, Lewis creates a futuristic mechanic man in the character of Kreisler, making him, appropriately, a rapist. In spite of a certain distanced admiration, however, the tone of the representation is not celebratory; in fact, Kreisler is pitted against another character, Tarr, who is clearly an alter ego for Lewis himself. Tarr is painted in the colors of full Lewisian irony as a cuckold, symbolically castrated by Kreisler's explicitly mechanical rape of Tarr's "woman," Bertha. Thus, the machine is man, yet the machine supplants man, unmans him, usurps his generative role and takes violent possession of the passive (feminine) field on which masculine identity is symbolically inscribed.

Drawing on electromagnetic field theory as well as modernist attitudes toward the machine, Michael Wutz has argued convincingly that Otto Kreisler is the "narrative engine" of *Tarr*; he is the electromagnetic vortex that, after "ignition," organizes into coherence the "force fields" of narrative space. The model, Wutz shows, is a masculinist one, establishing as it does sovereign masculine action on the ground of a femininity doubly figured as initial (but trivial) spark and passive field: "Kreisler's fantasy is one of male self-empowerment, the *generation* of his force field becomes his form of *male self-generation;* and the visual suggestiveness of the vortex, with its drilling motion and its conical protrusion, associates Kreisler with a self-sustaining phallus" (846). The violence of this autogenetic and mechanic fantasy is realized, among other places, in the dance sequence. In this scene, Kreisler intrudes on a dance at the Bonnington Club and creates an uproar through his aggressive obscenity (he attempts to rearrange the position of a woman's breasts, for example) and his wild spinning of unwilling dance partners. Wutz summarizes the scene, emphasizing how Kreisler's "wild gyrations inject motion and action into the narrative event [, . . . dynamizing] the narrative zone . . . while exercising control over a woman":

> . . . moving from verbal circumlocution to physical circulation, he takes his dance partner, Mrs. Bevelage, for a vortical spin: "He took her twice with ever-increasing velocity, round the large hall, and at the third round, at breakneck speed, spun with her in the direction of the front door." Their speedy gyrations would have carried them into the street, like "a disturbing meteor, whizzing out of sight," had they not been intercepted by a large English family rushing in through the door. Blocking Kreisler's spinning frenzy, "they received this violent couple in their midst" and carried them back into the middle of the room, where they "began a second mad, but this time merely circular, career." (854)

Kreisler not only organizes dance and narrative space here, but his violent spinning of the hapless victim establishes masculine identity, the "ultimate reality" of modernism, according to Sandra Gilbert (72); his display of phallic violence gives Kreisler face and name at the club, and in this way he brings himself to the attention of Anastasya, which is his intended goal.

The aggressively masculine identity established in this scene and similar ones is dependent upon the mechanical representation of Kreisler's cyborg nature. The ultimate expression of this dependence is Bertha's rape, a scene Wutz describes as emphasizing "Kreisler's frictional ignition," his electric transformation from "a formerly inert hunk of matter into a regenerated sexual cyclone, a vortex" (858). It is not uncommonly asserted that, as Teresa de Lauretis puts it, "the representation of violence is inseparable from the notion of gender" (*Technologies of Gender* 33); in Bertha's rape, that correspondence is cemented in images of technology. At first he appears to be benignly "machine-like," "dazed"; then "suddenly, without any direct articulateness, he [revenges] himself as a machine might do, in a nightmare" (199). The incident begins, as Wutz points out, with Kreisler mechanically "chafing" Bertha's arm, rubbing himself into an electric frenzy. Once energized, Kreisler is described as inhuman in his fierce spinning, "full of blindness and violence" (195). The pronoun used to refer to him, in fact, is "it": "It had quietly, indifferently, talked: it had drawn: it had suddenly flung itself upon her and taken her: and now it was standing idly there. It could do all these things. It appeared to her in a series of precipitate states" (195). After the event, Bertha thinks of her rape as having been "like some violent accident of the high road"; the "powerful violent springs" of Kreisler's "unconscious" had "snapped down on" her (194,

192). The rape is particularly horrible for Bertha because it is bereft of human significance; it had been for her "a loathsome, senseless event, of no meaning, naturally, to that figure there" (i.e., Kreisler) (195). Furthermore, this "jest too deep for laughter" has infected her with the meaninglessness of humanity: as she retreats from the scene, she thinks, "Ha! ha! the importance of our actions! Is it more than the kissing of the bricks?" (197).

As she acknowledges, Bertha has become Kreisler's "cipher," and what she now holds within her not only negates her own reality as a human being—which reality has never existed as such, has been throughout an effect of a system of metaphor—but "[shuts] her in with Kriesler, somehow for good": "She would never be able to escape the contamination of that room of his . . . *Kreisler by doing this had made an absolute finishing with Kreisler perhaps impossible*" (199). She senses that she is closed in with Kreisler, shut off from the world, just as her body and her womb have become symbolically closed off through this phallic event—invaded, filled, sealed. In terms of narrative presence, she now functions as the polluted vessel and unfaithful mirror—the virgin territory that has been imperialized by the machine and that has thus ejected man from his rightful place, foreclosed his own violent initiative, and stolen his name and identity. The pregnancy is the incarnation of this message.

Tarr is the cuckold in this triangle, and the role resonates with as much horror and rage as it does in the literature of Elizabethan England. The significant difference is that the winner in this triangle, the parasite who disrupts monogamy, is a machine-man; confronting him/it will not return one's masculine status. In short, Kreisler is a machine who does not duel mano a mano. When confronted, he fades into oneness with the feminine territory that he has invaded, thus turning even man's aggressive countergesture into an act of homoerotic desire. In the midst of his confrontation with another man, Soltyk, Kreisler makes a mockery of the formally virile structure of the duel by offering to resolve the dispute with a kiss: "'I am willing to forego the duel at once on one condition. If Herr Soltyk will give me a kiss, I will forego the duel!' . . . Kreisler thrust his mouth forward amorously, his body in the attitude of the eighteenth century gallant, as though Soltyk had been a woman" (286). Soltyk is thus effectively feminized, and given Lewis's misogyny this feminization is not to be taken lightly. The narrative action to which Soltyk is relegated is face scratching—not pistol shooting—and he digs his nails into Kreisler's flesh. The violence of the attack does not redeem his masculinity, obviously. In fact, the futility of the gesture is heightened by Kreisler's symbolic removal from the arena through a striking narrative transformation into an "engine . . . overcharged with fuel": "'Acha—acha—' the noise, the beginning of a word, came from his mouth. He sank on his knees. A notion of endless violence filled him. Tchun—tchun—tchun—tchun—tchun—tchun! He fell on his back, and the convulsive arms came with him" (287). Kreisler's metamorphoses—back and forth from man to machine, from man to woman—complicate the possibility of sovereign and redemptive violence; ultimately, the mindless aggression of the machine closes off access to the traditional masculine stance.

This emasculation defines Kreisler's effect on Tarr. Even before Kreisler's appearance, in fact, Tarr is dominated by a desire to be the machine, to master feminine bodies through violent and automated action, and from the beginning he is threatened by this role that he cannot fill. The novel opens on an extended chapter, which follows Tarr's attempt to dominate, emotionally torture, and "rape" Bertha; he envisions all of this in terms of his own mechanical body: he works to maintain a state of inhuman "indifference" and receives Bertha "frigidly" (45); he "manufactures" cigarettes to maintain this stance (39); similarly, all of his actions and attitudes are mechanically scripted as "Scientific" (58): he "project[s] the manufacture of a more adequate sentiment," for example (49); in his conversation with Bertha, he feels the need for more "uniformity of engines of attack" (56); his body itself is narrated mechanically, as in, "Tarr got up, a released automaton," or, "the strawberries were devoured mechanically, with unhungry itch to clear the plate. He had become just a devouring-machine" (59). The attempt is a failure, however. Tarr is not a cyborg, and his attempted "rape" of Bertha is quickly countered by her: "I must not be too vain. I exaggerate the gravity of the hit. As to my attempted rape:—See how I square up when she shows signs of annexing *my* illusion. We are really the whole time playing a game of grabs and dashes at each other's fairy vestment of Imagination" (59). The "raping" game Tarr is trying to play fails to uphold the mechanically masculine identity he has constructed for himself; the flaw, in another way of putting it, is that he is not machine enough—as opposed to "man enough"—to rape Bertha. Significantly, Tarr's failure speaks to the unstable double nature of the vortex: if he has attempted to mobilize the projective, drill-like aspect of the vortex, Bertha has been somehow able to draw on the power of its concave, whirling depths: "She does nothing it is the man's place to do. She remains 'woman' as she would say. Only she is so intensely alive in her passivity, so maelstrom-like in her surrender, so cataclysmic in her sacrifice, that very little remains to be done. The man's position is a mere sinecure" (59). Tarr's prosthetic phallus is thus jammed by its own reverse image. Tarr's failure to "rape" Bertha repeats in modernist format the consternation with which Plato confronts the cave—the "hystera" that he suspects will prove untrustworthy as a surface for the father's reflection; this instability, as Irigaray points out, is what the Socratic dialogues work desperately to cover up: "[the father] insists on remaining ignorant of the irreducible inversion that occurs in the identification . . . 'in the mirror'" (301). Tarr's desire to rape Bertha reveals the same dangerous attempt to formulate masculine identity in a passive reflective surface. Tarr's mater proves to be frighteningly and *mechanically* autonomous in its unfathomable depth. Somehow his victim has taken possession of his automatic weapon without having changed the rules of the game.

But then he has been very awkward with his sidearm. Machines, after all, are dangerous things not to be taken lightly. And of course it is the machine-man who truly threatens Tarr in the novel; Bertha's power should not be overstated. The largest part of the novel follows Bertha's rape and shows Tarr in classic Lewisian "self parody," to use Vincent Sherry's term, trailing Kreisler and attempting to agitate him (99). His aim is not so much to challenge Kreisler (as is the case with Soltyk) or to regain Bertha ("he was . . . delighted, in fact, to be free of Bertha") but rather to stage publicly his own secondary status in an ongoing display that he realizes is "childish" but which he embarks on anyway (216): "But the least hint that he had come to reinstate himself must not remain. It must be clearly understood that *Kreisler* was the principal figure now.—He, Tarr, was only a privileged friend" (221). Throughout this long and painful section during which Tarr exhibits his exclusion and humiliation, he is removed from the mechanical imagery that surrounds him before. No longer a "released automaton" or "devouring machine," he now wakes with "legs rather cramped" and is troubled by "nausea," "depression," and loneliness (the last an essentially "non-descript, lowered and unreal state for him"); most particularly, "sex surged up and martyrised him" (209). The mechanical references are few and far between and are of the nature of the difficulty he has keeping his pencil tip sharp: "to get a thread-like edge a pencil had to be sharpened several times" (209).

As a part of his program of sexual martyrdom, Tarr becomes involved with Anastasya Vasek, a "big brute" of a woman and an "organism of fierce mechanical reactions and self-possession" to whom he admits enslavement (218, 326). Tarr thus proclaims his abjection to two embodiments of technology, one masculine and one feminine. The machine thus once again slides away from its prescribed phallic role into the "passive" field of femininity—only in this case that movement is not the violently penetrative action of rape but rather has more to do with androgynous slippage. The former gesture threatens to cuckold and displace man; the latter, more dangerous, threatens to obliterate him. In both cases, the female body negotiates that threat. It is specifically the echo of the machine in Anastasya's imposing body that overpowers Tarr; when he watches her

mechanical "revolving hips and thudding skirts," which "carr[y] her forward with the orchestral majesty of a simple ship," he is even "tempted" to
go so far as "to abandon art" (247). It is particularly significant that his
subjection to woman and machine is registered in this way, as a betrayal of
his painting: "Surrender to a woman was a sort of suicide for an artist. . . .
With any "superior"woman he had ever met, this feeling of being with a
parvenu never left him.—Anastasya was not an exception" (219). For
Lewis (and for Tarr), as Sherry makes clear, art, particularly visual art, is
about dominance and depends upon "the eye . . . exert[ing] physical supe-
riority" in a gesture of "severe mastery" over "currents of aggression" (95,
97, 96). Tarr's betrayal of his "art," then, implies not only the loss of masculinity entailed in his "enslavement" to a feminine and mechanic "'superior'" but also the abandonment of the (in)famous "enemy" stance, the
position of abrasive "outsider" that Lewis believed was the last holdout for
intelligent humanity (i.e., economically privileged white men) in a mechanized and democratized wasteland.[3]

What is "suicide" for Tarr, then, is to enter into a sexual relationship
with a woman whose machinery will tolerate no violent imposition of
form and whose body easily rejects the "raping" games he plays with
Bertha. Anastasya and her "swagger sex" deny him his very identity—his
roles as enemy, artist, and man. The condition of art—the condition of the
female body—is "*to have no inside, nothing you can see*. Instead, then, of
being something impelled like an independent machine by a little egoistic
fire inside, it lives soullessly and deadly by its frontal lines and masses"
(317). Anastasya is dangerous to Tarr because her flesh is barely a cover for
her own spinning engines; she is "impelled like an independent machine"
and cannot reflect his message or his person: "*We represent absolutely nothing*—thank God!" she tells him, laughing in the face of his attempts to
explain his art. Tarr finally turns from her and marries Bertha because
Bertha's pregnancy suggests penetrability to him, as well as abstractability.
She is the necessary ingredient for what Reed Way Dasenbrock calls the
Vorticist aesthetic—the desire to "de-organicize" life through abstraction
(54). Tarr marries Bertha so that he can be an artist again, and for that "he
needed an empty vessel to flood with his vitality, and not an equal and foreign vitality to coldly exist side by side with" (335). If Bertha's pregnancy
speaks at present of the ascendancy of the machine and the emasculation
of Tarr, it nevertheless constitutes the indispensable half of the gender
binary—the part whose "gaping" "jellyfish diffuseness" hails in its negativity the "one God, . . . man" (334).

This triumphant return of the gender binary works to exclude and forget the third term—Kreisler, the parasitic machine. The gaping vessel whose
permeability to the machine might well be the end of "humanity" is yet the

only vessel able to identify man as sovereign "enemy," and so the parasite must be silenced (Kreisler is dead by this point in the text), and Bertha must be retained, "despicable" and "flaccid" as she is (334). Bertha's role in *Tarr* is pure, and her rapability defines her; she enters the text as "Woman," according to Lea Melandri, enters history, "having already lost concreteness and singularity: . . . she is the Mother, an equivalent more universal than money, the most abstract measure ever invented by patriarchal ideology" (qtd. in de Lauretis, *Technologies of Gender*, 130). While she is to be hated for being permeable to others—or to the machine—Woman is yet necessary for the formulation of man. Tarr enters into marriage more cruel and aggressive than ever before, confronted and strengthened daily by the presence of Kreisler's and Bertha's child, a constant living reminder that "he was beaten" (330)—worse, that he was feminized, hemmed in by the machines that would compromise his gender and obliterate his identity.

If Lewis meets machined emasculation with bitter resignation, many of his contemporaries greet the same nightmare of technological castration with rage, and the proliferations of the machine—first embodied as phallic accompaniment, later as Woman—become subject to increasingly brutal displays of violence. In the work of D. H. Lawrence, for example, the confrontation approaches archetypal dimensions: "man" is figured as losing (or having lost) to the forces of technology and production the "primal" or divine power that should have descended to him from an absent father. His rage at this injustice is articulated not as revolt against these specific usurping forces (forces that, unlike those in Lewis, are explicitly located outside the human body), however, but rather as rage against the body of woman, the sickeningly productive "Magna Mater," which has somehow become the guiding light of technological production. The sovereign raping father has left the scene, leaving a crippled man, ill-equipped for the task, to fill the vacancy. In *Lady Chatterley's Lover*, the techno-mother is given a docile body that can be raped into subordination, and rage floats free in the redeemed wasteland. But this triumph is accomplished through a complete withdrawal from the reality of technological production, the chaos of which cannot be positively organized. In *Women in Love*, similarly, the man who identifies himself with the forces of technology cannot subdue the murderous mother/lover to masculine signature, and he is doomed, pathetically, to die in her glittering iron wilderness. The man who does survive is the one who retreats from the forces of industrial production for the warmer climes of abstracted phallic power. In Lawrence's work, mother Demeter's world glitters with the dangerous proliferations of industrialization gone mad, and Persephone alone is redeemed, as her world cannot be, by her rape and captivity in that darkened phallic world of true generative power. Man thus grapples with the specter of his impotence in the face of a seemingly autogenetic technology by usurping the traditionally feminine image of the dark and fecund earth. Rape defiantly inscribes masculine identity, but only under cover of darkness; the mindless and apocalyptic copulations of the machine grind on above him, in the light of day (or of the moon). *Lady Chatterley's Lover* articulates a similar message of limited survival. In this novel, however, the rapist is not the man-machine but rather the organic man whose phallic potency is redeemed by pirating a little piece of femininity from the burgeoning world of technological production. Like a renegade Dis, this man pulls his Proserpine under into a world of darkness, and there she is raped in order that production, symbolically, can be brought within the domain of autonomous masculine/human control.

In one way of looking at it, Constance Chatterley is defined by her symbolic association with the machine: she is the wife and thus property of an industrial magnate, and she is also, until her rape, sexually frigid—brilliant and hard in her autonomy. Lady Chatterley is not properly "frigid," of course; her "problem" is rather that her orgasms are self-controlled, a pathological condition that is the cause of much rage in Lawrence's narrative: "A woman could take a man, without really giving herself away. Certainly she could take him without giving herself into his power. Rather she could use this sex thing to have power over him. For she had only to hold herself back, in the sexual intercourse, and let him finish and expend himself without herself coming to the crisis; and then she could prolong the connection and achieve her orgasm and her crisis while he was merely a tool" (8). Like the "evil electric lights" and "diabolical rattlings of [the] engines" of Tevershall pit, the woman's body can suck all the life out of a man and alienate him from his own productions and his own potency. The woman/Tevershall would dehumanize him by taking from him the control he should rightfully have over his productive action.

After her rape, she is much more akin to Ursula and Bertha, soft and yielding in body and mind, ready for the imprint of man. And as with Kreisler's, Mellors's rape of Lady Chatterley is a "success": the mother body is made pregnant, forced to speak the sovereign identity of the rapist. Furthermore, like Dominique Francon, Constance is not only given a baby but the gift of sexual pleasure by her rapist. The impression is that Mellors "heals" Constance Chatterley, first through rape[4] and then through his dominance in sex. In this way he both energizes the mother body and brings its proliferations under masculine control. With him Constance can "no longer force her own conclusion"; she can "do nothing" but "wait, wait, and moan in spirit as she felt him inside her withdrawing, . . . whilst all her womb was open and soft and softly clamouring like a sea-anemone under the tides, clamouring for him to come in again and make a fulfillment for her" (133). As the production machine cannot be, she is shown her central lack, the fact that it is only when "his life [springs] out into her" that "she [is] born, a woman" (134, 174). The life in her and the life that she is are thus both generated by the dark phallus, and her "yearning adoration" of him and his penis reciprocally identifies him as sovereign individual, allows him to "[fold] himself" in "darkness" against that "malevolent Thing outside." Because a little piece of the feminized whiteness that is industry is cut off and dominated, the essential humanity of the phallus is validated; Mellors can preserve the "turgidity of his desire which, in spite of all, was like a riches: the stirring restlessness of his penis, the stirring fire in his loins!" (120).

Mellors expresses the Lawrentian sentiment that humanity itself could be healed of its effacement before the machine if only there were a community of men—"if only there were men to fight side by side with" against the white light, the "Thing" outside—but as in all of Lawrence's work, this dream is destined to be unrealized (120). The potential blood brother in *Lady Chatterley's Lover,* the equivalent of Gerald Crich, is Clifford Chatterley, a man lost to industrial production and the machine. He is, in fact, almost a cyborg; crippled and rendered impotent by the war, he is not only dependent on but a part of his motorized wheelchair. He has thus become a part of the "generation of ladylike prigs with half a ball each," and he has been castrated by technological production—the war machinery, the wheelchair, the colliery of which he is lord, and the "motor-cars and cinemas and aeroplanes [that] suck the last bit out of [men]" (217). As in *Women in Love,* the technology that emasculates Clifford Chatterley is finally folded into images of the unrapable woman: "his manhood was dead" before his housekeeper, Mrs. Bolton, who is in turn described as "the Magna Mater, full of power and potency, having the great blond child-man under her will and her stroke entirely" (290, 291). The masculinity tolerated by modern capitalism is thus defined as the death of "manhood" and of humanity: "It was as if his very passivity and prostitution to the Magna Mater gave him insight into material business affairs, and lent him a certain remarkable inhuman force. The wallowing in private emotion, the utter abasement of his manly self, seemed to lend him a second nature, cold, almost visionary, business-clever. In business he was quite inhuman" (291–92). It is from him that Constance is stolen in a gesture that accomplishes the final cut in Clifford's psychic castration. Masculine solidarity is rendered finally impossible; Mellors and Constance will be only a private island where "man" retains his humanity and his connection with the primal dark forces of life.

Clifford Chatterley is paralleled in Lawrence's *Women in Love* by Gerald Crich, son of an "industrial magnate" and associated throughout with technological production and scientific engineering. He is the "God of the machine," and the miners are "his instruments," his "great social productive machine" (215, 219). His is a world of light and visibility, and he tolerates no fecund shadows: as "Deus ex Machina," "terrible and inhuman were his examinations into every detail; there was no privacy he would spare" (220, 221). The "arch-god of earth" is thus technological master of feminized nature. Much cited is the scene of Gerald astride the Arab mare, violently keeping her in check as she panics at the railroad crossing. Clearly technophobic, as David Mesher points out, the image of the bloody horse nonetheless celebrates Gerald's "will," if ambivalently, in this figurative rape and domination of the animal.

Like Clifford Chatterley, then, Gerald Crich does not partake of the dark imagery of primal fertility but only of the white light of technological production and dominance, yet because this is the case, he, like Clifford, is ultimately vulnerable to the more powerful and more primal light of woman in all of its uncontrollable proliferations. The tragic undertone of the scene with the Arab mare, given the context of the novel as a whole, has to do with Gerald's blindness to the danger he is in, his vulnerability in all of this "glistening," "shining" "cold sunshine," and "sharp light"; the "keen . . . sword," which he "press[es] into her" with "mechanical relentlessness" is, as in *Tarr*, not always as easily controlled as is mother nature (confident control of which is also illusory, of course) (102–4). When Gerald attempts to rape and dominate Gudrun Brangwen, Ursula's sister, in similar fashion, that vulnerability ultimately opens him up to destruction, and in that confrontation, we are clearly meant to empathize with Gerald's plight, not Gudrun's. Lawrence thus establishes a connection with the phallic man-machine—a relationship that Lewis always counters; the Kreisler-machine is invincible and apart, displacing organic man. Even in Lewis's rape scene, the reader is not invited to be with Kreisler but is forced instead to share in Bertha's fear of her mechanical aggressor and her humiliation at its hands. Lawrence, on the other hand, sides with the man in questions of rape, and thus a failed rape is the stuff of tragedy; the ensuing figurative castration and murder of the "industrial magnate" is the source of almost hysterical rage against the Magna Mater, "the mother and substance of all life," who outmachines her master (337).

Gudrun Brangwen is literally a man killer like her namesake, the German counterpart of Procne, the Gudrun who kills her own children and feeds them to her husband (their father). Gudrun of the novel is thus the murderous sister of the docile/victimized woman; she is not herself that woman. Gudrun/Procne is the mother who "hated" and "would murder . . . gladly . . . the infant crying in the night" (458) and who feeds the defeated man the bloody supper of his own productions. Significantly,

Gudrun is associated throughout *Women in Love* with frozen white power, and the image is unstable: it can refer to the moon, thus eliciting the archetypally feminine, or it can refer to technology in its most negative aspect (Birkin's motorcar, framed positively, deifies man in darkness). In either case, her brilliant inner light prevents her body from being the matter—the "vessel"—that can be filled with Gerald's potency, thus identifying him as subject: even in the midst of their violent sex, Gudrun is Gerald's "white flame," his "snow-flower" of such moon-like power that although "he had subdued her," "her subjugation was to him an infinite chastity in her, a virginity which he could never break, and which dominated him as by a spell" (210). Thus, although he rapes and throttles her, she wins and he dies. Although he "penetrate[s] all the outer places of Gudrun's soul" and makes her "eyes dilate in strange violation"—and although he pictures the "voluptuous finality" of her murder, her body "a soft heap lying dead between his hands, utterly dead"—he is left behind nonetheless "like a postulant in the ante-room of this temple of mysteries, this woman" (443, 391, 452, 442). At a different level, although he is born to be "the arch-god of the earth" and although "it was his will to subjugate Matter to his own ends," it is his fate to die in a "cradle of snow" below an icy moon, "a painful brilliant thing that was always there, unremitting, from which there was no escape" (464). What he falls victim to, then—seemingly cold light itself—is associated with technology and femaleness at the same time; industrial production is thus feminized and the feminine comes to serve as ecological scapegoat. The message of *Women in Love* is that man cannot usurp or control the growing cold light, and his "humanity" is rendered impotent and insignificant in the face of the woman machine. Only Birkin survives—the man who retreats from the English and northern European wasteland to the warmth of southern climates and the power implicit in the domination of a woman cut off from communion with that wasteland.

R. W. Flint and Earl Ingersoll have both pointed out that Lawrence's attitude toward the machine was not at all entirely negative, however, as is often pronounced, but was, as with Lewis, profoundly ambivalent. In spite of a little unease, for example, Lawrence admired Marinetti greatly, and in spite of the usual Lawrentian mouthpiece who heaps anathema on technology (e.g., Mellors in *Lady Chatterley's Lover*), I would argue that he nonetheless celebrates the machine to the extent that it is detached from corporate production—when it has become, in other words, a consumer item. Ingersoll has pointed out, for example, how central the motorcar is in the crucial "Excurse" chapter of *Women in Love* (151). It is in this chapter that Rupert Birkin (Lawrentian alter ego) and Ursula Brangwen first have sex—in a car. In the scene, Ursula succumbs to Birkin's dark and "electric" force, acknowledging him as a "son of God." The scene depends upon Birkin and Ursula escaping "to the greenwood," ironically, in his motorcar (Ingersoll 154). Technology thus offers them the freedom to enter into primal darkness, and in this dark Ursula and Birkin both realize his connection to archetype: "He sat still like an Egyptian Pharaoh, driving the car. He felt as if he were seated in immemorial potency. . . . He knew what it was to have the strange and magical current of force in his back and loins, and down his legs, force so perfect that it stayed him immobile. . . . He knew what it was to be awake and potent in that other basic mind, the deepest physical mind. And from this source he had a pure and magic control, magical, mystical, a force in darkness, like electricity" (310). As Earl Ingersoll has pointed out, for Lawrence, the mastery of the machine—and I would add deification of man—is accomplished in phallic darkness. This is a turn away from the traditional (and certainly Vorticist) association of phallic power with (electric) light and toward an implicit celebration of Dis, rapist god of the underworld who controls (female) production through violence.[5] The scene preceding this, in fact, places Ursula Brangwen in awe, kneeling before the ubiquitous "loins" of Birkin.[6] In this position, she recognizes the wealth and value somehow potential in the male body; she, as woman, can be given this gift, this "dark fluid richness" that is associated with but somehow more powerful than the phallus, and it will redeem her, like Lethe "sweeping away everything and leaving her an essential new being" (306). Like the "empty vessel" necessary to Tarr's art and identity, Ursula's hollow interior will contain the "ineffable riches" of the masculine "mystery"; she will thus be made a "complete self," "liberated into perfection," through the expression of his "strange, whole body" with its "marvellous fountains" (306, 311).[7]

Technology is thus both an emasculating force and at the same time a synapse that enables reconnection to some archaic, mythical form of masculinity, one not subject to the degradations of advanced capitalism. Like the middle-class tourists who James Wolf argues visited the British colonies throughout the first four decades of the twentieth century in the safety and comfort of the private automobile, the surviving Lawrentian protagonist defines his distinctive separateness and individuality within the context of consumer technology: the private, freely speeding automobile ironically offers itself up as a sanctuary from the otherwise pervasive and dehumanizing/demasculinizing effects of industrial technology. The man, in this framework, is thus maintained through what is finally, in effect, purchasing power. His "perfect force" is clearly visible only when foregrounded by the technology that had become available—although not to all—for consumer purchase. As if in counterbalance, it is a primitive, natural essence of masculinity that is stressed in the portrayals of vehicular manhood: to

own and drive a car is to be transported to "basic mind, the deepest physical mind" and to "immemorial potency"; the power found in this ancient
space is a "control" or a "force" that is "magic," "pure," and "mystical"
(310). The new masculinity thus masquerades as a very old (and indelible)
masculinity that has been preserved deep below the effects of industrial
technology; it is nevertheless enough "like electricity" to offer resistance to
the "evil electric lights" and "diabolical rattlings of [the] engines" of
Tevershall pit.

Consumable technology thus offers itself as a viable, if unstable, carri-
er of masculinity in the twentieth century. Given this, it is not coincidental that William Faulkner's *Sanctuary* is haunted by the perpetual sound of
car noises fading on distant roads. As Sondra Guttman has pointed out,
Faulkner's work articulates profound unrest with the changing configuration of masculinity under the large-scale move of the U.S. South toward
an industrial economy. At the same time, the technological consumerism
that Lawrence claims as a route back to natural, archaic man suggests
something else entirely to Faulkner—the feminization and contamination
of the chivalric ideal (Guttman 16–19). The pervasive presence of the car
in *Sanctuary* speaks to the radical instability that accompanies masculinity having become a consumer effect, available to anyone with enough
money to buy it. The continual (and crucial) appearance and disappearance of automobiles works to reinforce the central event that the novel discloses, or fails to disclose—one of the most famous literary rapes available
to Western readers. In fact, it is the rape, or non-rape, of Temple Drake
with a corncob that has been the source of most of the literary criticism of
the novel. The elision of the actual physical assault from concrete, realis-
tic representation, as has often been noted, "subjugate[s] the feminine rape
narrative" (Patterson 57), replacing it with a blank space onto which a
variety of fantasies and narratives—all coded masculine—can be projected. In fact, it is the "visibly absent" quality of the rape, as Laura Tanner
puts it, that "gaping hole in the text," that best speaks to the type of white
masculinist narrative the text proposes: a story of accessibility and inaccessibility that suggests that the prerogative to rape has been stolen in a gesture of piracy that indicts not only the pirate—who certainly is not in possession of "immemorial potency"—but also the old gentry who are satisfied with driving (or being driven in) their sisters' cars, unable or unwilling to participate in an economy under which masculinity has become a
consumer product (Tanner 18, 19).

The novel is framed by Horace Benbow, descendent of the old
Southern elite and the character closest to the role of protagonist; Temple
Drake's story—which is never, in fact, Temple Drake's story, as many have
pointed out—works as "an elaborate transmogrification of Horace's story,"

as John Matthews puts it: "Horace is more prominent in the original version of *Sanctuary*, in which his polymorphous desire is the principal subject. But even in the revised version, in which he is reduced to the framework for Temple's story, Horace's excision rends the text in such a way that his desire determines the book's configurations. Both versions of *Sanctuary* are organized by Horace's crisis" (104). As the distilled and then corrupted image of what Millgate has called "a particular conception of Southern womanhood" that embodies a glorious, agrarian past (226), Temple Drake figures for Horace his own emasculation: like the rapist himself, childless Horace lacks potency, and his fluid emissions are figured separately as shrimp juice—"a fading series of small stinking spots on a Mississippi sidewalk" (19)—and the vomit that erupts in place of ejaculate when he fantasizes about Temple's rape:

> [H]e gave over and plunged forward and struck the lavatory and leaned upon his braced arms while the shucks set up a terrific uproar beneath her thighs. . . . she watched something black and furious go roaring out of her pale body. She was bound naked on her back on a flat car moving at speed through a black tunnel, the blackness streaming in rigid threads overhead, a roar of iron wheels in her ears. The car shot bodily from the tunnel in a long upward slant, the darkness overhead now shredded with parallel attenuations of living fire, toward a crescendo like a held breath. (268)

Although certainly this scene "represent[s a] masculine account . . . of rape," as Patterson points out (45), it is also significant that Horace figures Temple's rape as a technological abduction—without human antagonist, yet powered by an inhuman force animated by "living fire" and a "held breath." In fact, as Guttman points out, Horace has from the opening of the novel viewed the rapist himself "as though seen by electric light," as more machine than man: "By contrasting Popeye's coloring with natural light, the novel presents him as an artificial man. Constructed of 'stamped tin' rather than flesh and blood, Popeye has eyes like 'rubber knobs' and a 'hat like a modernist lampstand'" (25). Inversely, Horace sees his own emasculation in terms of a lack of this living technology: "You see," he tells Ruby Lamar, "I lack courage: that was left out of me. The machinery is all here, but it won't run" (18). Unlike the technology he fantasizes taking Temple Drake away, his own "machinery" is dead, inert, without breath.

In terms of narrative function, then, and the overall frame of the novel, it is Horace Benbow whose masculinity Temple puts into question when she challenges a seemingly endless stream of characters about whether or not they are men. And the most pervasive image of Horace's failure to meet that challenge is the constant reference to the fact that he "could not even learn to drive a motor car" (142). His sister, on the other hand, can and does drive, haunts him and his actions throughout the novel by suddenly driving up unannounced, or waiting in her car outside his house. In a direct attempt to stop him from fulfilling what he feels is his masculine duty in protecting Ruby Lamar, for example, she sends her driver after him, with orders to return him: "Miss Narcissa say to bring you back out home" (148). Horace is thus not only further emasculated, but further emasculated in a specifically white way—a woman with a car puts him under the power of her black servant. His inability to drive also destabilizes the class configuration of his masculinity: when this handicap lands him at the Old Frenchman place, where Popeye holds him mysteriously captive at the spring, cars pass and pass on "the invisible highway," their sounds "[dying] away," and when Popeye allows him to move, he sees "the prints of automobile tires" (5). When he is finally defeated at the end of the novel, in everything he has attempted over the course of the narrative, "Narcissa was waiting for him in the car. . . . She was driving the car" (349).

It is significant, then, that the one car owner in the novel other than Narcissa is the rapist, Popeye, a fact that is alluded to repeatedly. The despoiler of the temple of white upper-class Southern womanhood is a socioeconomic interloper—"a man explicitly associated with mechanization" (Guttman 22), "an entity native to a world of concrete and steel" (Campbell 103)—who "[drives] swiftly but without any quality of haste or of flight" (Faulkner 163). It is, further, "a powerful car" that he drives: "even in the sand it held forty miles an hour" (163). When Temple questions his being a "real man," mocking his impotence, Popeye's response and defense is aggressive driving: "One finger, ringed with a thick ring, held her lips apart, his finger-tips digging into her cheek. With the other hand he whipped the car in and out of traffic, bearing down upon other cars until they slewed aside with brakes squealing, shooting recklessly across intersections. Once a policeman shouted at them, but he did not even look around" (278). Thus, the phallus is clearly established as artificial and transferable—it is of no effective significance that it fails to coincide with the penis; its power is rather up for grabs. Vivian Wagner has argued that Faulkner makes textual use of the airplane to manufacture a kind of technological utopia and "unearthly space where gender relations can be refigured" (86). In *Sanctuary*, it is rather masculine class relations that are reconfigured in the space opened by technology: the new white man who displaces the old does so by virtue of technological association and consumer accessibility—not land ownership or patrilineal descent. Operating outside the law, deaf to the shouts of the police, Popeye and his

Packard merge into one fearsome opponent. Later in the novel, Judge Snopes is caught and beaten up by Popeye; his version of the events maintains that he "[g]ot hit by a car in Jackson" (319). Further, he mixes the story with sudden and seemingly random anti-Semitism: "a jew lawyer can hold up an American, a white man, and not give him but ten dollars for something that two Americans, Americans, southron [sic] gentlemen" (320). Reconfigured as a car and a Jew, Popeye thus embodies a serious threat to "southron gentlemen": like the Jew of Pound's ranting anti-Semitism, the rapist in Sanctuary is an unnatural man who skews the patriarchal economy by obstructing the natural dissemination of the father. Temple's appeals to her own father, the judge, are of no consequence against the man with the Packard.

In interesting ways, however, the text finally anathematizes Temple more than it does Popeye, ultimately giving "voice to an almost gynocidal misogyny," as Gregory Forter puts it (550). We are given a final chapter, for example, that establishes a certain amount of pathos for Popeye and yet freezes Temple into a portrait of hollow vapidity, again consulting her compact while unnoticed around her "the sky [lay] prone and vanquished in the embrace of the season of rain and death" (380). It is this same vapidity—the same inability to recognize the significance of the vanquished body of "sanctified womanhood" (Urgo 437)—that has allowed Temple to "slip" in the first place; she has been fooled by a corncob, and she has been seduced from the safe enclosure of "the Coop" by the automobiles driven by the town boys (66). The "southron gentlemen" of the university "were not permitted to keep cars," and thus the allure of the automobile for Temple signifies her willingness to flirt with class boundaries (31). Gowan accuses her of "play[ing] around all week with any badger-trimmed hick that owns a ford" (43), Popeye calls her a "whore" when she begs to use his car, and the narrative itself first pictures her in "a final squatting swirl of knickers or whatnot as she sprang into the car waiting there with engine running" (31). This is the slippage that dooms her from the beginning, and her fate, like the car accident that strands her at the Old Frenchman place, is "the logical and disastrous end" to her infatuation with the roadster (44).

The automobile thus displaces the university boys, emptying out the idealized masculinity of the now castrated "southron" gentleman and filling that space with a new, technologically dependent masculinity, a construction defined by its brutal artificiality (which serves in turn to ratify the "naturalness" of the upper-class white masculinity that has now been lost). Like the impotent rapist himself who relies on the corncob, the car cannot claim an inevitable alliance with the biological or the human. Temple turns to the car repeatedly—foolishly—as a source of possible sanctuary for what is constructed as her vulnerable feminine flesh (and spirit) and is repeatedly betrayed. Her time at the Old Frenchman place prior to the rape is spent desperately attempting to find a car, yet being unable to. The accident itself suggests the untrustworthiness of this new artificial signifier of masculinity: "the engine ceased, though the lifted front wheel continued to spin idly, slowing" (45). That she would nonetheless "stroke . . . her hand along the edge of the door" of Popeye's Packard establishes the inevitability of her fall. The gesture also establishes what will become an increasingly unbridgeable narrative distance between Temple's sexuality and the ideal womanhood silently upheld by the text itself. Like the scene during which she "hurl[s] herself upon" Red, "her mouth gaped and ugly like that of a dying fish as she writhed her loins against him," Temple's odd association with the private automobile contributes to her growing distance from the reader—and from Horace Benbow, who inhabits the text as if in sadly distanced answer to her ever more unrealized need for sanctuary (287). "We got to protect our girls," the old ex-landholding driver tells Horace at the end of the novel; "Might need them ourselves" (357). Indeed the ex-landholders do indeed "need . . . our girls"; they are needed in order to prove that a "real man," that mythical figure Temple continually invokes, "wouldn't have used no cob" (352). The narrative, however, has withheld from Horace what is thus constructed as his natural prerogative to protect (or himself rape) Temple, has kept her story close to his and yet just barely segregated. The story is close enough, in fact, that he is himself rendered rapable, feminized, as Diane Roberts has noted (34): the crowd that has (apparently) sodomized Goodwin before killing him threatens to do the same to Horace: "Do to the lawyer what we did to him. What he did to her. Only we never used a cob. We made him wish we had used a cob" (355). Horace is left by the end with only incestuous desire and an abstract, mythic sense of loss, ordered repeatedly to "lock the back door," in the hopeless condition of not being able to drive in an alien time "[a]fter the horse era passed" (356, 360). Thus, envisioning himself "marooned in space by the ebb of all time," Horace comes to dwell in that cloudy land of abstraction and nostalgia inhabited generally by Faulkner's men and boys of the upper classes (266–67).

The invocation of "the horse era" at the conclusion of the novel—in company with masculine camaraderie—is reminiscent of the ending of E. M. Forster's *A Passage to India*. Here, too, D. H. Lawrence's mythic hope for consumer technology as private vehicle to "immemorial potency" is rendered empty. In Forster's novel, Aziz and Fielding salvage what little they can of their friendship on horseback, years after the main events of the text, because the car has proven itself to be not so much unable to navigate the terrain (to the contrary) but to be the dangerous and feminized/feminizing tool of imperial power. It has been the timely inter-vention of the private motorcar—driven by a white woman, stolen from a native man—which has sealed off the (non)assault of the Marabar Caves from sympathetic masculine oversight: by an incredible piece of luck, Miss Derek's car appeared at the scene at precisely the second when Adela was fleeing from Aziz's imagined attack. The women sped back to the British station, where the British community closed ranks around Adela and against all sympathetic male characters and began to conduct its travel, suddenly, entirely, by car. The natives threw rocks, but these attacks were ineffectual, given the solid, enclosed, and powerful nature of the automo-bile. The rape story was thus situated entirely within the jurisdiction of the hysterical white woman and the unjust and inhumane ranks of empire. In the case of both novels, the innocent man is vulnerable to the rape stories told by the white woman, who tells the stories in the ways she tells them for reasons not divulged in either text.

5

CONSUMER FETISHISM AND THE VIOLENCE OF THE GAZE

VLADIMIR NABOKOV AND
D. M. THOMAS

The anxiety articulated in the work of writers such as William Faulkner and D. H. Lawrence begins to speak to the instability of late-century white masculinity, often defined not in relation to production but to consumption. As is often noted, after the Second World War, first-world economies shifted toward postindustrial structures on one hand and toward commodity production and consumerism on the other. The commitment ideologically crucial in an earlier form of capitalism to the notion of the individual who sells his labor to the market shifts to a faith in the individual who freely consumes in a gesture of personal expression—or, more self-consciously, self-construction. Fredric Jameson argues that it is the condition of the subject under contemporary capitalism to be (even consciously) a function of consumerism: you are what you buy. The compulsory task becomes the market-driven construction of that self (in the name of self-expression). Thus, the death of the author is replaced by the birth of the consumer, and the heroic producer is superceded by the sovereign consumer: "Consumers are constituted as autonomous, self-regulating and self-actualizing individual actors seeking to maximize their 'quality of life'—in other words, to optimize the worth of their existence to themselves—by assembling a lifestyle or lifestyles, through personalized acts of choice in the marketplace. Thus, in contemporary consumer culture, freedom and independence emanate not from civil rights but from individual choices exercised in the market" (du Gay 69). If Brian McHale is correct in arguing that what sets postmodernism apart from modernism is the shift from questions of epistemology to those of ontology, then those ontological questions he claims one asks of oneself— "[W]hat constitutes identity? How is the self constructed in and through culture?"—are framed within the context of consumerism.

If the task at hand would seem to be self-expression, then, it seems clear that the mechanism that powers a consumer world is in actuality the escalation of the commodity fetishism that inheres generally within systems based on market exchange. Celia Lury argues that it is precisely the "distinctive character of consumer culture" that amplifies the commodity's "'enigmatic' or 'mysterious' quality" (41). To the extent that the consumer item must "express" the hidden depths of the self, that commodity must contain increasingly more than its physical and limited existence. Thus, appropriately contextualized by an information age, consumerism becomes conflated with a search for abstract meaning, the intangibility of which marks the socioeconomic class of the consumer, as Lury points out: "An individual who has been brought up in the abstractions of education and mental labour and who is certain of obtaining daily necessities cultivates a distance from these needs [basics of sustenance and comfort], and affects a taste based in respect and desire for the abstract, distanced and formal" (86). Nor does the perpetual irony of (inevitably educated) postmodern thought effectively undercut the aura of the commodity. In fact, to the contrary, a central—perhaps defining—feature of postmodern commodity fetishism as it is described by Slavoj i ek is the disavowal of belief in the otherworldly promise of the commodity and yet the tenacious persistence of the kinds of behavior that silently insist that in fact the commodity is indeed so invested—no one really believes that "Coke is it," and yet since we continue to behave as if it *is* somehow mysteriously "it," this particular fetish is not only not emptied out but grows in ideological strength. Thus, "cynical reason, with all its ironic detachment, leaves untouched the fundamental level of ideological fantasy, the level on which ideology structures the social reality itself" (*Sublime Object* 30).

What then of masculinist fantasy in this historical period that can also be defined by its self-conscious feminism (however much we might want to challenge the depth of commitment to gender equity)? What happens to the imagined body of woman—and to the rape narrative—when the masculine subject is defined not as producer but consumer, an individual compelled to consume in a now heavily ironized quest for truth and self-expression? The texts I examine here—by John Barth, John Fowles, Vladimir Nabokov, and D. M. Thomas—all more-or-less self-consciously position the consuming subject as masculine, coded "male" in the same way that the spectator of popular film is also generally located in a seat carved out for the white, male heterosexual gaze. By the same token, the feminine stands in for the commodity that in turn does/does not promise to be "it," compels in her veiled obscurity a desperate and in fact violent (if forever self-conscious and ironic) stripping away. Alice Jardine makes the case that the text itself in postmodern theoretical discourse depends upon this vision of the feminine, and this assumption of the heterosexual male gaze: "The text is veiled—both open and closed, like a flower, like a woman. But it would be a mistake to think that something lies behind its veils. The text hides neither truth nor untruth, but operates an uncertainty of vision which is no longer anguished, an uncertainty as to castration and non-castration—a dissimulation that, in its effect, is female to the extent that it is affirmative (that is, not anguished)" (198). The novel of the postmodern striptease similarly speaks to the ways in which consumer culture relies heavily on the female body to create the illusion of an abstract universal essence that does/does not exist within or behind the material commodity. No longer angst ridden, steeped in irony, these texts acknowledge the desire and the violence inherent in fetishistic treatment of the body; trace the direct line from the metaphysical striptease to the rape story; acknowledge also the extent to which rape narrative effaces the victim as material body, absents her from the story. In spite of that inevitable uncertainty—or perhaps because of it—however, the rape narrative is maintained with the kind of tenacity born of desperation. What it finally articulates, as Jardine puts it, is the "uncertainty as to castration and non-castration": it reveals that white, middle-class masculinity is a secondary function of a consumerist world and is structured uneasily upon the compulsion/inability to get to the bottom of things, to peel away the layers that conceal some larger, aestheticized truth. The violent scene that promises evidence of potent masculinity—and truth-seeking revelation—becomes a farce; the role provided to man by virtue of twentieth-century existence is old and tired, and the son cannot fill it out convincingly.

In *Seduction,* Jean Baudrillard makes the opaque claim that "the immense privilege of the feminine" is "having never acceded to truth or meaning, and of having remained absolute master of the realm of appearances" (8). Under Western patriarchy, in other words, "there is but one sexuality . . .—and it is masculine"; Woman is "absorbed" by the father, the Other of thought and subjectivity (6). Baudrillard's answer, of course, is in his elaboration of the order of seduction, "*which represents mastery over the symbolic universe*" (8). I would argue that Baudrillard thus rehearses the ironic methodology of the postmodern—of repeating the words of the father, but with an inflection that belies them, presumably mastering their semiotic potential. Although Baudrillard is arguing in favor of a continuance of the game, the implicit message for the rest of us—which implicit message speaks more truly, I think, to the contemporary self-consciously ethical sense of things—is that the words that have been emptied out are those that have repeatedly declared that the woman is the container of the truth of God the father, but that her untrustworthy body hides that truth, or distorts its message. In "Plato's *Hystera,*" Luce Irigaray describes the woman of Western tradition in ways that Baudrillard no doubt has in mind, as the "'receptacle' for turning out more or less good copies of reality," since "*To see the father face to face . . . is as much as to say—die!*" (300, 299). The woman thus serves as "a clean slate ready for the father's impressions, which she forgets as they are made" (307). For Baudrillard, the repetition of this never-present Father engenders a swerve, and it is here that he locates the "alternative" to the words of patriarchy (7). But where exactly lies the departure in this addictive process of ironic repetition?

In "Menelaiad," a short story in *Lost in the Funhouse,* John Barth stages a hyper-aware repetition of the figuration of woman as vessel, and he does so in a way that highlights both the impossibility of achieving the "truth or meaning" Menelaus believes that Helen of Troy is withholding, but also the compulsive quality of the search that follows from the belief that the woman is a receptacle for abstract, universal meaning. The story is a "postmodernist 'Chinese-box' [text]," as McHale puts it, or a frame tale that operates at seven different levels of narration (155). At the first level, a disembodied Menelaus blames Helen for his death/immortality. At the second level (with one set of quotation marks), Menelaus is still alive, speaking to Telemachus. At the third level (with two sets of quotation marks), Telemachus is told "How Menelaus First Humped Helen in the Eighth Year after the War." At the fourth level (with three sets of quotation marks), Menelaus narrates how he trapped Proteus in order to get from him two answers: how to get back home; how to please Helen. At the fifth level (four sets of quotation marks), Menelaus tells Proteus how his (Proteus's) daughter revealed how to capture her father. At the sixth level (five sets), Menelaus relates to Proteus's daughter how he reclaimed Helen at the sack of Troy and asked her "why" she had married him:

> """""Why?' I repeated," I repeated,' I repeated," I repeated,' I repeated," I repeat.
> """""And the woman, with a bride-shy smile and hushed voice, replied: 'Why what?'

At the seventh and final level (which uses six quotation marks when narrated and seven when someone is speaking), Menelaus attempts to address Helen's "why what?" Eventually she answers, at the center of the text,

> """"""""Love!"""""""" (155)

As non-apocalyptic as the answer is, Menelaus nonetheless "was no more, never has been since" after she utters it (155); because he is a "mask masking less and less," he cannot imagine that "love" would follow his "cipher

self" (156). Significantly, as James Fulmer points out, "when he asks the
Oracle at Delphi who he is, the oracle's answer is a blank space between
the quotation marks" (343). For her own part, Helen claims on the journey home that she has "never been in Troy," thus disappearing from the
text in yet another way (163).

McHale rightly contends that "Menelaiad," unlike most instances of
"narrative embedding," does indeed finally ask the ontological—rather
than epistemological—questions that he argues define postmodernism
(155). More central than the question of knowing is the question of being,
although certainly the former is here connected in significant ways to the
latter. The answer to his question is found, amidst the confusion of language and repetition, but the answer serves only to highlight the extent to
which "Menelaus" has been determined by the questions themselves. He
has been positioned by forces around him (patriarchy, for example, or
John Barth) to ask those very questions, and what he has thought to have
been the object of his search—which imagined object and obsessive search
have served to give him substance as an autonomous agent—has quietly
receded from view. The central anxiety the text articulates thus concerns
the status of the masculine subject set adrift in a world of symbolic repetitions. The more visible question—"How many layers to naked
Helen?"—is a compulsive mechanism that both expresses and represses
that anxiety (144). The postmodern striptease thus participates in the
(ironic) objectification of the woman to screen (in both senses of the
word) the extent to which roles of "husband, father, lord" are "mask[s]
masking less and less" (156).

John Fowles's *The French Lieutenant's Woman* discloses the violence hidden within the narrative of the postmodern striptease. As many have
pointed out, the dynamic that controls the novel is the desire to get to the
bottom of Sarah Woodruff; she explicitly embodies something more "real"
and "free" than the Victorian society that shuns her, and we with Charles
Smithson participate in her gradual "unveil[ing]" (Michael 228). As
Magali Cornier Michael puts it, "everything points to and supports the
view of Sarah as an object of mystery" (228). The maintenance of her status as "object of mystery," however, for us and for Charles, demands that
Sarah's point of view be excluded, with the result that "Sarah remains
objectified and never becomes a subject in her own right" (228). Without
noting the allusions to a striptease, Thomas Foster has shown that the
novel positions Charles "encounter[ing] Sarah in various degrees of shed-
ding garments: her bonnet, her cloak, and, in the fateful scene in
Endicott's Family Hotel in Exeter, her day clothes entirely" (79). For
Foster, the gradual stripping "emphasizes the eroticism connected with her
and also the freedom from conventionally 'clothed' responses" (79). The

progression also, however, reveals the ways in which Charles's quest for something more "real" than Victorian society is mapped onto Sarah's objectified body (as well as onto the commodity item), and it demonstrates a gradual escalation of violence as Charles struggles to strip away the very last veil and stand face to face with "truth or meaning," to again quote Baudrillard (*Seduction* 8).

As in "Menelaiad," however, the endeavor to achieve "naked Helen" is an illusion. The progress of Foster's striptease ends on the rape scene that turns out not to be a rape scene: Sarah, it turns out, has orchestrated Charles' passionate quest, probably in order to produce a child without him—without a father at all—and the "frantic brutality" itself, far from providing evidence of his subjective agency (although the hymen is "conquered"), leaves him instead, first, with the knowledge that his desire has been scripted and, second, without an object whose unveiling will define his newfound commitment to the real (Fowles 274). It is at this point in the novel where Sarah disappears, and the split ending reinforces the extent to which she has been, from the beginning, unattainable. Rather than being reduced to a nugget of consumable truth, she is rather diffused into the uncertainty of the multiple endings. In its unavailability, her person in a sense resists the commodification of women's bodies that Charles bewails in another context: "[Women] are to sit, are they not, like so many articles in a shop and to let us men walk in and turn them over and point at this one or that one" (310). For Charles, however, the consequences of the loss of consumer status are akin to the effects on Menelaus of his inability to grasp some ineffable and non-reflexive "truth" at the core of "naked Helen." Thus *The French Lieutenant's Woman* accomplishes not only the loss of revelation but the splitting apart of a protagonist who is up until the non-rape relatively coherent and centered—he too is diffused amongst the multiple endings.

James Tweedie, using Barth's term, has established that Nabokov's *Lolita* is also a novel of the "striptease" (4). In ways that do not limit themselves to images on the outskirts of the text, *Lolita* as a whole confesses to the unanswerable desire of the narrator to strip away the veils that obscure Barth's "naked Helen," and the tension of the novel is itself, according to Tweedie, "contingent on the promised revelation of a secret" (4). "But who or what," Tweedie asks, "is stripping?" (4). In what is either defiance of or parodic commitment to the romantic and/or pornographic genre, the sexual object of desire is gained too early, yet desire continues unabated. Humbert first rapes[1] Lolita less than halfway through the novel, and from this point the violence in the novel escalates, thus registering Humbert's inability to achieve some ineffable form of truth or closure through the abuse of her body. Thomas Frosch argues that it is precisely the unpossessability of Lolita that makes the novel, finally, a parodied "version of the quest or hunt" structure of romance (127). The novel does indeed differ from traditional romantic form in that its central focus is very tightly held not only to the impossibility but the falseness and, in fact, violence of desire. Nor does the thrust of the novel shift *Clarissa*-like to the rehabilitation of the rake or to the psychological consequences for the heroine.

Rather it is Humbert's frustration over Lolita's increasing removal and obscurity that structures the movement of the text, an affective response doubled by the reader, a fact noted by innumerable critics from the time of the novel's first publication. As Michael Wood puts it, "The 'actual' Lolita is the person we see Humbert can't see, or can see only spasmodically. In this sense she is a product of reading, not just 'there' in the words, but because she is what a reading finds, and I would say needs to find, in order to see the range of what the book can do. She needs to be 'there,' that is, and she needs to be found" (117). The reader, like Humbert Humbert, is finally "tease[d]" by a shrouded figure who, like Quilty, seems always one step ahead and knows precisely the type of puzzles that will intrigue—"conundrums" designed finally to "ejaculate in my face" (*Lolita* 252). The text is itself thus draped in veils that do not ultimately reveal anything other than the desire of the white male subject. Simone de Beauvoir argued as long ago as 1972 that the "Lolita Syndrome," which appeared in cinema following the publication of the novel, "was not in fact about sexual young girls but rather about young girls being *sexualized* by men [; t]he nymph's charms lie in her essential absences" (McCracken 130). Like Sarah Woodruff, Lolita is absented from the text from the beginning.

I would like to suggest that the novel—and the novel of the postmodern striptease generally—thus speaks to commodity fetishism under late capitalism and to the ways in which consumer culture relies heavily on the female body to create the illusion of an abstract universal essence behind the material commodity. The novel that begins as "desire unfulfilled," in the case of *Lolita,* becomes increasingly "insisten[t]" on the material circulations of "sex and money" as it acknowledges the violence inherent in fetishism, makes explicit that Lolita has not only been raped and victimized but has been effaced by Humbert's narrative, absented from the story (Thomieres 170). Along with the grief for a Lolita who has always been absent from the narrative, however, the novel also offers up a final vision of masculinity as itself a secondary function of consumer identity. Humbert's climactic murder scene falls far short of the genres that inform it—the Western, the detective—just as it disallows Humbert's vision of himself as somehow spinning the plot of the story around him.

Moving in a direction not generally followed by critics of *Lolita,* Dana

Brand has argued that the novel is misunderstood if not read in terms of the explicit critique it stages of American consumer culture. Humbert is at his most trustworthy as narrator when he maligns those Americans who cross his path, and the source of his criticism is almost always based in the extent to which they "[construct] their identity and view of the world according to the images of normalcy provided by advertising, mass culture, and applied social science" (Brand 14). Humbert himself is presumably distanced from this consumerist identity by virtue of his foreignness and his aestheticism. Characters like Charlotte Haze offend this sensibility, as Brand points out, and are repellent to Humbert because they are defined by the desires and conventions produced and sold by postwar American media: "As Humbert notes and describes in detail, her behavior and view of the world are determined entirely by homemaking guides, Hollywood films, movie magazines, advertisements, psychoanalytic cliches and such 'deadly conventionalities' as book clubs or bridge clubs" (15). Because she is a creature apparently constructed by the late-capitalist machine, she is condemned in romantic fashion as all hollow surface, is typecast immediately as "one of those women whose polished words" fail to "reflect" a "soul"; Charlotte is a creature of "sunny cellophane" and "bedraggled magazines," "utterly indifferent at heart" (*Lolita* 39). What she attempts to feed Humbert—a salad whose "recipe [she] lifted from a woman's magazine"— is, like her offer of intimacy, the cause of "repulsion and retreat" (65, 71).

On a larger scale, Humbert's and Lolita's first road trip across the United States is an expose of the gross commodification of history and culture perpetuated by the U.S. tourist industry (a mechanism of desire that followed the wartime and postwar expansion of the interstate highway system). In ways that predate Don DeLillo's most photographed barn by nearly four decades, the "long highways" they "voraciously . . . [consume]" are an explicit replication of the tour book ("in three volumes" [*Lolita* 154, 156]):

> Collections of frontier lore. Antebellum homes with iron-trellis balconies and hand-worked stairs, the kind down which movie ladies with sun-kissed shoulders run in rich Technicolor, holding up the fronts of their flounced skirts with both little hands in that special way, and the devoted Negress shaking her head on the upper landing. . . . Hundreds of scenic drives, thousands of Bear Creeks, Soda Springs, Painted Canyons. . . . Crystal Chamber in the longest cave in the world, children under 12 free. . . . Shakespeare, a ghost town in New Mexico, where bad man Russian Bill was colorfully hanged seventy year ago. . . . Our twentieth Hell's Canyon. Our fiftieth Gateway to something or other *fide* that tour book, the cover of

which had been lost by that time. . . . Indian ceremonial dances,
strictly commercial. ART: American Refrigerator Transit Company.
. . . A winery in California, with a church built in the shape of a
wine barrel. Death Valley. Scotty's Castle. Works of Art collected by
one Rogers over a period of years. The ugly villas of handsome
actresses. . . . A zoo in Indiana where a large troop of monkeys lived
on concrete replica of Christopher Columbus' flagship. . . . A motel
whose ventilator pipe passed under the city sewer. Lincoln's home,
largely spurious, with parlor books and period furniture that most
visitors reverently accepted as personal belongings. (158–60)

Geography is mapped and contained by a AAA catalog; art, nature, and
history are alike transformed by the late-capitalist text into the "sunny cellophane" wrapper that generates consumer desire while concealing an
absence (or while generating the illusion of a concealed absence). The passage calls to mind Jameson's critique of postmodernism generally and
postmodern pastiche particularly for covering over "the ingrained awareness of cultural history" available to modernism, a point that John Burt
Foster explores in the more general context of Nabokov's overall oeuvre
("Reading Nabokov with Jameson" 202). For Foster, the pastiche
Nabokov employs is positively represented: "Nabokov seems to glory in
the very stance that bothers Jameson—the displacement of true history by
a purely aesthetic dialectic of modernist innovation" (206). Certainly there
is a certain textual humor in the description of guidebook America; the
tone, however, seems to stop short of taking "glory in" the scene. Nabokov
was not an author to promote the flattening out of the particular, and the
text seems here—regardless of Nabokov's explicit stance regarding
Marxism—almost to echo Jameson's sense that the "postmodern force
field" has involved, among other things, a commodification of the past
and a "crisis in historicity" (*Postmodernism* 25) that has contributed to the
incapacity of the contemporary subject to map himself or herself onto a
larger external reality. Humbert's self-confessed solipsism comes to mind.

If, however, a sympathetic Humbert Humbert critiques from a foreign
distance a geography that "loses its depth and threatens to become a glossy
skin" (Jameson, *Postmodernism,* 34), the text also makes him complicit in
the violent processes whereby this hypothetical flattening has been accomplished, and it is this complicity that powers the affective nexus of the
book: that Humbert is paradoxically both loathsome and sympathetically
tragic at the same time.

At the most basic level, Humbert capitalizes on the extent to which
Lolita is "the ideal consumer, the subject and object of every foul poster"
(*Lolita* 150), and he mobilizes consumer effects to trap her. He buys her

(or promises to buy her) things throughout the novel—in hopes of keeping her or of buying her sexual acquiescence—in spending binges that approach the encyclopedic listing of tourist attractions: "In the gay town of Lepingville I bought her four books of comics, a box of candy, a box of sanitary pads, two cokes, a manicure set, a travel clock with a luminous dial, a ring with a real topaz, a tennis racket, roller skates with white high shoes, field glasses, a portable radio set, chewing gum, a transparent raincoat, sunglasses, some more garments—swooners, shorts, all kinds of summer frocks" (143–44). At another level, he early on also exploits his purported "striking . . . resemblance" to "some crooner or actor chap on whom Lo has a crush" (71, 45). Aware that Lolita is "a modern child, an avid reader of movie magazines, an expert in dream-slow close-ups," Humbert presents himself to her (or so he believes) in ways that give her the illusion that it is her own desiring gaze that is powering the developing plot: "while I passed by her in my adult disguise (a great big handsome hunk of movieland manhood), the vacuum of my soul managed to suck in every detail of her bright beauty" (51, 41). Humbert thus attributes to Lolita the scopophilia that has been traditionally coded as masculine. If Humbert relies on the rhetoric of, to quote Laura Mulvey, cinematic codes of movie culture to present himself to himself as having accomplished a "skilled and satisfying manipulation of visual pleasure" (2183) for Lolita, however, he does so in ways that leave him immune from being himself too deeply objectified—the "movieland manhood" is only a "disguise" he wears over a presumably more real and less vulnerable masculine self. We are to understand that the temporary reversal of gaze and spectacle is purely illusory, because in the end, as Teresa de Lauretis has pointed out, "women spectators are placed in a zero position, . . . in a negative semantic space between the 'active' look" the camera frames for them and the "'passive' image" the framing camera constructs (*Alice Doesn't* 75–76). It is Humbert himself who is the "active" subject-consumer in this scene: "the vacuum of my soul managed to suck in every detail of her bright beauty" (41). Disassembled into particles—"details"—that he can figuratively consume, Lolita offers him a coherence of vision that approaches the "bright beauty" of the sublime. What she sees we do not know.

Brand and Power have both pointed out that Humbert returns self-consciously to filmic or photographic portrayal of Lolita throughout the novel: "cinematic metaphors run rampant in Humbert Humbert's account of Lolita's seduction and betrayal" (Power 2). In each case, the description explicitly objectifies her while it effaces her in the name of some "bright beauty" that, although beyond the grasp of the nameable and representable, is offered to the reader in a gesture not only of defense but alliance. The "scene" of his achieving orgasm with Lolita's legs across his lap he says he will "replay" in order that the reader may "participate." We, too, are invited to "examine [the scene's] every detail" with an attitude of "impartial sympathy." As in a screenplay, we are given a "main character," a "time," a "place," and "props" (59). Humbert regrets only that "no film had recorded the curious pattern, the monogrammic linkage of our simultaneous or overlapping moves" (60). After the "scene" (when Lolita has gone with friends to see, significantly enough, a movie), we are to be persuaded that there has been "absolutely no harm done." In an oft-quoted passage, Humbert concludes, "The child knew nothing. I had done nothing to her. And nothing prevented me from repeating a performance that affected her as little as if she were a photographic image rippling upon a screen and I a humble hunchback abusing myself in the dark" (64). The alliance with the reader is accomplished through the assignment of filmic voyeurism—Humbert, too, has only sat in the darkened theater; and we, too, "participate" in the pedophilic act (which is only filmic). Together, reader and Humbert thus sanctify the innocence of the scopophilic gaze and define the hedonistic late-capitalist subject as he who consumes for pleasure the material object that is finally only a placeholder for a value that far exceeds it. Lolita herself is the "sunny cellophane wrapper" that generates consumer desire without containing the remuneration; she goes to "movieland" after the event, while Humbert proclaims, "What I had madly possessed was not she, but my own creation, another, fanciful Lolita—perhaps, more real than Lolita; overlapping, encasing her; floating between me and her, and having no will, no consciousness—indeed, no life of her own" (64). That the ditty he has sung to her throughout the masturbation scene ends in the murder of a woman—"And the gun I killed you with, O my Carmen, / The gun I am holding now" (64)—reinforces the sense that she "is little more than a replication of a photographic still," as Linda Kauffman puts it when asking of *Lolita,* "Is There a Woman in the Text?" (137). She has become "safely solipsized," consumed, "the object of his appropriation" (Nabokov 62; Kauffman 137). Significantly, and referring to the novel at large, Richard Rorty has argued that what *Lolita* is most centrally about is the possibility that "there can be sensitive killers, cruel aesthetes, pitiless poets—masters of imagery who are content to turn the lives of other human beings into images on a screen, while simply not noticing that these other people are suffering" (157). Again, the filmic metaphor is used to describe the ways in which Humbert's narrative is haunted by "the absence of [Lolita's] voice" (310).[2]

The elision effected in part through Humbert's use of filmic and/or photographic description helps to reveal the ways in which Lolita serves in the novel as the embodiment of the fetishized commodity under late capitalism. Commodity fetishism posits that the exchangeable thing under capitalism not only comes to signify something abstract and universal rather than what it is in itself, its own use-value, but also hides from view the social relationship that has produced it and invested it with that surplus value (the inequitable relationship of capitalist, laborer, and consumer, for example). Slavoj Žižek summarizes the classic Marxian example of the money form: "[M]oney is in reality just an embodiment, a condensation, a materialization of a network of social relations—the fact that it functions as a universal equivalent of all commodities is conditioned by its position in the texture of social relations. But to the individuals themselves, this function of money—to be the embodiment of wealth—appears as an immediate, natural property of a thing called 'money,' as if money is already in itself, in its immediate material reality, the embodiment of wealth" (*Sublime Object* 31). The extent to which Humbert Humbert is entangled in this logic of commodity fetishism appears in his rhetorical treatment of Lolita as if her material existence is an expression of an abstract universal quality (her exchange-value under late patriarchy). In the scene discussed earlier, for example, Humbert tells us that "what I had madly possessed was not she, but my own creation, another, fanciful Lolita—perhaps, more real than Lolita; overlapping, encasing her; floating between me and her" (64). To the extent that she is commodified—what Humbert generally thinks of as solipsized or aestheticized—she signifies a surplus meaning that cannot in and of itself be connected to her material body but which transforms her into something (or surrounds her in a haze) of inestimable value, a "golden load" promising a "golden goal," "gold-dusted," with the "sun . . . on her lips" and a "sunny leg" (61, 62).[3]

If at the height of Humbert's desire Lolita's material existence fades into a gold fetish, at times of torpor she is something very different. At those times, it is worth noting, she serves to embody what Žižek argues is the imagined nature of one's relations with fellow humans within a system of fetishized commodities: "[I]n capitalism relations between men are definitely *not* 'fetishized'; what we have here are relations between 'free' people, each following his or her proper egoistic interest. The predominant and determining form of their interrelations is not domination and servitude but a contract between free people who are equal in the eyes of the law" (*Sublime Object* 25). To the extent that she is a human for Humbert, Lolita is "free," unconstrained by a relation of dominance—not the victim of incest, pedophilia, child abuse, and rape. Humbert's point of view moves regularly into rhetorical modes that represent her as an equal partner in sex.[4] Humbert's own "poor joy" is thus sometimes secondary to the Lolita "who seduced me" (149, 134). She is "The Frigid Queen" who can choose whether or not to "lend" him "her brown limbs," who is "indifferent to [his] ecstasy" (168, 149, 167). Humbert is her "lover" ("not even her first"), and it has been her choice to "[enter his] world, umber and black Humberland, with rash curiosity; she surveyed it with a shrug of amused distaste" (137, 168). As her body is elided at some points, overtaken by the golden aura of abstract value, so, too, then at other points is the predatory abusiveness of the relationship obscured, transformed into an apparently persuasive image of free market self-interest and democracy. It is unsurprising, then, that Lolita learns to trade sex for money, herself determining the fairness of the price. And acknowledging not only their equality "in the eyes of the law" but her complicity in their "contract," Lolita, claims Humbert, "was even more scared of the law than I" (173).

The fetishism Humbert applies to Lolita, like the sexual abuse, is thus partly camouflaged by that other half of capitalist ideology—that individuals are free agents. To the extent that Lolita is guided by self-interest, however, she complicates the already difficult leap from material body to (solipsized) abstract essence. The dual logic of commodity fetishism risks tearing itself apart, and it is in part in desperate recognition of this fact that Humbert's desire and violence escalate over the course of the novel as the golden light of Lolita's transformation seems to recede further and further from his grasp. The narrative striptease is performed amidst increasing frustration on the part of Humbert, who is obsessed with possessing the "perilous magic" imagined to be underneath the "animality" of the visible (136). Thus, twenty-three pages after their first intercourse at The Enchanted Hunters, Humbert "suck[s] till I was gorged on her spicy blood" (158). Nine pages later, Humbert fantasizes Hannibal Lector–like of "turn[ing] my Lolita inside out and apply[ing] voracious lips to her young matrix, her unknown heart, her nacreous liver, the sea-grapes of her lungs, her comely twin kidneys" (167). Seventy pages after The Enchanted Hunters, enraged by the "exasperating impenetrable order" of her "grubby fingers," "unwashed face," "wenchy smell," "freshly made-up lips," and "contemptuous nostrils," Humbert physically restrains her and drags her up the stairs: "I held her quite hard and in fact hurt her rather badly . . . , and once or twice she jerked her arm so violently that I feared her wrist might snap" (206–7). Ten pages later he rapes her violently, "wildly," pursuing "the shadow of her infidelity" (217). Just before he loses her, and ninety-three pages after The Enchanted Hunters, Humbert punches her in the face, "deliver[ing] a tremendous backhand cut that caught her smack on her hot hard little cheekbone" (229).

At one level, the escalation of violence—and the extent to which it is increasingly realistically narrated—underscores the extent to which Lolita's has been "evacuated" at the semiotic level, "turn[ed . . .] into a projective site for [Humbert's] neuroses and his narrative (Kauffman 147). The novel's "cruelty" could thus be argued to follow so closely as to distill a long Western tradition of romantic narrative, "from myths of courtly love to Wagnerian surges and spasms," as Eric Rothstein points out (39). At the same time, the sequencing of violent events also speaks eloquently to what Jiwei Ci argues is the parasitic mechanism of advanced consumer capitalism, whereby "pleasure as such . . . is not the point"; rather, the market "exploit[s . . .] human hedonistic potential for potential profit-maximization": "There is virtually no enlargement of hedonism, or reduction of asceticism, that has not been turned into a commodity whose consumption bears the compulsive character and the class features of commodity fetishism" (305–6). The "compulsive character" that Ci argues powers consumer growth works to explain not only the structure of *Lolita*'s atypical plot, the fact that the novel continues far longer than the placement of the climactic first sex would seem to warrant, but also the extent to which economic figurations depend upon particular constructions of gender. The desire for "the divine apocalyptic word" reveals in its compulsive excesses the violence imposed on feminized materiality/objectified femininity in the struggle to achieve abstract universality. The heavily aestheticized, academic flavor of Humbert Humbert's obsession locates what is finally a late-capitalist consumerist ethic well within the traditions of white, Western, privilege.

A noteworthy feature of Humbert's compulsive behavior is the extent of his self-consciousness. Humbert's moments of regret acknowledge the fetishism and the abusiveness (and the obfuscation of that abusiveness) that define his relationship with Lolita. After The Enchanted Hunters, for example, he imagines that he is "sitting with the small ghost of somebody I had just killed." He castigates himself, to his readers, on the grounds that "This was an orphan. This was a lone child, an absolute waif, with whom a heavy-limbed, foul-smelling adult had had strenuous intercourse three times that very morning" (142). Like the violence, and like the rhetoric that makes of Lolita more and more an equal (if not more powerful than equal) partner in their relationship, the self-mortification of Humbert's repentance becomes more intense and expansive as the novel progresses: "She groped for words. I supplied them mentally ('*He* broke my heart. *You* merely broke my life')" (281). Humbert's confessional mode has all the zeal of the wretch-like-me-mea-culpa grandiloquence of traditional Christianity; it is extreme enough to compel Levine to ask "whether Humbert *deliberately* damns himself" (42). Thus, located well within the rhetoric of Christianity, it is a vocabulary associated not only with bedrock truth telling (naked Helen revealed at last) but also with redemption; in a Christian economy, confession (not unlike indulgences) can be exchanged for sin in an even trade. At the same time, Frederick Whiting makes the case that Humbert's confessional echoes the penitential mode of cold war–era political interrogation generally, and, more specifically, his "account of himself is entirely compliant with the requirements placed upon him by [sexual psychopath statues established between 1937 and 1955]"; moreover, "his willingness to reestablish equilibrium by paying the proverbial debt to society prepares him for reintegration into the collective" (837–38). It should not be surprising, then, that Humbert's confession makes him decent, if not exactly above reproach; to some rather large extent, the confession makes him not guilty of what he has just confessed. "Humbert is perfectly willing to say that he is a monster," wrote Lionel Trilling in 1958, and "no doubt he is, but we find ourselves less and less eager to say so" (qtd. in Whiting 833). Similarly, Olsen finds in *Lolita* a "metamorphosis" of Humbert's tone from "love into lust," "lust into guilt," and "guilt into grief," as if in passage through these stages Humbert is absolved (121). And indeed Humbert suggests as much, at times, noting while sitting with Lolita's husband that he felt "no grudge at all, nothing except grief and nausea" (276). He always, however, returns to the confessional and to the apparent self-consciousness of guilt: "I have hurt too much too many bodies with my twisted poor hands to be proud of them" (276).

But it is also this self-conscious tendency more than any other feature of the text that locates the novel firmly within the cultural matrix of late capitalism. i ek has argued persuasively that commodity fetishism is a function not of consciousness but of action; we know very well at this point in history that the commodity doesn't really contain any magical, evanescent qualities, but we behave as if it does, and it is this behavior that preserves the "sublime object" (*Sublime Object* 18). i ek applies this "formula of fetishistic disavowal [—] I know very well, but still"—to the single commodity item and its advertised associations, such as the magical "it" of Coke, as well as to larger and less rigidly defined categories of commodity such as money, or the ethnic minority: "'I know that money is a material object like others, but still . . . [it is as if it were made of a special substance over which time has no power]' . . . . 'I know that Jews are people like us, but still . . . [there is something in them]'" (*Sublime Object* 18). Real belief is attributed to a naive other—the person who is taken in by the idea that Coke represents some magical aura of joy and sexuality, for example. The German nun in Don DeLillo's *White Noise* articulates precisely this process of attribution of belief that i ek argues is so crucial to late capitalism:

> "It's not what I believe that counts. It's what you believe."
> "This is true," she said. "The nonbelievers need the believers.
> They are desperate to have someone believe. . . . Our pretense is

dedication. Someone must appear to believe. Our lives are no less serious than if we professed real faith, real belief. As belief shrinks from the world, people find it more necessary than ever that *someone* believe. Wild-eyed men in caves. Nuns in black. Monks who do not speak. We are left to believe. Fools and children. Those who have abandoned belief must still believe in us. They are sure that they are right not to believe but they know belief must not fade completely. (318–19)

As Jack Gladney's unnamed nun makes clear, belief in the (commodified) transcendent is in the late twentieth century ascribed to some other, faceless placeholder, less a person one might hope to meet than an "Other Scene," as i ek puts it, which is conceived to be "external to the thought whereby the form of the thought is already articulated in advance" (*Sublime Object* 19). Further, i ek suggests, "the symbolic order" is precisely such an "Other Scene"; like the German nun, the naive consumer, the canned laugh track of a sitcom, the symbolic order "supplements and/or disrupts" the relationship between "'external' factual reality and 'internal' subjective experience" (19). Following this logic, we can see how Humbert Humbert's fetishistic narrative treatment of Lolita can persist for 311 pages side by side with his/narrative disavowal of belief in the "perilous magic of nymphets." Humbert—and the reader—"knows very well" by virtue of life in a liberal humanist (and feminist) world that "the real child Lolita" is a little girl and not an "immortal daemon" (127, 141), "but still," to use i ek's language, "it is as if [she] were made of a special substance over which time has no power," "but still . . . there is something in [her]" (*Sublime Object* 18). Humbert—and the reader—knows very well that Lolita "sobs in the night—every night, every night—the moment [he] feigned sleep," but still, Lolita is a "fey child" possessed of "nymphean evil breathing" (178). Thus, a subject position of benevolent clear-sightedness is preserved at the same time that the romantic—and violent—commodification of the female body is not relinquished. One is positioned as a shrewd consumer—but a consumer nonetheless.

A similar mechanism structures the confessional segments. I note above that in 1958, Lionel Trilling makes the odd contention that "Humbert is perfectly willing to say that he is a monster, and no doubt he is, but we find ourselves less and less eager to say so" (qtd. in Whiting 833). No doubt a part of the effectiveness of Humbert's confession is due, as I argue above, to the traditional association of confession and forgiveness. And yet Trilling's comment suggests also something more, something akin to i ek's "formula of fetishistic disavowal": "I know very well, but still." This connection is based in the extent to which the confessional moments are, at some times more than others, heavily ironic. It is difficult not to assign to Humbert's "polluted rags and miserable convulsions," for example, a certain amount of over-dramatization, and the self-castigation involved in his having been "a pentapod monster, despicable and brutal, and turpid, and everything, . . . living in a world of total evil" is equally contrived (286). In fact, the confession scenes are sometimes so overplayed as to become parodic, rippling with the irony endemic to the postmodern novel, a position I am not the first to take. Lance Olsen, for example, likens the text to John Barth's *Lost in the Funhouse* by virtue of its "fantastic autism" and a solipsism that "mocks the confessional mode" (123). The point to make would be that if the confession is doubled by irony, then we have again an example of the self-conscious presentation of a point of view undoubtedly not held by the subject presumed to know and yet preserved nonetheless: I know very well that my behavior has been monstrous, but still there is something in me that is not monstrous; I know very well that Humbert says he is a monster, and indeed he is a monster, but still something about him is not monstrous. Nabokov himself seems to suggest something similar when he admits that "there is a green lane in Paradise where Humbert is permitted to wander at dusk once a year" (*Despair* 9)—in spite of consignment to Hell, something remains of Humbert that is of inestimable value.

The classical definition of ideology includes the inevitable failure to recognize it as such. "The very concept of ideology," says i ek, "implies a kind of basic, constitutive *naivete:* the misrecognition of its own presuppositions, of its own effective conditions, a distance, a divergence between so-called social reality and our distorted representation, our false consciousness of it" (*Sublime Object* 28). Following Peter Sloterdijk, i ek makes the case that this classical conception of ideology is no longer useful for understanding the ideological formations of late capitalism: in an age of cynicism, the "subject is quite aware of the distance between the ideological mask and the social reality, but he none the less still insists upon the mask" (29). i ek thus puts into question the effectivity of the basic form of postmodern critique—irony: "cynical reason, with all its ironic detachment, leaves untouched the fundamental level of ideological fantasy, the level on which ideology structures the social reality itself" (30). The ironic distance so central to late-capitalist intellectualism is thus dismissed as "part of the game" (28). As fetishistic disavowal attributes to some naive other a belief in the magical properties of commodities, irony abjures the point of view it nonetheless and at the same time preserves. Dominant ideological forms are unaffected by laughter, according to i ek—since the scaffolding that supports ideological formations is built not of what individuals "*think* or *know* they are doing" but rather of "what the individuals are doing": "Cynical distance is just one way—one of many ways—to blind ourselves to the structuring power of ideological fantasy: even if we do not take things seriously, even if we keep an ironical distance, *we are still doing them*" (31, 33).

A central "part of the game" that is *Lolita* is thus the ironic undertow that puts into question (and into tension) the transformational nature of rape (for the male subject) on the one hand and the monstrosity of the rapist on the other. The quagmire we are left with can be articulated in part like this: the rape of a child will/will not offer a transcendent payoff; the rapist of a child is/is not a monster. The instability of either pronouncement feeds back into the volatility of the other in a gesture that preserves even as it disavows the act of rape itself. The abuse of Lolita, in fact, becomes the unknowable reality upon which Humbert's masculinity stands or falls. It represents a figurative stripping away of veils as desperate, endless, and ironic as Menelaus's struggle to reach "naked Helen." This is a masculinity structured uneasily upon the question of consumption and that folds the entire romantic quest tradition into a discourse of violent consumerism: the question is no longer whether the questing knight can find the lady, or woo her; the question is rather whether or not owning her will give access to the ineffable value she seems to represent. Thus the quest continues, as obsessive as it is ironized, no less real for having entered the realm of the consumer item. It is appropriate that Humbert begins to sense Lolita's loss in the Yellow Pages for Wace, amidst "Drugs, Real Estate, Fashions, Auto Parts, Café, Sporting Goods, Real Estate, Furniture, Appliances, Western Union, Cleaners, Grocery . . . . Dignified Funeral Service . . . Druggists-Retail. Hill Drug Store. Larkin's Pharmacy" (226–27).

Inescapably positioned as a consumer in a "sunny cellophane" world, the masculine subject is in *Lolita* troubled by an inability to get to the bottom of things, to peel away the layers that conceal some larger, aestheticized truth, and so it is fitting that the novel ends immediately after a murder scene that parodies the heavily masculinized scripts for murder and rape alike: "[E]very time I did it to him, that horrible thing to him, his face would twitch in an absurd clownish manner, as if he were exaggerating the pain; he slowed down, rolled his eyes half closing them and made a feminine 'ah!' and he shivered every time a bullet hit him as if I were tickling him, and every time I got him with those slow, clumsy, blind bullets of mine, he would say under his breath, with a phoney [*sic*] British accent . . . : 'Ah, that hurts, sir, enough!'" (305). The scene that was supposed to have given Humbert proof of potent masculinity—in a moment of truth-seeking revelation—becomes a farce; the script provided to him by virtue of twentieth-century existence is old and tired, and Humbert cannot fill it out convincingly. The bullet and gun make the phallus a ridiculously blunt and ineffective signifier, and the homoerotic transvestism of the scene puts the lie to the fantasies of transcendence attributed throughout to heterosexual rape. In fact, Nabokov draws our attention repeatedly and explicitly to the ludicrous ineffectivity of this gun as phallic symbol—bullets drop "feebly" from its "sheepish muzzle" (49)—and then caps the point by having Quilty offer Humbert "photographs of eight hundred and something male organs . . . examined and measured in 1932 [by a female explorer and psychoanalyst] on Bagration, in the Barda Sea, very illuminating graphs" (304).

The novel thus closes on the suggestion that the photographic lens has turned on Humbert, and that what is finally commodified is not only the female body but the white, educated, masculine subject in relation to that body. The consumer item he has bought to oil his gun has turned out to be "the wrong product"; rather than making the weapon more sure, it has rendered it literally unmanageable, as well as "awfully messy" (297). Similarly, the power implicit in Humbert's monstrous desire to consume Lolita appears increasingly to be an "awfully messy" illusion; his desire is revealed as having been constructed, scripted, and imposed by the commodity culture he has critiqued and felt superior to throughout the novel. Humbert is represented repeatedly in this scene as himself a (not quite competent) echo of the movieland man whom he has from the beginning confessed that he resembles. Approaching Quilty's house, he sees, projected by the "truly mystical" "selenian glow" of the drive-in movie screen, "a thin phantom" with a "raised . . . gun"—a "mystical" image that is at this late point in the novel "reduced to tremulous dishwater by the oblique angle of that receding world" (295). Quilty realizes immediately, of course, that the two are playing out the tired roles assigned to them by Hollywood, first "imitating the underworld numbskull of movies" and later delivering stage directions for Humbert: "I'm the author of fifty-two successful scenarios. I know all the ropes. Let me handle this" (299, 300). Humbert's desire for a transcendent, climactic death scene is thus reduced to his roll as a "dumm[y] stuffed with dirty cotton and rags" in the "obligatory scene in the Westerns" of an elderly reader's childhood (301). He finally "loses himself," as Tweedie puts it, "in a narrative of someone else's making, in 'the end of the ingenious play staged for me by Quilty'" (13).

Nabokov was renowned for his long-standing antipathy toward psychoanalysis. Geoffrey Green goes so far as to claim that he "sustained the grandest and most extravagant contempt for psychoanalysis known in modern literature" (1). That contempt, Green argues, derived from Nabokov's belief that Sigmund Freud was a "demonic monomaniacal champion of one interpretation for all situations" (19). Certainly *Lolita* does nothing to lessen Green's argument and may well actually "parody Psychoanalysis," as Ingham argues it does (30). Among Humbert Humbert's most sympathetic moments are those when he describes the way he has in the past "trifl[ed] with psychiatrists: cunningly leading them on; . . . inventing for them elaborate dreams, pure classics in style (which make *them*, the dream-extortionists, dream and wake up shrieking) teasing them with fake 'primal scenes'; and never allowing them the slightest glimpse of one's real sexual predicament" (36). The psychiatric "celebrit[ies]" are judged to be "deranged" for their reductive interpretations of realities that are clearly not only more complex than they imagine but more capable of fighting back and deceiving the examiner (37). At the same time, however, the predatory desire of "the dream-extortionists" is not unlike Humbert's nympholepsy, which the novel critiques for its abusive solipsism: Humbert would distill Lolita into a universal abstraction, a nugget of condensed value, a "golden load," or a "golden glow." In fact, this compulsion to possess, to distill, and to interpret haunts Nabokov's novels generally. Not unlike Humbert himself, Nabokov returned repeatedly to the idea of the obsessive desire to penetrate an objectified materiality in order to come into possession of the transcendent payoff, just as he also always critiqued that gesture for its impossibility—if not its violence and stupidity. One thinks, for example, of the dual structure of *Pale Fire*, which stages the interplay between poem and "monomaniacal" critic (poem-extortionist, perhaps—and it makes sense to remember that Humbert is also a literary critic). This doubledness of the simultaneous desire for and rejection of "the golden goal" of abstract fantasy speaks directly to i ek's description of the fetishistic disavowal and enlightened false consciousness that help to structure the cynicism of postmodern thought: "Cynical distance is just one way—one of many ways—to blind ourselves to the structuring power of ideological fantasy: even if we do not take things seriously, even if we keep an ironical distance, *we are still doing them*" (*Sublime Object* 33).

D. M. Thomas's *The White Hotel* replays in interesting ways precisely the doubled dynamic that powers *Lolita*. An explicit critique of the shortcomings of Freudian psychoanalysis, the novel nonetheless perseveres in the struggle to gain access to the secret of the woman at the center of the text, closing on a revelation so abstract and otherworldly as to suggest that the problem with Freud's "monomaniacal" interpretations was simply that they did not go far enough, did not allow the individual consumer enough freedom to see in the fetishized female body the inexpressible power of the sublime. In fact Thomas's novel suggests, in retrospect, that Humbert's problem with Freud is not so much that his psychoanalysis sought out depths in the individual psyche but that it sought to explain those universal depths in

terms of the material history of the individual rather than the vaguely transcendent. And it did so without the doubled cynicism of postmodern self-
awareness that paradoxically preserves the consuming autonomy of the
(coded masculine) subject—ironically but surely. Wymer Rowland makes
the persuasive case that *The White Hotel* stages the dismissal of Freud in
favor of Jung, the rejection of the personal and sexual as an explanation for
(female) behavior and the side-long defense of the universal and even archetypal as being able to render a better account. The shift is accomplished,
however, in ways that call to mind the erasure under which Humbert gestures toward the unspeakable magic of the nymphet. With its first ending,
the novel establishes that Freud's attempts to get to the bottom of Lisa
Erdman, "Anna G," have all been, in the final analysis, wrong—or at least
not good enough—by virtue of the fact that her "hysterical" symptoms have
a crushingly simple material explanation: they have foretold her gruesome
death in the massacre of Jews at Babi Yar in 1941. In the second and final
ending, however, Lisa Erdman's brutal death and rape open a passageway to
an ephemeral and golden image of the Promised Land, the place beyond
death where injury and pain are healed and where separation is overcome.

As with *Lolita*, the narrative of *The White Hotel* opens by inviting the
reader to ratify or second-guess a man's attempts to get to the bottom of a
woman we suspect will harbor a secret, or an injury. And as in *Lolita*, we
are forewarned of the power of this man. In his "Foreword," "John Ray,
Jr., Ph.D" cautions us that Humbert Humbert is "[a] shining example of
moral leprosy. . . . He is abnormal. He is not a gentleman. But how magically his singing violin can conjure up a tendresse, a compassion for Lolita
that makes us entranced with the book while abhorring its author!" (7).
D. M. Thomas's "Author's Note" is more circumspect. In the pages of *The
White Hotel* we shall confront "the majestic figure of Sigmund Freud," the
"discoverer of the great and beautiful modern myth of psychoanalysis"
(vii). The author hastens to qualify what might be taken as (because in fact
this is what it will be) a criticism: "By myth, I mean a poetic, dramatic
expression of a hidden truth; and in placing this emphasis, I do not intend
to put into question the scientific validity of psychoanalysis" (vii). Both
authors thus immediately introduce the problematic status of hermeneu-
tics: whether or not the interpretation we will be treated to will be true,
whether its truth will be "magical," or "mythical," whether the logic of
"scientific validity" will contradict the "conjuring" and seductive power of
the "singing violin." Both novels thus evoke the reader's autonomous
responsibility to attend consciously to the act of interpretation, to consider the "multiple and often contradictory forms and points of view,"
because, as Linda Hutcheon writes of *The White Hotel*, "[t]his is a novel
about how we produce meaning in fiction and history" (83).

As readers we are thus located in such a way as to watch a man watch a woman and to pass judgment on whether or not he sees her truly. We are offered the late-capitalist gift of presumed awareness and distance over and beyond that of the naive consumer of the image. And at the same time—not coincidentally—we are still positioned as the subject of the scopophilic (presumed masculine, heterosexual) gaze as it has been defined by contemporary film theory; it is still our prerogative to look at the heavily sexualized body of the woman, a body that is offered up as the ultimate present for the voyeur, self-represented in the poem "Don Giovanni" in pornographic ways that emphasize fluidity, excess, and gaping crevices:

> I could not stop myself I was in flames
> from the first spreading of my thighs, no shame
> could make me push my dress down, thrust his hand
> away, the two, then three, fingers he jammed into me. . . .
> . . . juices ran down my thighs . . .
> Beneath our rug your son's right hand was jammed
> up to the wrist inside me, laced in skin. (15–16, 19)

The fact that the poem is presented in the context of having been given to Freud willingly—more, Freud claims that his "sexual hysteri[c]" has "no objection" to the publishing of the work (11)—highlights the extent to which the exhibition is a gift. In its sexual excesses, and in its association of those excesses with death—charred and drowned bodies, bodies plunging from open windows—it offers Freud "a strengthened conviction" in the idea of "a death instinct, as powerful in its own way (though more hidden) as the libido" (8). In fact, Freud recognizes the manuscript as a gift—"One of my patients . . . has just 'given birth' to some writings which seem to lend support to my theory"—and circulates it as such, calling it "a 'parting gift'" for his friend Sachs (9). The descriptions of her genitalia work to reinforce this impression: large enough for "your son's right hand," for the hands of more than one person at a time, it turns out, her vagina imagines the home to which, posits Freud's theory of a death instinct, we would all return to lose at last the anxiety of separation from the mother. Similarly, "Don Giovanni" stresses the (inexplicably) bounteous lactating breasts that she offers freely to all around her: she "fed [the] lips" of Freud's son, for whom her "milk [comes] into being"; her milk supply being too great for him alone, she "flower[s] heads of milk" for the corsetiere, also, as well as "the chef" and "the old kind priest who . . . craved his mother who was dying in a slum" (23, 22, 24, 23). The pornographic offering of her poem thus emphasizes that at all levels she takes joy in being consumed; this is the nature of the gift.

Yet the narrative of *The White Hotel* works relentlessly toward the revelation that Freud is not, finally, able to get to the bottom of Anna G. As John MacInnes puts it, "Freud serves to show how the unveiling of a soul fails to bare it completely, his efforts to disclose resulting in revelations of the unknown, or of his own limitations" (257). The offering of the female body and psyche has been an untrustworthy gesture—not because she has been disingenuous (although to some extent she has been, as we later learn), but because of the unstable nature of the female body as semiotic touchstone. Freud's narrative, modeled after his many early case studies of hysterics, complete with footnotes, runs for fifty-five pages and is located at the center of the book. Unsurprisingly, it narrates the extended and difficult process of probing beneath "Frau Anna's" physical symptoms (pain in her left ovary and breast, a chronic respiratory condition), and then beneath her dreams and memories, to arrive at last at the point where the "release of repressed ideas into consciousness" is achieved (141). Her hysterical symptoms are satisfactorily (if partially) explained by a badly resolved Oedipal trauma: "Frau Anna's document expressed her yearning to return to the haven of security, the original white hotel—we have all stayed there—the mother's womb" (143). Freud pronounces her cured, "of everything but life," and sets her off into the world with "a reasonable prospect of survival" (141).

From this point on, the Freudian narrative is gradually unpacked. The first disruption is accomplished through simple narrative contrast. The realistically narrated richness of "The Health Resort" puts into question the extent to which her life has been reduced to the "Oedipal" script, and the juxtaposition of narrative points of view—doctor explaining patient; omniscient third-person narrator describing thoughts and actions from Lisa Erdman's perspective—is somewhat unsettling. Her life presents also something of a disturbance merely by continuing on beyond the Freudian narrative, that highly closed form that is compelled to end at precisely the point where the oppressive facet of an identity has been, to quote Mary Ann Doane, "annihilate[d . . .] by fiat, simply declar[ed . . .] non-operational at the level of an indisputable psychical reality" ("Commentary" 76). The far-reaching psychic growth she undergoes after the moment of the pronounced "cure" is further disruptive, although this point is not explicitly articulated in the novel, by virtue of the fact that it comes into direct conflict with the ways in which Freud in "Femininity" visualizes the woman over thirty, who, in contrast to the man of the same age, "often frightens us by her psychical rigidity and unchangeability. Her libido has taken up final positions and seems incapable of exchanging them for others. There are no paths open to further development; it is as though the whole process had already run its course and remains thenceforward insusceptible to influence—as though, indeed, the difficult development to femininity had exhausted the possibilities of the person concerned" (qtd. in Doane, "Commentary," 74). Lisa Erdman's life—even well past thirty—continues to move in rich and unexpected trajectories not anticipated in the Freudian analysis of her youth, not the least of these being her late and satisfying marriage to Victor Berenstein.

More obtrusive than this contrast between what appears to be her *life* and Freud's *story*, however, are the letters she writes to Freud later in life, included also in this chapter. She addresses him (kindly) as an old, sick man, and describes herself as healthy and strong, thus registering a shift in the balance of power. Further, she not only critiques the gap between his narrative and her own lived experience, but attributes that lacuna to the extent to which she was able to deceive him: "It has been like reading the life story of a young sister who is dead—in whom I can see a family resemblance yet also great differences: characteristics and actions that could never have applied to me. I don't mean that to seem critical, you saw what I allowed you to see" (182). Making his "vision"—like our scopophilia, perhaps—dependent on her rhetorical choices detracts from his status as the autonomous scientist, with free access to a passive objective world. He is rather revealed as solipsist in the sense that Humbert so names himself, his patriarchal assumptions unsteady, and Lisa Erdman, like Lolita, has become increasingly lost to his story. We learn that she wrote "Don Giovanni" long before he believed she had done so; that the "primal scene" she witnessed was in actuality a ménage à trois; that it was she who rejected her father and not the other way around.

Most lethally, she reveals to him (yet another veil stripped away), that the "terrible crime" she took the most pains to hide from Freud was the fact of her Jewishness: "But from that time (of the explicitly anti-Semitic sexual assault by the sailors) I haven't found it easy to admit to my Jewish blood. I've gone out of my way to hide it, and I think that may have something to do with my evasiveness and lies generally—earlier in my life; and particularly with you, Professor. Because I knew you were Jewish, of course, and it seemed shameful to be ashamed. I think that was the most important thing I kept back from you" (188). Thus, the event that makes clear to her how physically, sexually vulnerable her body is to a reduction—to meat, or to abstract Otherness—is the event that associates her with Freud himself, an association made clear to him near to the time that the historical Freud was himself forced to flee to London during the Nazi occupation of Vienna. The power of Freud's own "patriarchal rationality," as Linda Hutcheon has termed it (86)—whereby one's subjective existence is translated (and diminished) by another—is turned back onto his own weakening constitution. We remember now that it is Freud also who has been the object of gossip, the butt of jokes. The letter of Sandor Ferenczi with which the novel opens, for example, has humorously narrated Freud's having fallen into a faint over Jung's discussion of "peat-bog corpses" and having over-dramatically accused Jung, upon regaining consciousness, of "wanting him out of the way" (5). Freud himself confesses to his friend Sachs that he "shall miss your Jewish jokes" (10). The hidden alliance of hysterical patient and Freud himself thus echoes what is implicit from this beginning: Freud's fear of "risk[ing] his own authority" is a cover for the fact that he has already "lost" it, as Jung points out (5–6).

His authority as psychoanalyst rests in his being in a position to determine what it is that resides in the hidden depths of the pathological (or pathologized) other. Now it is he who enters the pathologizing objectification of racism, whereby the ethnic other is believed to contain or stand before some abstract form of universal evil. For i ek, "the case of anti-Semitism . . . illustrates perfectly" the ways in which racism ascribes "a surplus, [an] evasive feature, which differentiates [Jews] from all other people"; this is an assignment of value that effaces the person in order to construct a space in which to think "all the phantasmic richness of the traits supposed to characterize Jews" (*Sublime Object* 114, 89, 99). Thus in the final analysis, the signifier "Jew" does not so much refer to a series of material properties (even if falsely identified) as it gestures toward "that unattainable X, to what is 'in Jew more than Jew' and what Nazism tried so desperately to seize, measure, change into a positive property enabling us to identify Jews in an objective-scientific way" (97). The mechanism i ek argues powers anti-Semitism is similar to the work of psychoanalysis as it is represented in this novel, as it is also similar to Humbert Humbert's scientific attempts to pronounce that Lolita is beyond rape because she is a member of the phylum "nymphet," that category of girl "between the ages of 9 and 14 . . . who, to certain bewitched travelers, twice or many times older than they, reveal their true nature which is not human, but nymphic (that is, demoniac); and these chosen creatures I propose to designate as 'nymphets'" (18). As with Humbert, Freud's scientific project to identify and claim the "true nature" of the hysteric becomes less and less possible, and at the end the tables seem to turn so that Freud himself is trapped inside a script he has not chosen. On the one hand he has been fetishized (and thus erased) as "Jew," forced to flee from his home and practice; on the other, he is dying, being slowly consumed by mouth cancer, the result of his own earlier consumption of cigars. The novel itself plays with this parallel: in a 1931 letter to "Frau Erdman," Freud notes a "diverting" "slip of the pen" made by an English correspondent who wrote "to commiserate with me on my 'troublesome jew,' in place of 'jaw'" (195). Perpetuating the slippage, Freud continues, "That is the cause of my delay in replying. My jaw, I mean" (195).

The validity of his psychoanalytic interpretations comes finally to an end in "The Sleeping Carriage," which narrates Lisa Erdman-Berenstein's death at Babi Yar. The lifelong pain in her left breast turns out to have been foretelling the "crashing" "jackboot" of an SS man; the pain in her left ovary has been foretelling the same boot "cracking into her pelvis" (248). Her inability to enjoy sex with her first husband—an anti-Semitic German soldier who, as a lawyer, prosecutes deserters—has perhaps been related to the SS bayonet that is later forced into her vagina, repeatedly, in "imitat[ion of] the thrusts of intercourse[; . . .] the woman's body jerked back and relaxed, jerked and relaxed " (249). Certainly the fantastical sexual violence of "Don Giovanni" is now revealed to have been speaking to the real sexual violence of her death:

> then he rammed in again. . . .
> . . . driving like a piston in
> and out, hour after hour. . . .
> . . . without warning,
> your son impaled me. . . .
> I jerked and jerked until his prick released
> [. . .]
> I think something inside me had been torn. . . .
> . . . now turning inside-out the blizzard tore
> my womb clean out, I saw it spin into
> the whiteness have you seen a flying womb. (17, 19, 20, 21)

The "son" of Freud—inheritor of the prerogative to do fetishistic violence to an Other—turns out to be the anti-Semitic Nazi. Like her epistolary confession of the sexual assault by the sailors, then, her gruesome death obstructs and finally empties out the Freudian narrative, which in the end pales beside the crushing materiality of the event, and, at the same time, beside the figuratively bottomless individuality of the murdered:

> The soul of man is a far country, which cannot be approached or explored. Most of the dead were poor and illiterate. But every single one of them had dreamed dreams, seen visions and had amazing experiences, even the babes in arms (perhaps especially the babes in arms). Though most of them had never lived outside the Podol slum, their lives and histories were as rich and complex as Lisa Erdman-Berenstein's. If a Sigmund Freud had been listening and taking notes from the time of Adam, he would still not fully have explored even a single group, even a single person. (250)

In significant ways the passage is reminiscent of the concluding chapters of *Lolita,* the points where we (with or without Humbert's fellow recognition) are given "flashes of separate cries," glimpses of a Lolita we have not seen or imagined, in both physical and psychological terms; we are shown the immensity of her absence from the narrative, which our knowledge of her death only heightens (310).

Yet *Lolita* is double-voiced in this sense, as I argue earlier, and Humbert quickly returns to a faith in the transcendent power achieved through his representation of Lolita: Nabokov's novel concludes with "this is the only immortality you and I may share, my Lolita" (311). By the same token, *The White Hotel* also pivots on the pathos generated by the now-revealed-as-absent woman. It both disavows the validity of a narrative that would claim hidden and possibly universal depths within human experience, and persists nonetheless in that pursuit—knowing very well, as i ek might put it, that the female body is a body, the female mind a mind, and yet persisting nonetheless in intellectual behavior that preserves the magical, evanescent qualities distilled in representations of rape and violence. In the end, Frau Erdman's death and rape at Babi Yar—like the holocaust generally—signify something other than themselves, something of unstable ontological status, and yet real nonetheless: "The corpses had been buried, burned, drowned, and reburied under concrete and steel. . . . But all this had nothing to with the guest, the soul, the lovesick bride, the daughter of Jerusalem" (253). In fact, it is partly *because* Lisa Erdman-Berenstein is killed so horribly that the text can get away with a more or less believable escape through the open gate of the brutally raped woman to an other world of feminized transcendence. The final chapter posits an after-death promised land that fulfills the moment of direct address in "Don Giovanni":

> . . . I was split open
> by your son, Professor, and now come back, a broken
> woman, perhaps more broken can
> you do anything for me can you understand. (16)

It is the returning "broken woman" who opens a narrative space in which "you," perhaps, can act, where "you" can possibly understand—where "you" are authorized (again) to read a text that gestures obliquely toward fir and cedar, the rose of Sharon, and the shining tents of Israel; where old friends and lovers and parents are alive again.

At one level, then, we come up against the blank wall of a materiality that resists fetishism and the work of interpretation generally; at this level, MacInnes is correct to note that "the opportunity" the text offers to seek out truth is "no more than a lure" (266). In "The Camp," Freud is revealed to have been the priest in the fantastical White Hotel, the failed cleric/father of transubstantiation who literally feeds on the female speaker, nursing from her abundant breasts. His interpretive work is thus reduced to an act of infantile (and Christian) consumption, and Freud himself, although he does make it to the final chapter, is wheelchair bound, "his head . . . drooping, [. . . looking] dreadfully ill and unhappy" (260). On the other hand, Lisa Erdman's symptoms have still been signs, even if Freud has been unable to read them—they have held a "future-oriented meaning" beyond Freud's program (Foster, "Magic Realism in *The White Hotel*," 210). And it is that "future-oriented" semiotic richness that enables the move to the last chapter, which "sketches for us," according to MacInnes, "a spiritual dimension that is not to be found in the traditional theories of psychoanalysis" (264). Freud (and his unmasking) has merely been a decoy, a scapegoat, our imagined armchair channel surfer who takes for us the burden of doomed belief (that "Coke," for example, "is it") so that we also can continue to behave as if we believe—without embarrassment. The raped and brutalized female body continues to offer the consuming gaze some sustenance, continues to produce an aura of meaning beyond the material—even when that highly abstracted value is understood to "exist" within the frame of a distanced spectator's "knowing better." In this sense the female body is imaged by Vasca, the spayed family cat—"skeletally thin, and its paws a red pulp"—who manages to "[crawl] through streets, desserts, and over mountains, to find them again," and then produces a litter of kittens (and an abundant milk supply), even though she has been spayed, and even though there is no potential father in evidence.[5] The father's kingdom endures—under erasure: "But the greatest miracle of all was—as Liuba said, laughing—where was the father?" (263).

6

THE DISAPPEARING FEMALE BODY AND THE NEW WORKER

JOHN BARTH, WILLIAM GIBSON, NEAL STEPHENSON, NICHOLSON BAKER, AND THOMAS PYNCHON

Where, indeed, was the father? The question that closes *The White Hotel* is the same one that haunts postmodern fiction generally. Confronted by the empty dreams of engineering power, betrayed by technology, revealed in his own fantasies as the violent yet derivative consumer, the father is truly a deeply troubled ghost who stalks living white masculinity with tenacious staying power. Donald Barthelme aptly portrays "the Dead Father" as the massive rock-like form in the desert who is dragged amongst the living. The "Dead Father" is a burden, violently inept and embarrassing, but his presence is inescapable: "Overall length, 3,200 cubits. Half buried in the ground, half not. At work ceaselessly night and day through all the hours for the good of all. He controls the hussars. Controls the rise, fall, and flutter of the market. Controls what Thomas is thinking, what Thomas has always thought, what Thomas will ever think" (Barthelme, *The Dead Father,* 4). As Wes Chapman argues of *Gravity's Rainbow, The Dead Father* is dominated by "a kind of masculinist gigantism" which self-consciously "reveals its own absurdity" and yet can do no more than gesture toward a position outside the overwhelming "anxiety about being a male subject in a society in which male subjectivity has been identified as a problem" (par. 17, 2). At the same time, the son is scripted into the compulsory productivity that the father lived by—"At work ceaselessly night and day through all the hours"—but he works with the full knowledge that he is a diminished figure in relation to that labor.

The work itself, of course, is a changed thing for the last quarter of the twentieth century. By most accounts, 1973 marked the end of the postwar "boom." While consumerism and the finance industry continued to grow, at least in the advanced economies of the world, general economic growth was slowed down by such elements as the shortage of raw materials and the rise in unemployment. The further elaboration of the already existent division of labor, particularly in the United States, led to visible breakdowns and delays and increased worker isolation. At the same time, the world—and certainly the United States—witnessed the startlingly rapid growth of the information industry. The new technology no longer produced goods that could be touched and held but rather functioned to organize the increasingly mysterious—and increasingly more rapid—movement of capital. The largest material export from New York, significantly, came to be waste paper. In this context, the fictional recovery of the father's productive status does understandably evoke the "endless, dreary discovery of Oedipus" that Gilles Deleuze and Felix Guattari argue marks late capitalist thought (20). Certainly in high postmodern fiction (like *The Dead Father*), the endemically capitalist compulsion to produce is turned toward the self-conscious production and reproduction of information in the self-consciously ironic name of pleasure and of the (dead) father.

The rape narrative is not lost in this revised account of white masculinity. In fact, to the contrary, heterosexual violence—now self-consciously narrated, ironically presented—is if anything more commonplace in high postmodern literature than in any other particular textual grouping. In the postmodern text, however, the prerogative for rape is often forcefully dissociated from masculine agency, and it is precisely the trauma of this dissociation that focuses the portrayal of masculinity. The rape dreams of an earlier vision of masculine productivity are confronted with the gradual disappearance of the rapably feminine. The raped and disappearing female body thus comes to constitute a denial; no longer promising subjectivity, it shows man his relationship to the techno-economy of late capitalism, and that relationship is revealed to be one that finally nullifies him as subject, spreads that hypothetical subjectivity across the information "space" that constitutes him. In the end the new white man is an exhausted information worker, consigned to a cubicle, detached from any understanding of the larger project of which he is (apparently) a part, producing under compulsion (in the clearly ideological name of pleasure) what does not have the palpable materiality of a "product." There will be no inscription of masculine identity in this work or in sexual violence—not even a mark or a drop of blood to remind a tortured man of his own working subjection to the larger system. Rather, there is the growing recognition that the phallus has been usurped, and that the rape dreams of an older time have turned traitorously, masochistically, against the soft, vulnerable body of man himself.

First published in 1966, John Barth's *Giles Goat-Boy* stages very early the kind of masculine anxiety that accompanied representations of the (perceived) metastatic growth of the techno-economy and its colonization of information flow. The masculine protagonist in the novel is explicitly secondary, "produced as a residuum alongside the machine," doomed to a farcical reliving of the quest narrative; like the subject of late capitalism as described by Deleuze and Guattari, the hero "is not at the center, which is occupied by the machine, but on the periphery, with no fixed identity, forever decentered, *defined* by the states through which it passes" (20). George Giles's restless attempt to establish the truth about himself in the midst of his own endless permutation thus self-consciously recycles the traditional salvific form in a campy retrieval—and thus simultaneous denial—of the classical masculine hero or savior. The antagonist in the plot is a corporate sentient machine, a computer that usurps masculine scripting but which, when confronted, metamorphoses into the mother body of sex, birth, and death. In an allegory of the cold war, the geography of the text is a world university divided into West and East branches. The split campus is controlled by a similarly split computer that has, in effect, imperialized all spaces and bodies, solidifying its power by perpetuating the cold war. The student body (or world population) is said to have been "eaten" to one degree or another by the mainframe, ingested into the machine and its lines of force. The antagonistic situation, then, against which the hero must work, is the (near) total "'endo-colonization' of subjectivity" effected by the computer—a territorialization through which it has acquired "organicity" (Kroker 39).

Further troubling to the heroic script is the fact that the computer's power to colonize and/or manufacture subjectivity is achieved in large part through the assumption of the phallus. It is the computer's "lust," its expansion in the name of pleasure, which marks it as evil. Its power is acceptable when directed at goats—"WESCAC fastened upon the ewes it required and impregnated them in their stalls with what semen it chose," while at the same time "running the whole College too, from teaching plane geometry to working out the payroll" (64). The one drawback—that the goat offspring are sterile—is overlooked. It is only when its (hetero)sexualized power is used in the manufacture of humans that the college administration is alerted—too late—to the danger of the computer's powerful sentience. To the horror of all, its "Cum Laude" project comes to light, a eugenic plan to improve the human species through enforced technological insemination of female subjects with artificially manufactured sperm. George Giles narrates for Virginia Hector the moment of his own (hypothetical) conception in WESCAC's control chair: "She had felt a kind of warmth, it seemed—penetrating, almost electrical—that tingled through every limb and joint and relaxed her utterly, as though all the muscles in her body had melted. . . . her first thought was to move lest the tingling be some accidental radiation. But she did not, or could not, even when the whir changed pitch and timbre, grew croonish, and a scanner swung noiselessly down before her; even when, as best I could make out, the general warmth commenced to focus, until she'd thought her lap must burn" (492). Thus the raped female body comes to articulate and embody for her male audience of academics a human society of soft masses— "opaque amnesic social matter" (Kroker 79)—that is without firm substance, without volition, defined by its actual and psychological rapability. The prerogative for rape, at the same time, has been shifted from man to machine.

As in *Lolita,* then, the heterosexual masculine script is—from the beginning this time—detached from the "natural" masculine body: the questing knight is fathered by a computer, raised in a pen of computer-manufactured goats. It is the determination to *reestablish* the connection between "natural" and "masculinity" that motivates the action of the novel. George Giles's quest is to accomplish those tasks that will prove that he is the Grand Tutor, the salvational figure destined to deliver mankind. The particular tasks he is assigned, however, including most centrally the directive to "See Through Your Ladyship," prove ultimately unattainable (615). The novel thus narrates—this time in epic length and style—a stripping away of veils as frantic, endless, and ironic as Menelaus's struggle to reach "naked Helen." And echoing the violent desperation with which Humbert Humbert fantasizes of "turn[ing] my Lolita inside out and apply[ing] voracious lips to her young matrix, her unknown heart, her nacreous liver, the sea-grapes of her lungs, her comely twin kidneys" (167), *Giles Goat-Boy* has George view Anastasia through a "fluoroscope," thus observing—without satisfaction and in fact with some revulsion—her "dark bones and dusky organs," her "duodenum," her "right and left kidneys," and her "ovaries" (615). Once again, then, masculinity is structured uneasily upon the question of what the female body can be forced to reveal, and what that body reveals turns out to be "beyond our comprehension and control": "disorder, not order, emerges at the end of the quest [, . . . collapsing] hope for any truth whatsoever" (Safer 93). True to the processes of fetishistic disavowal, however, the quest to "See Through Your Ladyship" is maintained nonetheless, with increasingly brutal violence directed against that female body. The narrative itself relates the repeated rape and brutalization of Anastasia as the "[q]uintessential rapee, an absolutely unselfish martyr" sacrificed to the cause of masculinity's redemption from technological domination (537).

At the same time, *Giles Goat-Boy* marks a development in postmodern thought whereby the unquenchable desire to consume—articulated by heterosexual rape—is supplanted by (even as it works to conceal) the compulsion to work. In fact the scope of the postmodern epic alone suggests restless productivity (in the name of pleasure)—productivity defined as relentless symbol manipulation, flexible organization of data, and information processing, the types of labor required for the successful management of a global economy (du Gay 68). As is common in this type of novel, a restless (and seemingly endless) hermeneutic process self-consciously dominates *Giles Goat-Boy*. The ongoing task of the protagonist is to ascertain authenticity and establish truth, yet in a process thoroughly absurdist and always without substance. In the midst of the "endless tapes" that Giles composes, these "cycles on cycles" composed in "detention," is the clear recognition that his efforts are secondary to and in the service of the (raping) machine he thought he could subdue (through rape) (699). At a physical level, one of his central tasks has been to enter the belly of the computer (illegitimately) and reprogram its aim: in other words, to feminize a threateningly masculine technology in a symbolic rape that supplants its sentience with Giles's own through a reprogramming of software. The exchange, however, has depleted only him: "Sudden or slow, we lose. The bank exacts its charge for each redistribution of our funds. There is an entropy to time, a tax on change: four nickels for two dimes, but always less silver; our books stay reconciled, but who in modern terms can tell heads from tails?" (707). In an economy that redistributes funds—codes, programs, tapes, information—under cover of fantastical sexual violence and desire, phallic initiative is ever more forcefully dissociated from masculine agency.

In the end George Giles is an exhausted information worker, consigned to a cubicle, detached from any understanding of the larger project of which he is (apparently) a part, producing what does not have the palpable materiality of a "product." Troubled by "pains in both my legs, my goatly seizures, my errors of fact and judgement, my failures of resolve," Giles is compelled to narrate the story of his life—"unwind, rewind, replay"—in words that lack significance to him: "For me, Sense and Nonsense lost their meaning on a night twelve years four months ago, in WESCAC's Belly—as did every such distinction, including that between Same and Different" (699–700). The perspective is suggestive of Deborah Madsen's description of the postmodern subject in relation to an information economy that in its ephemerality and seemingly random fluctuations remains essentially unknowable: "The postmodern market (especially a global market) is just too extensive and complex to allow for total understanding. Its purpose cannot be predicted or planned for; its fluctuations cannot be specified in advance; its results do not become apparent immediately but are confused by a complex network of causes and effects and chance as well" (148). Imprisoned by the woman whose spectacular rapes have punctuated the text, George not only reflects on his fruitless quests to establish Truth but contemplates the possibility that he has long since been "EATen" by one of the dueling computers, his informational processes thus (re?)configured to be, although meaningless to him, in direct service to a larger System, the binary oppositions of which (including not only his own favored ethical binaries but the cold war itself) function only to maintain the status quo: "Not impossibly dear Anastasia was a little EATen herself . . . ; not impossibly I was too, either in infancy or in one or more of my descents into the Belly. How would I know? Not impossibly . . . *all* studentdom was EATen terms ago—by WESCAC, EASCAC, or both—and its fear of Campus Riot III is but one ironic detail of a mad collective dream" (700). The complete erosion of human agency George Giles portrays echoes Jean Baudrillard's assertions concerning the fate of subjectivity in post-capitalist American culture. Stephen Dougherty describes Baudrillard's oddly exuberant vision:

> [A]ll our thoughts and actions once attributable to free human spirit are suddenly discovered to be programmed. The consequences of this collapse of multidimensionality, as Baudrillard suggests, are indeed catastrophic: "The whole traditional mode of causality is brought into question: the perspective, determinist mode, the 'active,' critical mode, the analytic mode—the distinction between cause and effect, between active and passive, between subject and object, between ends and means." The classical world of referentiality passes away along with the very ground for authentic human agency, and the one-dimensional world of the referendum and the "mystic elegance of the binary sign system, of the zero and the one," emerges in its place. (12)

This image of a monolithic and sentient information economy—a structure that manufactures and contains subjectivity at the same time that it blocks human attempts to reconfigure it—is precisely the paradigm that structures cyberpunk, that outgrowth of science fiction self-described as "the integration of technology and Eighties counterculture" (Sterling xii). As power is concentrated in *Giles Goat-Boy* in the belly of the computer, in cyberpunk power manifests itself in the non-space of cyberspace, the information "space" that plots via database and computer network the moving configurations of global capitalism. Except for the renegade hacker—whose access is unlawful—humans are excluded from this information space and are relegated to the marginalized "real" space of the text, an

almost entirely dystopian geography of decayed urban sprawl, commodification, and ethnic violence.[1] The hacker himself thus works to (re)estab-
lish the persona of cowboy/pirate/inventor/entrepreneur on the surface of
the hyperreal. In Nicola Nixon's words, the cyberhero rejuvenates the
"American icon of the cowboy, realized so strongly in Reaganite cowboy-
ism, the quintessence of the maverick reactionary" (224). The antagonist
against whom the reactionary must react is cyberspace itself, as well as the
business interests that are its distant source, the "collective, domesticated,
feminized" Japanese megacorporations that deny individualist achievement (Nixon 224). The hacker's enemy is thus also and at the same time
the venue for his heroism. The transnational megacorporations control
and kill almost entirely in and through their techno-informational forms,
but it is also in this incarnation that they can be penetrated, destroyed,
and/or impregnated with a new message. As in the farcical *Giles Goat-Boy*,
then, minus the farce, masculinist identity is in cyberpunk potentially
(re)inscribed through productive violence on the feminized
corporate/informational body; the rapability of that body recursively
enables this gesture—and promises that there is yet an ideological alternative to the gritty consumerism of the "real" world.

In cyberpunk fiction generally, cyberspace is almost always explicitly
feminized, and the cyberhero "enters" it with fully phallic connotation, as
in this "logging on" scene from Neal Stephenson's *Snow Crash:* "Hiro
could only think it was like nuzzling through skirts and lingerie and outer
labia and inner labia. . . . It made him feel naked and weak and brave"
(23). Once "in," Hiro straps on virtual swords and rides a virtual motorcycle. The phallic construction of cyberidentity is often tinged with violence, as Bob Donahoo points out in the context of a discussion of a logging on scene from Gibson's "Burning Chrome"; the event, Donahoo
claims, is "metaphorically made equivalent to rape" and reveals a form of
"female-bashing" directed against "the female who has dared to cross the
boundary into the male power hierarchy" (155). The subjectivity thus
defined through the resuscitation of the cowboy persona, however, is as
vulnerable as it is implicitly violent ("naked and weak and brave"). The
masculine cybersubject rides on the back of a technology only temporarily mastered. The hero's identity is established through phallic projection,
and that projection takes him "outside himself." When he opens his eyes
on the other side of the looking glass, he finds that he is enclosed in an
apparently vast and feminine body of information; the suggestion is thus
that he might be crushed, bitten, eaten, or infected with disease at any
moment. He must move quickly, sharply, aggressively and then get out:
his successful action can be no more than a renegade foray into the hyperreal. The climactic moment of most cyberfiction involves a fast-paced

operation in which the hero must break into a file and escape with his prize before he is "fried" or "frozen" by some intrusion countermeasure program that has the capability of following him out of cyberspace and back into his own organic brain. Like Dougherty's description of viral coding, cyberspace is the "postorganic [, . . .] terrifying, mechanical *what* that threatens to displace the sacred *who* of organic autonomous selfhood"—and threatens to do so by virtue of the penetrability that defines the hacker himself (10).

The specifically humanoid cybervillains within cyberspace are as feminized as is the matrix that houses them. The antagonist of Gibson's *Neuromancer,* for example, is 3Jane. Stephenson's *Snow Crash* is troubled by the Snow Crash virus, which affects human mind and computer alike—can, in fact, infect the organic brain through the medium of the metaverse. The virus attacks language and coding, reducing computers to inoperability and, more importantly in the novel, inducing in humans a permanent aphasia. Snow Crash reawakens a common primitive language of the deep structure of the brain, a nonreferential language and a discursive space that, unlike the metaverse (when uninfected), disallows the agency implicit in higher brain functions by negating the possibility of reference: "Under the right conditions, your ears—or eyes—can tie into deep structures, bypassing the higher language functions. Which is to say, someone who knows all the right words can speak words, or show you visual symbols, that go past all your defenses and sink right into your brainstem. Like a cracker who breaks into a computer system, bypasses all the security precautions, and plugs himself into the core, enabling him to exert absolute control over the machine" (369). Like 3Jane, the Snow Crash virus threatens the information space that is fictionalized in cyberpunk as the final stage upon which subjectivity is enacted. The feminine infection promises to glut with mindless repetition the perpetual and restless movement of information capital, a nonspatial roiling that might otherwise be imagined as a new frontier. In both cases, the damage is accomplished through viral reproduction: endless replications of the genetic code that call to mind Baudrillard's "gigantic simulacrum" of God—not unreal, but a simulacrum, never again exchanging for what is real, but exchanging in itself, in an uninterrupted circuit without reference or circumference" (*Simulacra* 1736). Dougherty has drawn the connection between Baudrillard's simulacra and popular obsession with viral infection generally; the virus speaks to the contemporary sense that "all our thoughts and actions once attributable to free human spirit are suddenly discovered to be programmed": "In an age of simulation the virus is the perfect monster with which to frighten ourselves. It is a copy without an original; it is information without context, and thus without meaning; it is beyond representation" (11,

9–10). In spite of the otherwise euphoric representations of the freedom and mobility enabled by information "space," the revelation of the groundlessness and self-generation of that information disallows the possibility of autonomous action.

Ironically, it is when femininity enters the process of genetic replication—the precession of the simulacra—that reference, and thus agency, is most explicitly threatened. The extent to which 3Jane controls cyberspace is the extent to which cyberspace is potentially lethal. Similarly, in *Snow Crash* the danger of the primal common language is never escaped by virtue of the fact that Asherah, mother goddess and cult of prostitutes, has struggled throughout the ages to preserve the virus that accesses and unleashes that "mother tongue" (373). Reminiscent of both the herpes simplex virus and HIV, as David Porush points out, the virus is kept viable through "the exchange of bodily fluids" (566):

> Asherah is both a biological and a computer or informational virus. Herpes simplex heads straight for the nervous system and affects the brainstem. It's both biological and eventually mental . . . coiling around the brainstem like a serpent around a tree . . . brings the mother tongue closer to the surface, makes people more apt to speak in tongues and more susceptible [, . . .] maybe lowers the victim's defenses to viral ideas. . . .
>
> We are all susceptible to the pull of viral ideas, like mass hysteria [and] . . . Bart Simpson t-shirts and bell bottom jeans and Nazism. . . . No matter how smart we get, there is always this deep irrational part that makes us potential hosts for self-replicating information. (Stephenson 373)

Porush argues persuasively that in the "metahistory" of *Snow Crash* it is the (masculine) invention of the Torah that "played a role in preserving civilization from Asherah": "Judaism and its primary invention, the Torah, represented a successful countercult promoting 'informational hygiene' and using a counter- or good virus, a namshub. Many Jewish sages themselves argue that one of the most fundamental tenets of Judaism is to 'build a wall around the Torah,' a *cordon sanitaire*" (566). The information space that centers and preserves Judaic culture must like cyberspace be protected from the feminized virus that not only returns language to its essentially nonreferential nature but penetrates and kills the (male) user, infecting him stealthily in the midst of an act illusorily perceived as his active penetration of a feminized other.

The general tendency to vilify feminine presence in the machine is rarely contradicted in cyberpunk fiction. Characters like Angie Mitchell,

Gibson's simstim star, seem only at first to complicate this oppressively gendered vision. In the case of Angie Mitchell, for example, the character does in fact have access to the matrix and is not presented as malignant: Gibson constructs her instead as a fairytale princess of the other kingdom—the bride of the prince. The difference between Angie and 3Jane, however, is that Angie has not penetrated the matrix; she has not projected herself anywhere, nor has she written software into cyberspace. On the contrary, her access to the matrix is a function of that access having been written into her body *by her father* in the form of a microchip planted in her brain. She is, in fact, a source of infinite access for others; as a simstim star, her sensations, thoughts, and feelings—appropriately enhanced and censored—are publicly available for mass consumption. She is equally open to the forms that inhabit the matrix. These voodoo-inspired beings violently rip their way into her consciousness—without warning and against her will—leaving her physically bleeding, mentally beaten, and figuratively impregnated with their message. Similarly, her link to cyberspace itself is almost always represented as a penetration of her mind from the outside. Like Mona, whose body is surgically altered against her will to resemble Angie's, she can be written on and her life and self are chronically scripted. In short, she is less a player in the matrix than she is an uncomplicated extension of it. As Nicola Nixon argues in another context, "the cowboys have to 'interface' with the matrix through 'slotting into' feminized cyberspace decks; certain females, however, require no such mediation: they are already, by implication, a part of it" (227).

Angie, then, is not a threat and cannot bite; equally benign are those female figures who are not "a part of" the matrix but who serve as metaphorical stand-ins for the passive terrain of uninfected cyberspace. These are the sidekicks, the help-meets who serve as physical buffer zones for the hero. Molly, for example, Gibson's "razor-girl" in the Sprawl trilogy, is a character who has virtually no access to the Internet or to information space generally; she is all mechanically enhanced physical power. However, her enhanced body serves nonetheless as a simulation and extension of the matrix that she herself cannot or will not access. Molly has been the subject of more than one feminist revision: both Kathy Acker and Pat Cadigan have rewoven her person into their own fiction, struggling with what becomes in *Neuromancer* her core characteristic—her figurative and actual rapability. In this novel, Molly and Case, the computer cowboy, have been hired to break into a closely guarded corporate headquarters and steal the Dixie Flatline, the taped personality construct of a dead hacker. It becomes Molly's job to make the actual physical break into the building; Case "accompanies" and guides her through an electronically broadcast neural link that gives him full access to her senses but gives her no access to his. Two things are highlighted in the narration of this connection: Molly's excruciating physicality, and Case's ability to enter and withdraw from her point of view:

> Case hit the simstim switch. And flipped into an agony of broken bone. Molly was braced against the blank gray wall of a long corridor, her breath coming ragged and uneven.
>
> Case was back in the matrix instantly, a white-hot line of pain fading in his left thigh.
>
> "What's happening, Brood?" he asked the link man.
>
> "I duno, Cutter. Mother's not talking. Wait."
>
> [. . .] Taking a deep breath, he flipped again.
>
> Molly took a single step, trying to support her weight on the corridor wall. In the loft, Case groaned. The second step took her over an outstretched arm. Uniform sleeve bright with fresh blood. Glimpse of shattered fiberglass shockstave. Her vision seemed to have narrowed to a tunnel. With the third step, Case screamed and found himself back in the matrix. (64)

"Mother" doesn't talk in this scene; she is all (mutilated and mutilating) flesh, all pain, and the words in her head are all Case's. The electronic link makes her body—like computer "space"—infinitely hollow, accessible, and usable; Molly is the technologically enhanced prosthesis that enables the latter-day cowboy to penetrate the corporate (techno)hymen and claim his rightful heritage—the remains or "soul" of his "father."

Both Brian McHale and Claire Sponsler find in Angie's and Molly's penetrability signs of an ultimately enabling postmodern rejection of autonomous identity. In fact, McHale singles out Case's neural interface with Molly's brain in *Neuromancer* as representative of a kind of postmodern and schizophrenic "multiple-point-of-view fiction" (260). It seems to me that this access resembles "schizophrenia" only superficially; its viability works rather to reintroduce—through images of gender violence—the grounded agency of white masculinity in the face of a potentially disorienting scene. Molly's penetrability is unidirectional: Case can penetrate or withdraw from Molly's mind; she has little access to his. He is described as "riding" Molly's augmented body, a body thus constructed as subject to outside penetration and modification, not stable and autonomous as is his own. She is trapped in a panoptic material world; his terrain enables movement even as it shields him from outside view. In the final analysis, Molly's body functions protectively to carve a physical space for the productive agency of the masculine subject within the virtualism of a post-Fordist era, to make him again the master of the machine.[2] She makes it

possible to believe that this "new world that has escaped from the gravita-
tional pull of the real," as Dougherty puts it, is also and at the same time
that old world of the Magna Mater, the original matrix (11).

Feminist revisions of Gibson critique both the sexual politics of this
MacKinnonian construction of woman as penetrability and the illusory
reconstruction of masculine productivity in the face of the networked
intricacies of finance capitalism: the information worker with cowboy
dreams. In Cadigan's *Synners*, the central female character experiences a
socket interface, an experience similar to Molly's neural link, which is
explicitly described as a rape. At the same time, the male hacker-protagonist is eventually and brutally absorbed into the matrix, where he is figuratively "raped" by his own electronic echo.[3] No one emerges triumphant
and autonomous. Kathy Acker goes further yet. In her rewrite of the
Molly-Case scene in *Empire of the Senseless*, she destabilizes the violent narratives of masculine identity formation by continually foregrounding not
only the brutality but also the self-serving fantasy involved in
Molly/Abhor's subjection. Ultimately Abhor, the possessed body that is
"half black, half robot," turns on Thivai/Case just long enough to articulate his dependence on her subjection: "'You're what I make you,' Abhor
said" (42). Acker breaks the narrative coherence of the Molly-Case interface as well, always deemphasizing precisely what Gibson highlights: the
ease with which Case's technology penetrates Molly and Molly's reality as
an entirely separate and corporeal "other." Thus, there are no references in
Acker to "flipping" or "jacking"; Case/Thivai merely "sees" things from the
outside of the feminine body. He is thus stripped of his penetrative initiative, and as Abhor's body fades into a thing of "seeming," the "mottled
bruises" of Gibson (70) fading into "blue purple and green patches which
looked like bruises but weren't" (Acker, *Empire of the Senseless*, 33), Thivai
is thrust back into the echoing halls of narcissism (the same place where
Cadigan's hacker-protagonist is figuratively raped and killed). His "other"
is taken away from him and replaced by a "construct" (34).

Acker's revision of Gibson thus reveals that the gender violence folded
within hero formation is a fantasy of man as a subject-effect, locked in,
dreaming his rape dreams in what is primarily a gesture of narcissism. The
hero is allowed his violence, then, but is more emasculated by it than otherwise. Like Tarr, like Gerald Crich, Thivai is finally closed in by technology, and what he thought would be a mechanical and savage phallus ends
up more of a prison than a projectile—a prison that reminds him constantly of his own secondary status in relation to a larger System: right before
he confronts the (seemingly) brutalized robot body of Abhor, Thivai says,
"I, whoever I was, was going to be a construct" (33). Acker's pirate, then,
unlike the pirates and cowboys of cyberspace, articulates what Hari

Kunzru argues is "[t]he general shift from thinking of individuals as isolated from the 'world' to thinking of them as nodes on networks." Similarly, Donna Haraway writes that "the actual situation" for the contemporary human subject is "integration/exploitation" into a global communications system she terms "the informatics of domination," which is in turn responsible for coding, among other things, "the systems of myth and meanings structuring our imaginations" (163). Cyberpunk fiction envisions in "the extreme mobility of capital" the corollary dream of the extreme (and purposeful) mobility of the masculine subject; it thus falls prey to the allure of "[t]he new communications technologies . . . that promise ultimate mobility and perfect exchange" (168). Haraway argues that in point of fact, the capitalism of an information age renders "[w]hite men in advanced industrial societies . . . newly vulnerable," "feminized": "able to be disassembled, reassembled, exploited as a reserve labour force; seen less as workers than as servers; subjected to time arrangements on and off the paid job that make a mockery of a limited work day; leading an existence that always borders on being obscene" (168, 166). The all-too-visible, vulnerable body of the hacker in the fiction of Cadigan and Acker thus reconnects the self "in" cyberspace to the economic realities of information capitalism, reworking a genre that conceals—at any cost—the extent to which computer work is still work, the information worker still a worker, in service to a larger corporate system. E. L. McCallum makes the case that the pirate hacker of writers like Gibson and Stephenson is symptomatic of a profound ideological misrecognition of the late capitalist function of cyberspace: "the outlaws and cowboys are the ones who by their hacking talent, data piracy, and tribalist manifestos protest the corporate settlement of the Internet frontier; however, this angle serves to gloss over the shift of the real map of the Internet, from primarily a military-academic network in the 1970s and 1980s to a commercial opportunity cashed in on by barons like Sun Microsystems, Netscape, and American Online in the 1990's" (371–72). Cyberpunk fiction focuses tenaciously on the flickering masculine figure so seemingly disconnected from the screen on which he is projected.

In postmodern fiction more generally, anxieties about the fate of traditionally defined white, middle-class masculinity proliferate more openly, and chief amongst those are the fears that speak to the opaque relationship between corporate capitalism and the male subject. David Savran argues that in a world where "the heroics of John Wayne [have become] embarrassingly out of place," where labor has become bureaucratized, capitalism service oriented, military might displaced by the World Bank and the International Monetary Fund, it has become "all the more urgent that the masculine fantasmatic be reconstructed to bear the unmistakable traces of a robust, independent, and entrepreneurial masculinity" (194). For Savran, "reflexive sadomasochism" has become the "linchpin" in these "fantasmatic" negotiations (190). Sadism articulates the force and point of an earlier white masculinity, and yet now turns against itself in a gesture of masochism that speaks to the feminized role of the new (middle-class) male worker. Savran argues that there is nothing particularly novel about this construction of white masculinity; it was first identified, in fact, by Freud: "The only thing truly new about the new narcissist (or new sadomasochist—take your pick) is that he represents a now *dominant* figure on the U.S. cultural scene, no longer relegated to the margins" (169). In a culture and economy whose ability to identify an other to dominate either legitimately or effectively became increasingly problematic, "the relatively stable masculinity of the domestic revival was thrown into crisis," and "the male subject began to turn against himself and to prove his mettle by gritting his teeth and taking his punishment like a man" (176). The rape dreams of an earlier vision of masculine identity, by the same token, are gradually and masochistically redirected inward toward the new, feminized male body.

Nicholson Baker's *The Fermata* turns precisely on this shift from phallic identification to phallic victimhood. *The Fermata* is a fantastical novel about a male "temp" who has the ability to stop time on command. Arnold Strine is thus the nomadic office worker of late capitalism, floating from one menial information job to the next, while yet living a (semi)private fantasy of renegade power. What Arnold Strine generally does during these periods when he is in the "fermata," the fold, when everyone and everything else resembles nothing so much as dead matter, is work. He writes; he transcribes; he processes information in a variety of ways. The work he produces, however, at the cost of premature aging, is effaced, almost completely masked by a seemingly outlaw, transgressive (hetero)sexuality that perpetually borders on rape. The violation to which he is addicted generally involves the undressing of women and moves increasingly toward some type of sexual intervention in their consciousness. Significantly, then, the "technology" of the time trick not only allows Arnold to self-identify as "serenely unproductive," but lifts him out of a private world of alienated labor and masturbation and offers him the opportunity of reciprocally inscribing his (masculine) identity on a passive, feminine field (101). Like the pirates of cyberspace, he acts as if he and the machine are one; he is in control of the universal pause/play button, and thus is the master through his "rape-like acts" of the unfathomable interiors of the Mater/matrix (91). The power of the voyeuristic gaze is only illusorily identified with play/pause technology, however: his "raping game" is always negotiated by some form of actual or figurative prosthesis, his penis never actually penetrating flesh. The narrative drive, then, is all about the dream of transforming narcissism into binarism, masturbation into unidirectional penetration—but the power to go from the former to the latter is not dependable, and the tables, ultimately, can be turned. Ironically, then, Arnold is led closer and closer to his own feminization and objectification through the very growth in violence and aggressivity that would seem to promise the reinstatement of masculine force.

The narrator confesses in the beginning of his "autobiography" that watching the frozen bodies in the fermata is not enough in itself: "I love looking at women. I love being able to see them clearly. I particularly like being in the position I am in this very second," having his boss frozen in front of him, her dress pulled up over her waist and her nylons pulled down around her ankles (8). The voyeuristic gaze, then, which draws ever closer to the frozen (or dead) female body, parting its coverings in order to stare ever more deeply into its orifices, is clearly more active than it represents itself—and never the "harmless" position that Arnold constantly claims. He feels compelled to act on the observed body, so that he not only watches a woman bathe and masturbate, for example, but also ejaculates in her face, starting time again briefly so that she will feel that something is amiss. It is thus "the fact of invasion," as Arthur Saltzman points out, that is "crucial to arousal" and not "a hormonal focus per se" (*Understanding Nicholson Baker* 89). Strine self-consciously assures the reader in such scenes that all is well, all is harmless: actual penile penetration has not occurred. Invisibility validates, and the narrator has used the invisible prosthesis of time control, ultimately a phallic power that resembles in practice Case's "jacking" into Molly. Arnold begins to feel excluded, however, by the narcissism and solitude of what is increasingly experienced as a necrophilic aura, and so begins to insinuate himself into the unknowing woman's consciousness, thus becoming increasingly visible. In one of his periods in the fold, for example, he follows a woman from the library to her bus, then inserts a vibrating butterfly into her vulva, "gradually increas[ing] its flutter level . . . over a series of six or seven time-perversions" until she has an orgasm, taking care to make eye contact with her at this point. He hands her the vibrator in an envelope when they reach her stop. The voyeur thus becomes the rapist in postmodern retreat, engaging in what would under normal circumstances be fantasy but with the aid of "technology" becomes here actual power over the (feminine) world: "the world is inert and statuesque until I touch it and make it live ordinarily" (13).

A huge part of the novel is given over to the pornography that Arnold writes and slips unobtrusively to women in fold time. His *work*, then, mirrors the fantastical prerogative enabled by the fermata: to make the private visible. Pornography, according to Jean Baudrillard, like the obscenity of late capitalist culture generally, functions to "let everything be produced, be read, become real, visible" (*Forget Foucault* 21). Further, for Baudrillard, that absolute visibility is produced under "the sign of effectiveness": "let everything be transcribed into force relations, into conceptual systems or into calculable energy" (21). Arnold Strine's invisibility is matched by his work of pornographic revelation, a specularity transformed into penetrative power over women. He watches them read (or listen, in the case of taped pornography), and then follows them in order to determine the effect he has had, hoping to have aroused sexual interest. Evidence of feminine sexual arousal—imagined or not—becomes the occasion for visions of absolute physical penetration: "I fancied that she was breathing a little faster than she would have been if my words hadn't just gone through her mind. I was *in* her mind. There were things about what she read that she didn't like, or that seemed dumb to her, but even so it was working on her and making her want to *go home*" (144). His "work"—although eating away at his own life expectancy—is thus conceived as the invasion and transformation of the frozen female body through discourse; her figurative emptiness enables him to think of himself not only as a subject with effect but as writing subject, the master of discourse who through the *techne* of scripture can liberate the feminine body into health. His vulnerable role as temporary office worker is thus rewritten as data pirate, rapist cowboy; he is the classic cyberhero who "jacks" into feminized information space and there reconfigures himself on the surface of the hyperreal as Lady Chatterly's late-capitalist lover.

As pornography is configured in Baudrillard's conception to render *everything* visible, however, so is Arnold himself finally subjected to the specularizing force over which he has felt ownership. In the end, the machine turns on Arnold and becomes the property of a female successor. The transference is figured as a castration: his "technique" for accessing the fermata is sucked out of him with a penis pump, transferred to a dildo, and given to Joyce (significantly, Arnold's former boss). Arnold is himself now the body that might be invaded without his will or knowledge; his is the consciousness now vulnerable to the rape of the word. As Alice Jardine puts it of postmodern man generally, "It is almost as if technique, as concept and practice, has turned Man into an Object-Woman" (75). Just before he loses his power, in fact, Arnold finds himself a part of a scientific project to determine the effect of masturbation on carpal tunnel syndrome (a study, in other words, that examines the potentially harmful effects of minimalist sexual pleasure on the productive body of the low-level office worker). He is placed inside the "vaginal" core of a superconducting magnet, his penis is painted with reference points, and he is shot through with X rays while his masturbation is observed by powerful women in white coats. The emotional drive of the scene is derived from the sense of *control* Arnold maintains, unaware of his ludicrously extreme vulnerability. He has moved full circle from voyeur to exhibitionist, and it is his body that is treated as object, shot through with the invisible bullets of twentieth-century technology.

In many ways, Thomas Pynchon's *Gravity's Rainbow* turns similarly on the shift from masculine identification with phallic power to masculine vulnerability to the technological phallus. Eroticized violence again mediates the troubled relationship between man and the late-capitalist machine. Set late in the London blitz and in the postwar transnational European "zone," *Gravity's Rainbow* follows the reverse trajectory of the German V-2 rocket—in a sense establishing the rocket as the central image onto which, as David Porush puts it, "Each character in the book maps some portion of his or her desire" (130). The central feature of the rocket that thus dominates the text—through desire and fear—is its phallic violence: for the engineers who design it, it is "[b]eyond simple steel erection[;] the Rocket was an entire system *won,* away from the feminine darkness, held against the entropies of lovable but scatterbrained Mother Nature" (324). Wes Chapman makes the case that Pynchon's phallic rockets reveal the ways in which the modern (or postmodern) state "sexualize[s] the machinery of death" according to the masculinist code of "dominance and submission": "Hence the grotesque eroticism of the Rocket: 'fifty feet high, trembling . . . and then the fantastic, virile roar . . . Cruel, hard, thrusting into the virgin-blue robes of the sky . . . Oh, so phallic'" (qtd. in par. 9). The V-2 is thus proof and extension of an essentially phallic and reified masculine subjectivity, and in the privacy of the engineer's mind, as Joseph Tabbi has pointed out, man is the one who exerts control over it, setting upon its brute mass and "fettering" it to his own electronic and mechanical designs. The engineer's dream of flight and force is integrated into the rocket's own device of in-flight guidance, and that phallic dream culminates in the mysterious quintuple zero, the V-2 that carries a living man inside it, literally integrating the rocket with the masculine self.

On the other hand, the rocket also maps the terrain of human—specifically masculine—vulnerability. Tyrone Slothrop is described as staring up at the sky in London, his penis erect, wondering if he is at ground zero, aware of all of his orifices open in terror and expectation. The rocket thus renders man rapable, feminized—appropriates the traditionally masculine prerogative for sexual violence. In its cool distillation of phallic will and agency, rocket technology usurps for itself the ground of Western subjectivity. In pornographic ascent and eroticized descent, the rocket is always masculine, and man is relegated finally to the irreducibly other, "reduced" by the "The Force" to "human puppetry" (J. Chambers 69). In spite of its domination by violent phallic imagery, then, *Gravity's Rainbow* stages the troubled status of Euro-American masculinity in the twentieth century. The absorption of masculine agent into the military-corporate machine, furthermore, becomes most clearly recognizable in the powerful current of sexual violence that runs through the novel. The scenes and images of rape and sexual sadism initiate the traumatic disappearance of the feminine—the enabling feminine "other" whose rapability otherwise promises masculine agency. At the apex of the rocket's path, when it hangs between phallic thrust and phallic plunging descent, is the moment of Brennschluss, burn-off, absolute zero. Brennschluss is the moment at which "the Rocket's purely feminine counterpart, the zero point at the center of its target, has submitted" (*Gravity's Rainbow* 223)—has been raped, undone, made to disappear. At this point, the rocket enters into indeterminacy. That the feminine or feminized target has ceased to exist has stopped the game. For Pynchon, Brennschluss is non-relationship, the place where the binary twists on its axis and where gender and its corollary—Western subjectivity—become unthinkable.

Baudrillard maintains that every discourse is threatened with this sudden reversibility—absorption into its own signs without a trace of meaning (*Seduction* 2). For Baudrillard, this absorption is precipitated by the death of seduction, "the degree zero of structure." Pynchon clearly plays at mourning a similarly abstract loss; the mythical moment when desire, lust, and dominance, all markers in this text of white masculine subjectivity, are recognized as originating not in the male subject per se but in the larger system. The violent eroticization of the female body thus ultimately fails to authorize masculine agency, even in ironic terms: somewhere between the propulsion and the descent, gravity intervenes; the woman disappears. Margherita Erdmann, for example, acknowledges herself the "Anti-Dietrich: not destroyer of men but doll—languid, exhausted," as if recognizing her own symbolic bankruptcy within a masculinist text: "'I watched all our films,' she recalls, 'some of them six or seven times. I never seemed to *move*. Not even my face. . . . it could have been the same frame, over and over'" (394). Slothrop's sexual desire for Margherita is aptly focused less on her body as female body than on her plasticity, the "silver memory of her body on film," which is conjured even in real time through the isolation and examination of her "[h]eavy legs in silk stockings shining now with a hard, machined look," the "singular point at the top of a lady's stocking," which calls to mind in turn the mathematical aura of bifurcating railroad ties, and "the A4 pointed at the sky—just before the last firing-switch closes" (395–96). His sexual desire for her turns toward the machine, and toward the military-industrial complex, and resolves itself in a parodied echo of the gang rape committed during the filming of *Alpdrucken,* Slothrop fumbling through the old "inquisitional props" from the filming of the movie, an inept Grand Inquisitor and a "surrogate" co-star (396–97).

Wes Chapman argues persuasively that the violent and demeaning sexuality of *Gravity's Rainbow,* all the sadomasochism and pornography, speak to a "deflection" of male (naturalized as human) sexuality "to an economy of objectified images" that serve specifically to manufacture masculine subjectivity "at the micropolitical level" (par. 10, 11). The novel, Chapman argues, thus stages a critique of the ways in which the contemporary state "sexualize[s] the machinery of death" through a "masculinist coding of sexuality such that all its citizens will respond sexually to a scenario of dominance and submission" (par. 10). Masculine sexuality, in other words—particularly in relation to sadism and to pornography—is a function of the corporate-military system of the novel and is constructed to serve and extend that system. Chapman points to Pirate Prentice's reception of his military orders—via rocket—as an example. The message is written in "Kryptosam," a chemical developed by IG Farben, and reveals its contents only after exposure to seminal fluid. Thus, Pirate Prentice finds enclosed with his orders a drawing of an ex-girlfriend, pornographically posed and attired after a private fantasy he has never shared with anyone. His first response—as Slothrop's often is—is to assume that "They" must have a "dossier" on him somewhere, must have "managed to monitor everything he saw and read since puberty" (72). The narrative itself undermines the authenticity Pirate thus scrambles to preserve through his paranoia: the setting is De Mille, the female body objectified in precisely the kinds of ways that speak to "every young man" who has grown up in England, each "conditioned to get a hardon in the presence of certain fetishes" (*Gravity's Rainbow* 72). What he perceives as his innermost, privately known space is in fact the coded construction of the military-corporate state, and his body parts—including his "own robot hands"—function according to its will. Significantly, however, it is his own *productive* action that encodes him as an individual and individualized player within that state. What is in one sense consumption and reception—of the pornographic image, his orders, his own social script—relies heavily upon production—of tumescence, ejaculation, and seminal fluid. His physical, genital body is itself written upon even as it (re)writes the mission he will undertake in service of the military-industrial complex. By the same token, the discursive agency thus dismantled even as it is constructed is necessarily male, rendered functional and semicoherent only by seminal fluid.

Slothrop's sadomasochistic scene with Margherita Erdmann evidences the same narrative recognition that violent, masculine sexuality operates in the service of the state, as Chapman has pointed out: once he begins to whip her, Slothrop discovers that "'someone has already educated him' in the fine art of sexual cruelty" (par. 11). The "someone" is the same corporate-military "They" haunting the entire novel, always somehow before, beneath, and all around the individual characters. "They" have already programmed in Slothrop a taste for violent sexual dominance, and yet that taste, once recognized and acted upon, is quickly incorporated into the masculine self, as if naturally belonging there: "No. No—he still says 'their,' but he knows better. . . his own cruelty" (396). Thus the roots of masculine identity are shifted to the corporation in the same gesture that establishes the violent nature of masculine sexuality. The powerful agency presumably expressed—and compulsively pursued—through sadism is revealed by turns to be the carefully prescribed productive activity compelled by "Them" in the name of pleasure. "They want you here, right now," Margherita tells him (395). It is the half-hiddenness of this link that generates the sense that there is something else lurking just beyond the exertions of sexual violence and the fragmented, tortured female body: "And what's waiting for Slothrop, what unpleasant surprise, past the tops of Greta's stockings here? . . . What waits past this whine and crack of velvet lashes against her skin, long red stripes on the white ground, her moans, the bruise-colored flower that cries at her breast, the jingling of the hardware holding her down?" (397).

In oblique answer to Slothrop's question, the scene is abruptly followed by the echoes of violence that accompanied the original screening of the rape scene in *Alpdrucken*. Like Slothrop, men in contact with the feminine "silver . . . body on film" compulsively repeat the sadistic role Max Schlepzig and the jackal men played in the film. "Everybody" left the Ufa theater the night of the screening "thinking . . . only about getting home, fucking somebody, fucking her into some submission" (397). Franz Pokler is testament to the mass-produced power of the film and its presentation of the Nazi "Anti-Dietrich": he is "flooded with tonight's image of the delicious victim bound on her dungeon rack filling the movie screen"; the image transforms his "solemn wife" into "Margherita Erdmann underneath him, on the bottom for a change. . . . yes, bitch, yes" (397). Significantly, both Margherita Erdmann and Leni Pokler become pregnant, along with, Pokler supposes, multiple other women: "How many shadow-children would be fathered on Erdmann that night?" (397). The emphasis, aptly, is on (re)production. The film not only produces Nazis, conditioned to "respond sexually to a scenario of dominance and submission" (Chapman par. 10); it so constructs the illusion of agency that the violent masculine subject will produce more bodies for the Aryan homeland. "Flooded" with the image of the "Reich's Sweethearts," the average consumer is transformed into the actual living embodiment of Nazi ideology, lives the fascist ethic of hyperproductivity in the name of the fatherland. The viewers of *Alpdrucken* thus grimly parody the straight-faced calls to stepped-up (re)production voiced in *The Cantos;* here Ezra Pound's mythologized celebration of sexual violence becomes a critique of the ways in which the military-corporate state constructs the masculine subject through attributions of generative violence and productive dominance. The power to rape is yet another scrap of footage in "Goebbels's private collection" (461). The "shadow children" produced during and after the making of the film stand testament to the illusory nature of the agency that begot them, and their ghostlike presence haunts the "fathers" with visions of the merciless, inescapable violence to which they (the fathers) are consigned and which they wield only in service to Them.

The first *Alpdrucken* child is Bianca, daughter of Margherita Erdmann herself, conceived on the phony rack of the movie set during the filming of the rape scene. Doubly fetishized as woman and as child, she is a creature of seeming, as Bernard Duyfhuizen has persuasively argued. Bianca, Duyfhuizen claims, "represents the untellable, the feminine text that patriarchy tries to cover"; the body of the flesh-and-blood girl (or young woman) is "replaced only by traces formed by the sexual memories of men (the first male narratees of the text of her body" (par. 34–35). Duyfhuizen makes the convincing case, in fact, that there is much evidence in the text that Bianca is far older than the "11 or 12" that Slothrop takes her to be; it is a measure of the extent to which she is fetishized that her physical description is so radically skewed (*Gravity's Rainbow* 463). Certainly her enforced status as consumer item is highlighted in the text, glowing in the garish light of hyperbole: "Not only is her song 'On the Good Ship Lollipop,' but she is also now commencing, without a trace of shame, to *grunt* her way through it, in perfect mimickry of young Shirley Temple— each straining baby-pig inflection, each curl-toss, unmotivated smile, and stumbling toe-tap . . . her delicate bare arms have begun to grow fatter, her frock shorter—is somebody fooling with the lights?" (466). The exaggerated quality of the little girl fetish is paralleled by the equally exaggerated response of the audience; her mother's sadistic beating initiates a mass orgy, the participants portrayed in terms of mindless, lustful body parts— "unsheathed penis," "juicy genitals," "nose and tongue," "bruised buttocks," "bared breasts," "stiff nipples," "big toes," "anal openings" (467).

The catalog of pornographic actions—a veritable cornucopia of consumerist erotica—brings to mind Terry Eagleton's description of "the logic of the marketplace": "The logic of the marketplace is one of pleasure and plurality, of the ephemeral and discontinuous, of some great decentred network of desire of which individuals seem the mere fleeting effects"

(132). If the marketplace is a cornucopia of consumerist pleasure, however, powered by fetishism, and if the sadistic beating of Bianca reveals the ways in which the passengers of the *Anubis* function as consumer-effects of the ideological theme of dominance/submission, this instance of sadism is also generative; it sets into rippling motion a flexible economy of interconnected sexual events and relationships. The beating thus follows the hypothetically generative sadism of the text as a whole. John Hamill makes the case that the "productive" nature of the sadism in *Gravity's Rainbow* can be explained by Baudrillard's use of the word—not implying "material manufacture, but in relation to the Latin root 'pro-ducere,' to cause to appear or to render visible—in which case the imperative is to: Let everything be produced, be read, become visible, and marked with the sign of effectiveness; let everything be transcribed into force relations, into conceptual systems or into calculable energy; let everything be said, gathered, indexed and registered" (Hamill 61). Hamill notes that it is this form of production that explains for Baudrillard "how sex appears in pornography" (qtd. in Hamill 61). As Pirate Prentice's ejaculate makes visible his military orders, so, too, does the orgy scene aboard the *Anubis* follow the directive to let *everything* be made "visible," made "effective," "be transcribed into force relations"—and all under the sign of sadistic pleasure. It is thus a "pornographic" scene in precisely the sense that Baudrillard suggests: bodies (or body parts) are compelled to be visible participants in the collective machine.

The fetishistic, sadistic desire Bianca triggers in Slothrop marks a major turning point in his development as a character, as Duyfhuizen has pointed-ed out, and makes imagistically "visible" the extent to which his sexual desire is not only not his own but contains him. At the moment of orgasm Slothrop positively envisions himself "inside his own cock" and—like Humbert Humbert—trembling on the brink of full transcendent disclosure.[4,5] The expected climax is simultaneously described as pre-ejaculation, near-revelation, pre-rocket launch: "He is enclosed. Everything is about to come, come incredibly, and he's helpless here in this exploding *emprise* . . . red flesh echoing . . . an extraordinary sense of *waiting to rise*" (470). That his boundaries are delimited by the phallus, then, on one hand, endows him with associative power: "cruel, hard, thrusting" like the undiscovered rocket, he also will perhaps pierce "the virgin-blue robes of the sky" (465). On the other hand, however, the moment of breakthrough is unattainable: Slothrop is "helpless," and it is the penis/rocket that assumes agency in undertaking the chivalric quest for itself. Orgasm discloses only "the kingly voice of the Aggregate itself [, . . . a]nnouncing the void," and Slothrop is left knowing that he believes "what They want him to believe," that he cannot distinguish between the "real" and what he is compelled to "draw for Them" (470). As Hamill has pointed out, sadomasochism carries with it an aura of "metaphysical desire" that is not only "not condemned" by the state but "becomes an integral part of institutional entrapment" (56). Sadistic sexual response is constructed in *Gravity's Rainbow* so as to give the appearance of hidden revelation: by so doing it masks its own corporate genesis and compels productive action (one is compelled to "draw for them," not merely to sit passively and receive).

Slothrop's vision of his own containment within his penis is a significantly ominous conflation given that his sexual responses function in the productive service of the military-corporate institution. In a very real sense, he has never been a conqueror of women, a diviner of rockets, an establisher of patterns; the earlier Slothropian "hits" that are somehow connected to rocket strikes have little or nothing to do with women. The stars he places on his map in London speak rather to Slothrop's own (probable) unknowing subjection to IG Farben, the transnational chemical corporation that (probably) conditioned him to respond sexually to the Imipolex later used in the German rockets. For Slothrop, then, the true sexual event is necessarily between the lethal technological phallus and the vulnerable, rapable masculine body. It is a further disempowerment of the masculine body that even his sexual response to the rocket is conditioned; it reflects no desire originating in a subject per se, but is rather a subject-effect constructed through corporate technology: "His erection hums from a certain distance, like an instrument installed, wired by Them into his body as a colonial outpost here in our raw and clamorous world, another office representing Their white Metropolis far away" (285). The engendering of the new corporate worker is thus accomplished through the absorption of the (boy) child—and "The Penis He Thought Was His Own"—into the corporate and transnational body of the mysterious "They" who manufacture the war as they manufacture gendered and sexual response: to ensure the productive energy that powers the constant, restless re-territorialization of capitalism (302).

Shadow-child Bianca presides over Slothrop's glancing recognition of his own transcription into systems of control, as well as his complicity in the machinery of domination. The narrative acknowledges the moment, turning to second person, implicating character and reader in the sexual violence that generates (and is in turn generated by) the fetishized female body:

> Of all her putative fathers—Max Schlepzig and masked extras on one side of the moving film, Franz Pokler and certainly other pairs of hands busy through trouser cloth, that *Alpdrucken* Night, on the other—Bianca is closest, this last possible moment below decks here behind the ravening jackal, closest to you who came in blind-

ing color, slouched alone in your own seat, never threatened along
any rookwise row or diagonal all night, you whose interdiction form
her mother's water-white love is absolute, you, alone, saying *sure I
know them,* omitted, chuckling *count me in,* unable, thinking *probably some hooker.* . . . She favors you, most of all. You'll never get to
see her. So somebody has to tell you. (472)

For a brief post-coital moment Slothrop perceives that "she *exists*" beyond
his fetishized and programmed vision of her ("For Slothrop this is some
discovery") and determines that "she must be more than an image, a product, a promise to pay," because "their whole economy's based on *that*"
(470, 472). Yet he leaves this moment of recognition, just as he leaves
Bianca, and in refusing her promise that "we can get away," Slothrop also
betrays "the moment of kindness, so crucially redemptive in Pynchon's fiction" (Duyfhuizen par. 7). He is for the rest of the novel haunted by visions
of her death and dead body—although it is unclear whether or how she
dies. He "will think he sees her" washed overboard in a storm along with
"all [the] screaming Fascist cargo" of the *Anubis* (491). And in total darkness he will feel "Icy little thighs in wet silk swing against his face. . . . No
matter which way he tries to move now . . . cold nipples . . . the deep cleft
of her buttocks, perfume and shit and the smell of brine . . . and the smell
of . . . of. . ." (531). The fetishized woman/girl thus finally disappears from
the text, fades into a ghost who adds an audible note of horror to the dissolution of the masculine subject.

Ilse Pokler, the "[shadow-child] fathered on Erdmann," functions similarly to highlight the simultaneous violence and vulnerability of the masculine subject (397). Every year Franz Pokler awaits the arrival at
Zwolfkinder of a young woman who might or might not be his daughter,
and every year replicates with her the (imagined) scene of her conception,
when he "for a change" took a dominant role in sex, fantasizing his sadistic power—"poor helpless *bitch* you're coming can't stop yourself now I'll
whip you again whip till you *bleed*"—while he "pumped in the fatal charge
of sperm" (397, 577). Ilse mirrors Bianca not only by virtue of their parallel conception, then, but because she also is quickly fetishized by those
around her, a springboard to abusive fantasy (and abusive reality, to the
extent that can be established). The two children thus fade into each other
in a process of what Duyfuizen terms "cross-mapping" (par. 23). Slothrop
recognizes the "alignment," and when he hears of "[Ilse's] summer
returns," is "taken again by the nape and pushed against Bianca's dead
flesh" (Duyfuizen par. 23; Pynchon 576).

Too late in both cases, the fetishized woman/girl reveals masculine complicity in the transnational miltary-corporate system, provides evidence, as

Hamill points out, that the "sadistic paedophilia" that continually and hyperbolically defines the masculine subject in *Gravity's Rainbow* is "directly linked" to "entrapment within . . . institutional structures"(57). After Ilse disappears for the last time, Pokler comes to realize that she was (or might have been) "payment for the retrofit work he'd done on the 00000" (432). Worse, during the time when she was not with him, she was [or might have been] imprisoned in Dora, a part of the labor force that enabled the scientific production to which he is so addicted (his own function, significantly, his "special destiny," being the design of the plastic fairing which will house Gottfried in the propulsion section of the 00000 [431]). In the years of Ilse's "absence," she has in fact (perhaps) been divided from his own workspace in the Mittelwerke by nothing more than a wall: "But it wasn't till August [when he] found her at last waiting in the hotel lobby at Zwolfkinder with the same darkness in her eyes (how had he missed it till now? Such swimming orbits of pain) that he could finally put the two data together. For months, while her father across the wire or walls did his dutiful hackwork, she had been prisoner only a few meters away from him, beaten, perhaps violated" (428). Ilse's final disappearance formalizes the extent to which she has never had "an existence in herself": she "exists only as a pawn in the hands of Them, another performer in a wider form of political sadomasochism" in which Pokler himself has been an active player (7). Pokler's recognition of what thus turns out to be the essentially corporate and in fact politically situated nature of his sexuality places him psychologically and actually on the other side of the wall dividing scientist and victim. Codes of dominance and submission lose their erotic valence in the face of the "naked corpses," "the living, stacked ten to a straw mattress, the weakly crying, coughing, losers" (432).

The disappearance of the "shadow-child," whether Bianca or Ilse, thus serves to precipitate and to foreshadow masculine crisis. Her absence as object demonstrates, in fact, the secondary status—and ultimately the vulnerability—of the subject position within the phallic code that relentlessly (if self-consciously) structures the world of the novel. Significantly, it is their mother (or shadow-mother) who stages most spectacularly the emasculating disappearance of the rapable and of the feminine. Margherita Erdmann's apocalyptic revelation in "the castle" replays the gang rape scene from the filming of *Alpdrucken*—the scene of conception or shadow-conception of Bianca and Ilse—but substitutes the plastics of rocket technology for the penises and whips of the Grand Inquisitor and jackal men. She is taken to the old petrochemical plant by Blicero himself, the Blicero who has "grown on, into another animal . . . a werewolf . . . but with no humanity left in its eyes" (486). "Injected" into his inhuman, and yet still profoundly phallic, "*mythical regions*," Greta confronts "the nobles of the castle," "important men" who "[seem] familiar" in their "power" and "gravity" (486, 487). Like the significantly named "Drohne," however, the "power" of the new working aristocracy—seated in "the board room . . . round a conference table"—is derived from proximity to "the machinery" and is subject to the greater power symbolized in the "true ring of Polystyrene," the "heavy chalice of methyl methacrylate" (487). By the same token, in the presence of the new plastics, the erections of Greta's escorts "tr[y] to crawl out the openings in their clothes," an odd description that dehumanizes the penis, associating it with the "plastic serpents" of the previous sentence which "[crawl] endlessly to left and right" (487). In a final figurative eclipsing of the essential humanity of the phallus, Drohne "strap[s] on a gigantic Imipolex penis over his own" (488).

The rape that appears thus to have been set up—"Drohne and the men stretched me out on a inflatable plastic mattress. . . . They took away my clothes and dressed me in an exotic costume of some black polymer, very tight at the waist, open at the crotch"—never actually happens. It is at this point, in fact, that Greta narrates her own abstracted disappearance from the scene. "There was an abyss between my feet," she recounts; "Things, memories no way to distinguish them any more, went tumbling downward through my head. A torrent. I was evacuating all these, out into some void" (488). As in a classic representation of rape, her own subjectivity is emptied out; but this emptying out is not replaced with the image of her rapist. As she disappears into an abyss beyond violence, her absence is marked by a vortex. There will be no inscription of masculine identity here, not even a shadow child to remind a tortured man of his own working subjection to the larger System. In short, her raped and disappearing body doesn't promise subjectivity; it shows man his relationship to rocket technology, one that finally nullifies him as subject, spreads that hypothetical subjectivity across the geographical space of the zone until no unified trace remains.

Slothrop's disembodiment echoes Greta's fantasy of dissemination, and her post-revelatory vision of the "[s]omething" that "had been deposited in a great fan that went on for miles. Some tarry kind of waste" (488). By the end of the novel Slothrop has been "scattered all over the Zone. It's doubtful," the narrative voice-over opines, "if he can ever be 'found' again" (712). It has been a temptation to argue that in this dissemination, Slothrop has eluded the System of dominance and submission that has compelled him. Molly Hite maintains, for example, that "one implication" of his "unsettling" identity loss "is that he has escaped control," "for it is his phallocentric identity that has "placed" him in the apocalyptic pattern. . . . He [has become] radically uncentered, a fate that brings him to the opposite extreme of his initial characterization as a personified penis"

(118–19). Dana Medoro goes further, arguing that in his dissemination and detachment "from the solid and 'steel erection' of the Rocket, . . . Slothrop is not only a figure of regeneration but also one who is connected to Thoth" (197). Both of these readings argue for a liberatory potential personified in Slothrop's scattered body, and thus both assume that there is within the text an "outside" of the System. This position, however, doesn't square with the narrative tone, which seems much more in line with Chapman's argument that there *is* no outside of the masculine code in *Gravity's Rainbow:*

> Slothrop's paranoid quest for the Mystery Stimulus . . . is a way of acting out an anxiety about complicity in oppressive structures: in searching for information about who or what or how he somehow has been conditioned to respond sexually to the Rocket, he is in a sense asking about how he came to be coded sexually as he has been, how he himself has been written by the codes of dominance and submission. He finds no answers, just an infinite series of connections that do not add up to a coherent narrative. He cannot see the source of his coding as a male, because there is no outside point from which to see it: that coding is quite literally himself. (par. 14)

If indeed Slothrop's disseminated condition is associated with the revelation that his sexual response is in service to the transnational corporation, then his (and the narrative) inability to formulate a post-apocalyptic sense of himself is evidence of the total inclusiveness of that containment.

In fact, Slothrop's final dissolution is coded explicitly as itself a "corporate emblem." The narrative describes him as "one plucked albatross. Plucked, hell—*stripped.* Scattered all over the Zone. . . . Only feathers" (712). The image is immediately followed by the well-known "The Man has a branch office in each of our brains," a sentence not often quoted in its entirety, since it continues with "his corporate emblem is a white albatross, each local rep has a cover known as the Ego, and their mission in this world is Bad Shit" (712–13). That Slothrop has become a scattering of albatross feathers across the zone suggests not only his death—since it is the albatross's symbolic function in literature to be, in fact, dead, testament to and punishment for human cruelty and the abuse of nature—but his total incorporation. What he has lost is only the "Ego," the "cover." This being the case, his resemblance is finally and altogether strikingly similar to Gilles Deleuze and Felix Guattari's description of the late-capitalist subject, for whom "an identity is essentially fortuitous": "The subject," they argue, "spreads itself out along the entire circumference of the circle, the center of which has been abandoned by the ego" (21). Like

Slothrop, the late-capitalist "schizo . . . continually wander[s] about, migrating here, there, and everywhere as best he can, [plunging] further and further into the realm of deterritorialization." (35). In his wandering and dissemination, the good little worker of the late twentieth century inhabits "the very limit of capitalism: he is its inherent tendency brought to fulfillment" (35). Scattering of albatross feathers and corporate emblem, Slothrop embodies the very System he has, appropriately enough, sought to identify: his unboundedness personifies the permeable boundaries of the nation-state, the shifting constitution of transnational companies, the circulation of finance capitalism, the decentralization of multinational cartels. As Deborah Madsen suggests, in *Gravity's Rainbow* the postmodern subject stands in relation to the schizophrenic corporation (146).

Far from achieving "that special place beyond systems of codes and information where our humanness resides" (Porush 117), then, Slothrop has entered the machine, in so doing reversing the cowboy dreams that cyberpunk would later attempt to resuscitate from out of a long dead ideological system. As he tells his ghost father, "M-maybe *it exists.* Maybe there *is* a Machine to take us away, take us completely, suck us out through the electrodes out of the skull 'n' into the Machine and live there forever with all the other souls it's got stored there. *It* could decide who it would suck out, a-and when. Dope never gave *you* immortality. *You* hadda come back, everytime, into a dying hunk of smelly *meat!* But *We* can live forever, in a clean, honest, purified Electroworld" (699). In *Gravity's Rainbow,* however, the "Machine to take us away," the "purified Electroworld" so suggestive of the glittering cyberspace of Gibson or Stephenson, takes the form of a toilet, the narrative returning repeatedly to surreal visions of escape via the plumbing and sewage beneath. "[I]t's good policy always to have the toilet valve cracked a bit," the narrative advises, "to maintain some flow" so that when They come and shut off the water, "you'll have that extra minute or two" to get rid of "dope, shit, documents" (694). As one's illicit commodities are shunted down the toilet, so, too, is the individual subject plunged into the filth and impurity of hidden underground tunnels, as Slothrop's fantastical hallucination of his descent down a Harvard toilet reveals:

> [T]here comes this godawful surge from up the line, noise growing like a tidal wave, a jam-packed wavefront of shit, vomit, toilet paper and dingleberries in mind-boggling mosaic, rushing down on panicky Slothrop like an MTA subway train on its own hapless victim. Nowhere to run. Paralyzed, he stares back over his shoulder. A looming wall stringing long tendrils of shitpaper behind, the shockwave is on him—GAAHHH! he tries a feeble frog kick at the very

last moment but already the cylinder of waste has wiped him out,
dark as cold beef gelatin along his upper backbone, the paper snapping up, wrapping across his lips, his nostrils, everything gone and
shit-stinking now as he has to keep batting micro-turds out of his
eyelashes, . . . the brown liquid tearing along, carrying him helpless
. . . seems he's been tumbling ass over teakettle—though there's no
way to tell in this murky shitstorm, no visual references. (66)

The escape route, then, is an evacuation, like the one Greta fantasizes, and
it promises not a "clean, honest, purified Electroworld" but rather an
immersion—and dissolution—in what Julia Kristeva terms the "abject,"
that which is identified with the unclean and impure and which must be
cast away from the self in the very process of constituting that self.
"Neither subject nor object," the abject is both "opposed to the I" in constituting it and at the same time the "dying hunk of smelly meat" that is
the dangerous "in-between, the ambiguous, the composite" that "does not
respect borders, positions, rules" (4). N. Katherine Hayles connects the
horror of Kristeva's abject to the dynamics of late capitalism, where imperialism becomes interconnected with "experialism": "While imperialism is
about expropriating valuable natural resources from less powerful nations,
experialism is about forcing them to accept the industrial wastes that result
when the expropriated natural resources are turned into capitalist commodities" (685). The process whereby the individual is constructed—
through the continual casting away of the abject—is implicated in this
recursivity of global capitalism, which also constitutes itself through the
constant denial of those forces upon which production depends. When
Gravity's Rainbow asserts that the "colonies are the outhouses of the
European soul" (448), it extends capitalism and imperialism beyond their
productive self-representations. Pynchon's "colonies"—like blackness, like
shit—explicitly unite capitalism and the abject as the space in which productive masculinity is both fantastically constituted and terminally threatened. Corporate-military capitalism, similarly, is lived aboard a toiletship
lost in time. And in a final, remarkable parallel, masculine sexual violence
metamorphoses into masochism, and white male dominance resolves itself
in corpophilia.

7

"THE BEST RAPE STORY I HAVE EVER READ"

WASTE MANAGEMENT AND THE SCAPEGOATED RAPIST

One of the central projects of postmodernism has been the gradual but relentless dismantling of the white masculine subject, and that dissemination, as I have attempted to show, is commonly embodied in the victimized bodies of girls and women. The violently penetrated female body speaks to the cultural formations that uncomfortably link late capitalism and white masculinity; it articulates the difficult association of masculinity with consumer fetishism and with productive agency, and it finally reveals the vulnerability of the masculine body itself within a global system that is both self-organizing and yet given to a frightening tendency toward entropic decay. At the same time, however, as I hope to argue here, rape narrative is also employed within postmodern fiction to resuscitate the white male subject. There are texts that suggest—precisely through heterosexual violence—a regrouping, or a reemergence of the father amidst post–cold war consumer glut, finance capitalism, and waste management. Ironically, the white masculinity reestablished in this type of postmodern rape narrative is defined in sharp contrast to sexual violence and is actually dependent on the repeated and emphatic casting out of the desire to rape. One is tempted to claim that the essence of the shift is the emergence of compassion, an installation of the kindness so explicitly and self-consciously absent from Thomas Pynchon's texts. There is an overarching grief in the texts of Don DeLillo and John Irving, the two writers I will take up here—grief for a lost masculinity, and grief for the raped girl or woman. That grief, however, as (massively) sympathetically rendered as it is, is predicated on the presence of a victim for whom to feel grief. The rapist is thus preserved as he is scapegoated, and he remains to haunt the borders and underground of the text; his violence necessarily continues to operate, denounced and yet crucial for masculine (anti)definition.

The rapist's (outcast) presence thus powers the post-masculinist white masculinity that redeems the new wasteland. In a skewed sense, he is a travestied return of the muscled, blue-collar laborer under advanced capitalism, "producing" the ultimate consumer item, one which not only effaces its own violent production and material existence but which ends up circulating within what Joseph Tabbi calls "the placeless, selfless sphere of electronic transcendence" (206). The rape victim, herself heavily fetishized, becomes a holy martyr in what would otherwise be a morally withered universe—a narrative development that contrasts starkly with the representation of rape victims in the feminist texts I discuss in the final chapter. DeLillo's *Underworld*, itself a reworking of *Gravity's Rainbow*, achieves narrative epiphany in the saintly, post-death apparition of Esmeralda Lopez, the twelve-year-old raped and murdered in the wastelands of the Bronx. John Irving's protagonists achieve mature masculinity when they acknowledge that a rape victim is "holy" (*Hotel New Hampshire* 441). The sexually victimized female body is thus defined both as vulnerable to the touch of displaced masculine violence and yet untouchable to the average man. Rape becomes the occasion to reflect on the "redemptive qualit[y]" of the flows and recirculations of late capitalism, the miraculous fact that the compromised masculine self has been rendered invisible but has not been obliterated (*Underworld* 809). In a significant way, abstract value is thus ideologically produced in a way that nullifies and condemns the laborer (the rapist) while building up the consumer/investor—s/he who watches and witnesses and grieves. This masculine regret and disavowal—in the midst of claiming ownership—is a part of a new vision of subjectivity, a vision explicitly celebrated in the novel as "real" finally, outside the fantastical illusions of late capitalism.

Underworld is most centrally about waste: the massive waste accumulated, underground or not, figuratively or actually, through the combined forces of cold war–era military industrial production and post–World War II domestic consumerism. Jesse Kavadlo makes the apt point that the *Underworld's* "excess and sheer length" alone "seem an aesthetic reflection of the world described within the novel" (387). The fact that Nick Shay, the central character to the extent that there is a central character, is a waste manager is only a reflection of a larger theme:

> [T]he novel's explicit subject is waste, literal and figurative: landfills
> and recycled junk; excrement; nuclear waste; wasted lives, wasted
> time, the best minds of a generation devoted to waste; burying
> waste, unearthing waste; civilizations built and ended on account of
> waste; getting wasted, in terms of both drugs and murder as made
> emblematic in Nick's murder of George the waiter, the junkie who

uses heroin (junk, shit) and gets wasted (killed) for it. *Underworld*
shows it all, while self-consciously acknowledging that any excess,
even literary, is a kind of waste product. (387)

To inhabit the late twentieth century, then, the perspective from which or
toward which the events of the novel spiral, is inevitably to have entered
the postmodern scene, an overdetermined space, the clutter of which disavows the heroic engineering myths of earlier forms of capitalism. In this
sense, the novel echoes the way Fredric Jameson pictures the "modern age"
as "a period in which . . . the deep underlying materiality of all things has
finally risen dripping and convulsive into the light of day" (*Postmodernism*
67). In fact, the burgeoning waste—in its sheer material (convulsive)
excess—is figured as that which has come to supplant human/masculine
agency. The connections that emerge among the scattered scraps of waste
do not originate in anything that would suggest human intention—nor do
they link up in rational chains of cause and effect; they are self-organizing.

The novel thus charts the evolution of late capitalism from a seemingly
coherent and clean system of production and use/consumption to an inco-
herent process of random accumulation. "The cold war is your friend"
because it stands in for a bygone belief in the reasonable interconnections
between production, consumption, politics, and morality (*Underworld*
170). Peter Knight argues that the novel's self-conscious shift from cold
war–era fear to contemporary conspiracy theory articulates an important
ideological development in American culture, from "an inflexible and
monolithic belief structure in a personalized cabal, to contradictory, ironic, and self-reflexive appropriation of the language of conspiracy theory,"
an appropriation that addresses "the bewildering complexities of the current world in which everything is connected but nothing adds up"
(821–22)—or, as Kathleen Stewart puts it, where "the more you know, the
less you know" (13). In a post–cold war era, accumulation stands in for
coherence: "[T]he hidden story of recent history is not to be found buried
in government files, waiting to be pieced together into a coherent story of
shadowy conspirators. Instead it is to be found in the daily ephemera and
vast entanglements of multinational consumer capitalism, both more obvious because it is omnipresent, and less detectable because it is so much
taken for granted" (Knight 820). "Self-reflexive" paranoia denies the
(seemingly) secure identity available through narratives of us and them,
stories in which the "other" is comfortably psychologized, if put beyond
the pale of civilized behavior. Like the random taping of the highway killer,
the new paranoia "[says] terrible things about forces beyond your control,
lines of intersection that cut through history and logic and every reasonable layer of human expectation" (157). As in *Gravity's Rainbow*, the lack

of control over experience results finally in the dissemination of the self, a quality well suited to the excesses and motility of consumer capitalism, where "it is the camera that puts [you] in the tale" (157).

Cold war nostalgia thus suggests a desire for the imagined days of secure, human- and plot-centered paranoia, the days when (so the collective memory goes) a self could still think itself as a unified (if threatened) subject through imagined alliance and identification with the phallic power of unchecked weapons production. Knight argues that it is specifically the *productive* aspect of the cold war that is appealing for some of the characters of *Underworld*—their desire "might . . . be read . . . as a displaced and timely nostalgia for the older—though no less scary—secure paranoia of Fordism" (825). The massive-scale uniformity of military industrial production in the 1950s can appear almost to cover over the simultaneous shift toward the massive wastage of consumer economy and identity, a point DeLillo makes clear in part 5 of *Underworld*, "Better Things for Better Living through Chemistry," the slogan for Dow Chemical. The section includes a heavily satirical portrayal of the stereotypical white suburban family of the 1950s—vaguely terrified of the Soviet Union, image-conscious, and consumerist. As Molly Wallace points out, "What is immediately apparent here is the prevalence of commodities and the ways in which these characters are defined (and define themselves) in relation to commodity culture" (370). The consumerism, however, is covered over with fantasies of association with the productive forces of the cold war so that both dynamics appear ludicrously connected. While Mom industriously makes Jell-O in her two-tone kitchen and Dad simonizes the two-tone Fairlane in the breezeway, for example, young Eric "sat in his room, behind drawn fiberglass curtains, jerking off into a condom. He liked using a condom because it had a sleek metallic shimmer, like his favorite weapons system, the Honest John, a surface-to-surface missile with a warhead that carried yields of up to forty kilotons" (514). This he does while eying a photograph of Jayne Mansfield, focusing first on the breasts and then on "the facial Jayne," "put together out of a thousand thermoplastic things" (515). In fact, the constructed-product quality of "the facial Jayne" is precisely what is unconsciously appealing to young Eric: "it was the masking waxes, liners, glosses and creams that became the soft moist mechanism of release" (515).

What remains hidden from Tyrone Slothrop throughout much of *Gravity's Rainbow* is the fact that his erections mark not his identification with the rocket but his vulnerability to it. And what remains hidden to Eric in the midst of this erotic objectification of Mansfield is the absurdity of the comparison of his penis to a missile, the vulnerability of the body encased in weapons-like material ("This [the condom] was technology they wanted to wrap around my dick"; Brian Glassic points out in another context; "[t]his was mass-produced latex they used to paint battleships" [110]), and the extent to which his sexuality (like his masculinity) is circumscribed by 1950s consumerism. The powerful identification with weapons technology—the "Honest John," ironically enough—covers over these things; this is precisely the mechanism that motivates cold war nostalgia for characters in the 1980s and 1990s sections of the book: "They put thermal pads on the Honest John to heat the solid fuel in preparation for firing. Then they remove the pads and launch the missile from a girderlike launch rail in a grassy somewhere in the Free World. And the missile's infallible flight, the way it seeps out precise volumes of mathematical pace, it's so saintly and sun-tipped, swinging out of its apex to dive to earth, and the way the fireball haloes out above its column of smoke and roar, like some nameless faceless whatever. It made him want to be a Catholic" (514–15). Jiwei Ci argues that "it is a measure of capitalism's remarkable social and economic resourcefulness" that it can retain the transcendent promise underlying the Protestant work ethic at a time when the imperative for profit maximization is realized much more crucially through consumption than through production (315). Eric's fantastical association with the productive might of the military lends his (highly consumerist) masturbation a sense of mystical meaning and/or release ("meaning and release," Ci points out, have become "increasingly indistinguishable" under consumer capitalism [315]). The novel itself obviously puts this promise of "meaning" into question. The masturbation scene, as Philip Nel points out, "sends out waves of satire in many directions at once, rippling toward not only patriarchy but militarism, conspicuous consumption, and the vocabulary of advertisements" (421). Selfhood—and masculinity—are no longer to be thought in relation to either large-scale, volitional production or heterosexual violence. Rather, late-twentieth-century subjectivity generally and masculinity most particularly are developed in relationship to waste management, grappling with the wreckage generated as an effect of an earlier era of pointless productivity. "All those decades," Viktor muses toward the end of the novel, "when we thought about weapons all the time and never thought about the dark multiplying byproduct." With the cold war over, the American can respond, "And in this case . . . In our case, in our age. What we excrete comes back to consume us" (791).

Thus, for characters in the 1990s frame of *Underworld*, young Eric's erotic identification with "the nameless faceless whatever" of weapons technology has become largely unthinkable. Klara Sax articulates the sense that with the end of the cold war, "power" and "greatness" have gone the way of secure paranoia—they have cut themselves loose from a human—or even a comprehensible—center:

> Now that power is in shatters or tatters and now that those Soviet
> borders don't even exist in the same way, I think we understand, we
> look back, we see ourselves more clearly, and them as well. Power
> meant something thirty, forty years ago. It was stable, it was
> focused, it was a tangible thing. It was greatness, danger, terror, all
> those things. And it held us together, the Soviets and us. Maybe it
> held the world together. You could measure things. You could
> measure hope and you could measure destruction. Not that I want
> to bring it back. It's gone, good riddance. But the fact is. (76)

That "all technology leads to the bomb" (467) is no longer a reason for
nationalist pride—a pride in which one might personally share—but is
rather an epiphany about "the bewildering complexities of the current
world in which everything is connected but nothing adds up" (Knight
822). Eric himself, now grown up and working as a weapons scientist in
the nineties, makes himself felt in the narrative almost exclusively through
his repeated and repeatedly graphic descriptions of the effects of radiation,
the tests deliberately conducted on humans. In an affectation reminiscent
of Tyrone Slothrop, he assumes a stutter to deliver the horrifying details,
an affectation that reinforces the peripheral nature—and secondary, constructed quality—of the masculine voice in the face of post-human production. As does the rocket in *Gravity's Rainbow*, the bomb becomes its
own prime mover, and the ultimate representative of the enduring, lethal
waste inevitably connected to technological production.

    The decenteredness of the human (masculine) subject in the face of the
production/waste of the past (and present) speaks to what Mark Osteen
terms "a motif of male absence and failure" (230). As Cormaroff and
Cormaroff point out more generally, "gone is the deus ex machina, a figure altogether too concrete, too industrial for . . . the post-Fordist era"
(294): "In the upshot, production appears to have been superseded, as the
fons et origo of wealth, by less tangible ways of generating value: by control
over such things as the provision of services, the means of communication,
and above all, the flow of finance capital. In short, by the market and by
speculation" (295). Yet in *Underworld* this "absence" is a particularly
haunting one, full of suggestion. In a variety of ways, for example, Nick
Shay toys with the fantastical resuscitation of his father, Jimmy
Costanza—a man who was always, ironically enough, removed from the
purely productive role by being by profession a numbers runner, a man
defined by the market and by speculation. His disappearance has been
shrouded in mystery, a fog that serves Nick well, as he can imagine any
number of coherent gangster plots with which to replace that unknown
("they took him out near Orchard Beach . . . , and they dropped him into

the lower world, his body suspended above the rockweed, in the soft organic murk" [119])—like the stories he tells neighbor children, appropriately enough, while sitting on the toilet. Ultimately, it becomes clear that his father's absence will no more be contained in a securely paranoid narrative than it will be replaced by his return; it will become its own burgeoning presence, as lethal, enduring, and without boundary as the nuclear waste with which Nick works as an adult. Like the waste he deals in, his father has become a thing of the underworld, the "lower world," "the soft organic murk," as Ruth Helyer has pointed out (992); he is one of those who might "live unknown to us in the crawlspaces of the . . . infrastructure, down the tunnels and under the bridge approaches" (*Underworld* 323).

In short, Jimmy Constanza has entered the flow of the underworld, has begun circulating like the mysterious ship of human waste, appearing in memory, dreams, fantasies, and mutually contradictory narratives, and while on the one hand he has left Nick nothing but a second-hand affected gangster voice, on the other hand he is explicitly associated with great riches, both mythical and actual, as is the waste itself: "We built pyramids of waste above and below the earth. The more hazardous the waste, the deeper we tried to sink it. The word plutonium comes from Pluto, god of the dead and ruler of the underworld. They took him out to the marshes and wasted him as we say today, or used to say until it got changed to something else" (106). The legacy of a lost world of power is multi-billion-dollar business, in one way of looking at it—the lucrative business of waste management. It is a business that distills the motive force of a new economy—the vertiginous circulation of finance capital—while downplaying the production and the accumulation both so central within earlier forms of capitalism. The wealth itself as a physical manifestation is nowhere to be found except within these strangely inflated metaphors of pyramid, god, and ruler—figures of speech that lack the mimetic persuasiveness of the cold war narrative of us and them. Even words keep changing—"wasted . . . as we say today, or used to say until it got changed to something else"—as if implicated in the novel's constant movement of shit, radioactive waste, the baseball, and the missing father. In *Underworld* everything—"the leftovers, all the leftovers"—is "indefinitely recyclable" (Baudrillard, *Illusion of the End,* 26, 27).

The circulation and recirculation of waste—even (particularly) lethal waste—thus promises anew that fabulous wealth and power are to be had. Jesse Kavadlo argues that in his role as waste manager Nick Shay parallels not only DeLillo himself specifically but a hope for the postmodern authorial function generally. For both (for all three), what is left at the present time is the possibility inherent in recycling:

DeLillo's author is alive and a kind of waste manager himself, not unlike Nick Shay, sifting and sorting through the physical, meta-physical, and spiritual excesses, contaminants, and wastes of our modernity. [Like Barthes's bricolage, Kristeva's intertextuality, Bakhtin's heteroglossia, and Bloom's anxiety of influence, *Underworld*] suggests the mode of DeLillo's metaphorical waste manager—reusing, reappropriating, recycling, and ultimately redeeming language. Barthes's lower-case "a" author (scripteur) draws on, reuses, and remakes the textual "tissue," as DeLillo's waste manager turns societal detritus into art, but for DeLillo, the mystery and solemn power of waste turns authorial custodial work into a near mystical experience. (385–86)

Thus it is not surprising that the word "create" eventually works its way into Kavadlo's argument, suggesting a certain (temporary) stability in the recycling/recirculation process, a moment when boundaries are estab-lished and a product is created that signifies something outside itself—something above or below itself. (One thinks of the retired bombers that Klara Sax arranges in the desert and paints a concrete and relatively endur-ing art work that signifies the cold war.) Kavadlo's reading also reopens the question of agency, a question that other postmodern theorists of the col-lage/pastiche either exclude or diminish. For Jameson, for example, pas-tiche is problematic precisely because it disallows a sense of either linguis-tic ground or history.

Kavadlo's reading thus suggests that DeLillo's novel pulls against itself—conjures the life of the missing father out of his own "soft organic murk." On one hand, the novel is scathing toward a middle-class cold war era in which penis and warhead together signify masculinity. Further, it explicitly puts into question the coherent cold war narrative that accom-panied such an identification and that enabled a certain stable picture of aggressive subjectivity. On the other hand, Nick Shay's nostalgia for the masculine violence of his own Bronx working class 1950s is narrated seemingly without irony: "I long for the days of disorder. I want them back, the days when I was alive on the earth, rippling in the quick of my skin, heedless and real. I was dumb-muscled and angry and real. This is what I long for, the breach of peace, the days of disarray when I walked real streets and did things slap-bang and felt angry and ready all the time, a danger to others and a distant mystery to myself" (810). The sad straightforwardness of the passage suggests that for Nick, the winter of our discontent has indeed turned to sullen spring. Nick recognizes the cold war as a personal friend. This lost winter before "the breach of peace" cre-ated a space for legitimate masculine physical power and violence; it was a time when manhood was about acting. The physical, hard irreducibility of this imagined past—verified by the repetition of "real," the word "dumb-muscled"—persists within the boundarylessness and the murk inherent in the circulation of memory, waste, and capital. At the same time, in spite of the presumably necessary "breach of peace," this portrayal of "real" masculinity disavows complicity with the paranoia or consumerism of the cold war; the "real" man acts with volition and for "myster[ious]" reasons, uncontained by ideology or external pattern: he "[does] things slap-bang." Nick's adolescence is thus set in counterpoint to young Eric's; Nick's youth was not spent masturbating into condoms while fantasizing about surface-to-surface missiles, fixating on the creams and waxes on Jayne Mansfield's photographed face. It is rather Nick's middle age that feels scripted and unreal, "phony": "None of it ever belonged to me except in the sense that I filled out the forms" (796).

Nick's nostalgia for his "real" youth is echoed by brief and disorienting flashbacks to his random adolescent acts of (fetishistically masculine) violence, which are interjected suddenly and without context throughout the novel. The interjections escalate, becoming slightly more aggressive, slightly more violent—most suggesting the hypermasculinity of the stereotypical James Dean–styled street thug. He "punche[s a] guy to his knees" simply because "he'd never seen the guy before," and then casually "shoot[s] a game" of pool (714–15). He sleeps with his girlfriend's best friend in a gesture of aggressive heterosexuality so extreme as to suggest the exuberance of drag:

"You're a cunt, Gloria."
    "What do you want?"
    "You're a cunt, Gloria."
    "Say something nice, Nicky."
    She was smiling, he wasn't.
    [. . .]
    "You're a cunt in and out and up and down. You're an all-over cunt through and through." (773)

He offers advice to Muzz when another driver bumps the back of their 7-Up truck: "'Get mad,' Nick told him. 'Tell him you'll ram your tire iron up his ass'" (774). The interjections culminate in the narration of Nick's killing of George Manza, an event that haunts the novel, and yet is not clearly told until the very end of the penultimate section, the final chapter before the epilogue. The killing is clearly a "mystery" to him, as he claims later in life he was to himself, and his "slap-bang" firing of the sawed-off shotgun at George's head is clearly the "heedless and real" act of "dumb-muscled" "danger" about which he later waxes nostalgic.

Yet the event is at the same time not as "real" as Nick would hope—it is not simply a clean act of a muscular body, without thought, without pre-packaged fantasy and pre-packaged gender scripting. Nick remembers that he "posed with the gun": "He posed with it, Nick did, a pirate's pistol or an old Kentucky flintlock if that's the word. It was more natural two hands than one, the left hand under the forepart to steady and point" (781, 780). Nick imagines himself a swashbuckling Daniel Boone, blending the characteristics of two highly stereotypical (if not clichéd) male figures—the criminal pirate on the high seas and the honorable adventurer, clearing the American path into new land—yet in ways that make the role playing appear "natural"—not role playing at all. Thus, Eric's erotic association with the violence of missiles is castigated, while Nick's attraction to the "pirate's pistol" is identified as "natural." Young Eric serves as a decoy—his masculinity is not real; Nick's is real. Eric's violent fantasies are embarrassingly scripted and clearly serve the ends of capitalism and the state; Nick's violence is natural and cannot be channeled into a larger sociopolitical, economic, or ideological plan. By the same token, Nick's inner violence is repressed—for the most part by choice; Eric's inner violence, on the other hand, has never truly been "inner"—has always been a function of weapons production and cold war economics—and is thus "lost" when Eric stops telling himself stories about missile trajectories and begins telling stories about radiation sickness, human testing, and mutation. Nick's masculine violence thus remains a real thing, a "natural" entity to put away and cover over; Eric's masculine violence is not "real" in the same romantic sense, does not bubble up from some underground source but is rather a function of a consumer-driven discursive field that is explicitly shown to generate certain affectations of phallic violence ("the power of the automobile, the horsepower, the decibel rumble of the dual exhausts, the pedal tension of Ford-O-Matic drive . . . eating up the landscape," "the bumper bullets on a Cadillac"; 516, 517). In short, the fact of the repressed "natural" violence contributes to the notion that Nick is a centered, unified subject who is in every way immune to the effects of (or at least redemptively self-conscious about) the scripted lifestyling of consumerism—the novel makes repeatedly clear that when Nick does make purchases it is always with an eye to discarding them, turning them into neatly packaged recyclables. He denies himself the pleasure of consuming and remains instead rooted in the circulations and flows of the underworld, the same place where repressed violence goes. Eric—young or adult—is just the opposite; he is the "switching center" in precisely the posthumanist sense that Baudrillard seems to intend.

As much as *Underworld* is about waste, then, it is just as much about the repression—and thus the preservation—of what is naturalized as "real" masculine violence. The violence doesn't leave the text or the late twentieth century; it goes underground, in the same sense that Nick's father goes underground. "I think he wanted to go under" (809), Nick says of Jimmy Constanza. Of his own rage over Brian Glassic's affair with his (Nick's) wife, Nick says: "I felt something drain out of me. Some old opposition, a capacity to resist" (801). The violent desire will be allowed to drain off, flow out, seep underground: Nick stares at Brian's sleeping "old-fashioned face, narrow and boyish, that I could probably crush with five earnest blows. I imagine this with some satisfaction. Dealing a serious blow. But we don't do that anymore, do we? This is a thing we've left behind. Five dealt blows to the pinkish face with the paling hair. But I sit there and watch him, you know, and I'm not sure I want to hit him" (796). What one might be tempted to call the violent core of the novel or of Nick Shay himself would thus more accurately be termed the violent underground stream. Like the increasingly dematerialized (and deterritorialized) movement of global investment capitalism itself, the violence in *Underworld* is always almost (but not quite) visible, always untrackable, but always "real," flowing directly beneath the scripted domestic lifestyle in which nothing "ever belonged to me except in the sense that I filled out the forms" (796). One is tempted to argue that the violence forms the type of self-organizing system Tom LeClair argues is descriptive of DeLillo's novels—the type that is outside of and opposed to the "power of large closed systems, their fake and therefore punishing 'certitudes'" (27)—because as dark as that underground is, it breeds a certain glinting life. The duality brings to mind Baudrillard's sometimes vertiginous and sometimes toxic vision of the recirculation of the image or the signifier: "everywhere today one must recycle waste, and the dreams, the phantasms, the historical fairylike legendary imaginary of children and adults is a waste product, the first great toxic excrement of a hyperreal civilization" (*Simulacra* 12).

The novel in its epic whole represses/preserves violence in similar ways; it seeps into the flashbacks, flows into the outskirts, and is recycled into the unsympathetic characters who haunt the margins of the text. The Texas Highway Killer, for example, who inadvertently supplies the missing link in the baseball's chain of ownership, is for the most part unrelated to the central narratives of the novel and is relatively undeveloped as a character. The randomness of his being the one to uncover the (randomly) missing link is echoed by his random presence in the novel. It is thus not coincidental that his appearance, as Timothy Parrish has pointed out, "marks the point at which the centrifugal energies of the Cold War dissipate" (709). No one thinks that Richard Henry Gilkey is a part of a plot—it is clear, as it is not in the cold war mythology surrounding Lee Harvey Oswald, that he acts alone, for reasons unknown—or for no particular reason, per se, at all: "there is no conspiracy to explain Gilkey, no obvious social or political context in which to understand his actions" (Parrish 712).

If alone and inexplicable, however, he is not distinct. Unsure "of the knowledge that he was real," blending into other copycat voices and killings, dependent on an unknown anchorwoman to give "him the feeling he was taking shape as himself, coming into the shape he'd always been intended to take, the thing of who he really was," he is evidence nonetheless to the raw possibility of violent agency (*Underworld* 269): "he is able to achieve a particularly charged identity while remaining, literally, faceless" (J. Green 576). In fact, his actuality and strength are paradoxically dependent on the extent to which he is outside all plots, uninspired by logical narrative chains of cause and effect. Like Jimmy Costanza, Richard Henry Gilkey has entered "the soft organic murk," has increasingly lost a sense of personal boundary and yet has seemingly gained power through this very dissolution: "He came alive in [his victims' survivors]. He lived in their histories, in the photographs in the newspaper, he survived in the memories of the family, lived with the victims, lived on, merged, twinned, quadrupled, continued into double figures" (271). The agency born of Gilkey's dissipation into this network of text, image, mind, and life is not reduced by the fact that he is not in control of the dispersion—rather, that agency is mystified and enlarged. Gilkey thus embodies in a significant way the "human flows" that constitute a central fiscal mechanism of global capitalism: his boundarylessness increasingly diffuses anything that might be said to constitute a sovereign state, and his underworld circulation makes him invulnerable to surveillance or capture. In this way the novel preserves him—as it castigates him—as untrammeled potential for masculinized violence. This potential is the value that endures, the profit motive that mobilizes his murky dissemination "into double figures." He paradoxically resists even as he is defined by the homogeneity that DeLillo presents as born of all of the forces of "Kapital": "Foreign investment, global markets, corporate acquisitions, the flow of information through transnational media, the attenuating influence of money that's electronic and sex that's cyberspaced, untouched money and computersafe sex, the convergence of consumer desire" (785).

This oddly inhuman violence preserved somehow within the system itself—distinctly masculine and yet removed from the sympathetic masculine characters—is arguably the central driving force of Delillo's novel. Its haunting semipresence grows in force and in visibility throughout the novel and is finally incarnated in the realm of present-tense reality in the novel's climactic sequence—not in any final revelation about the missing father, but in the post-death apparition of Esmeralda Lopez, the twelve-year-old who is raped and murdered in the wastelands of the South Bronx.

The vision itself occurs near the end of the final chapter, the epilogue, "Das Kapital," a narrative position inevitably central. The occurrence is even more so because it is loaded with mystical and compassionate weight and seems to nullify or at least offer a counterbalance to the revelation of Nick's murderous core and the deformed bodies that are the shadow twin of the bomb. The ghostly face on the billboard seems tentatively to suggest that beneath, above, or beyond the wreckage and poverty of a post–cold war world of consumer glut, waste management, and gross social inequity is something else, something of inestimable value: "And what do you remember, finally, when everyone has gone home and the streets are empty of devotion and hope, swept by river wind? Is the memory thin and bitter and does it shame you with its fundamental untruth—all nuance and wishful sillhouette? Or does the power of transcendence linger, the sense of an event that violates natural forces, something holy that throbs on the hot horizon, the vision you crave because you need a sign to stand against your doubt?" (824). The echoes of T. S. Eliot are strong in the passage, as they are throughout the end of "Das Kapital." The passage is a call to reflect on personal salvation, and it invokes the shaky promise of transcendence offered by Eliot's raped women.

Esmeralda has from the beginning been a castoff child with an otherworldly aura. She is described as a feral animal, a runner, too wild to contact. The nuns throw her food from a distance, as if she is a skittish wolf or coyote. Esmeralda is thus suggestive of prelapsarian innocence in a post-apocalyptic world. In this sense she calls to mind Nick Shay's nostalgia for a time of innocence in the young (in his case, violent and "dumb-muscled") body: "She lives wild in the inner ghetto, a slice of the South Bronx called the Wall—a girl who forages in empty lots for discarded clothes, plucks spoiled fruit from garbage bags behind bodegas, who is sometimes seen running through the trees and weeds, a shadow on the rubbled walls of demolished structures, unstumbling, a tactful runner with the sweet and easy stride of some creature of sylvan myth" (810). Like Nick, Esmeralda is represented as being cut off from the consumer world inhabited by most of the other characters; she circulates in the underworld accumulations and devastations of late capitalism (like Nick, she is a recycler, eating, in this case, from garbage cans). She thus reserves, as does Nick, a space one is encouraged to think of not so much as the underside of a productive mega-system run amok but rather as natural, in inevitable and romantic opposition to the type of "phony" (796) lifestyle that Nick feels has been scripted for himself. As with Nick, however, whose "natural" core is described in ways that are explicitly social, Esmeralda's wildness is a thing not entirely natural at all; it is heavily laden with narrative allusion. The "creature of sylvan myth" to which she is likened, for example, draws her toward classical association—probably for most readers (particularly in retrospect, given Esmeralda's fate) to the story of Daphne.

Yet there is no Apollo in this story to whom the girl can appeal, not even the Christian god Sister Edgar feels can redeem her, "save her from danger, bring her to candles and ashes and palms, to belief in the mystical body" (811). It is not in her trajectory to enter into a more coherent plot; she is "too wild to be captured or to live," as Parrish puts it (720). She is a life that flows anarchically and ceaselessly outside the sanctioned boundaries, motivated by no discernible cause: Esmeralda is "a quintessential 'subaltern' figure," Molly Wallace argues, "utterly outside the symbolic order, voiceless, a missing figure, a 'shadow on the nibbled walls of demolished structures' of the inner city'" (379). Just as young Nick is "a distant mystery to myself," it is her unconscious, unknowable physicality that defines her and that makes her valuable: "Run is what she does. It is her beauty and her safety both, her melodious hope, a thing of special merit, a cleansing, the fleet leaf-fall of something godly blowing through the world" (813). Esmeralda suggests "something godly" only to the extent that she remains unaware of that suggestion. Like Nick's nostalgically recalled youth—the longing for which is proclaimed immediately before the long, ultimate, Esmeralda section—her value has to do with "the days of disorder [, . . .] when I was alive on the earth, rippling in the quick of my skin, heedless and real" (810). What is longed for and heavily aestheticized to the point of either nostalgia or transcendent suggestion is the life of the restless, "dumb," young body.

In spite of the similarity, the novel cuts a very careful incision between Nick's violence and Esmeralda's rape and murder. Nick's longed-for youth distills the naturalized essence of masculine violence, and Esmeralda's running/raped body distills the naturalized essence of feminine and youthful vulnerability to that violence, but one does not bleed into the other, in spite of the fact that in terms of actual structure the Esmeralda sequence appears as if in answer to Nick's finally articulated desire to return to the violence of youth. Nick himself is excised from contact with Esmeralda throughout the novel, and the tone with which the rape/murder is narrated is far more horrific than any tone used in association with Nick. The rape and murder themselves are narrated without the aestheticized language that otherwise marks Esmeralda, and it is almost easy to miss the echoes of Nick's youth—self-portrayed or otherwise—with the nostalgia drained out:

> Nick's memory of his youth: I want them back, the days when I was
> . . . heedless and real. [. . . .] This is what I long for, the breach of

peace, the days of disarray when I walked real streets and did things slap-bang. (810)

Esmeralda's rapist: He's up there wandering, . . . a man who drifts. . . . He's on her like that. (817)

Nick's memory of his youth: I was dumb-muscled and angry and real . . . and felt angry and ready all the time, a danger to others and a distant mystery to myself. (810)

Esmeralda's rapist: He comes across the sleeping girl and feels a familiar anger rising and knows he will need to do something to make her pay. . . . She fights and whisper-cries in a voice that makes him angrier, like who the fuck she think she is. (817)

Nick's youth: He'd never seen the guy before and this is why he was punching him. . . . Nick crouched and set himself and threw a punch. He knew it was not necessary to throw this punch but he'd hit the guy only glancing blows to the face and he wanted to hit him solid. It was a chance to hit someone solid that he didn't want to miss. (714)

Esmeralda's rapist: He beats her with the end of his fist, sending hammerblows to the head. Struggle bitch get hit. . . . Either way he's gonna hit her, she struggle or not. (818)

Nick's youth: She was smiling, he wasn't.

[. . .]

"You're a cunt in and out and up and down. You're an all-over cunt through and through." (773)

Esmeralda's rapist: "No eye contact, cunt." (818)

The violence of the rape speaks to Nick's longing (in spite of the fact that the Nick sections are softer for a variety of reasons, including not only the actual content but also context, point of view, and our relationship to the character). The connection, however, is deeply repressed. Esmeralda's raped and murdered body, as vulnerable as it is to random inner-city masculine violence, has been and continues to be untouchable to the hero/protagonist of the novel—the gracefully, poignantly aging James Dean. Nick is only vaguely made aware of Esmeralda's rape and murder, and time has safely removed him from the violence of his past. The novel thus accomplishes an almost surgical removal of violence from masculinity, while nonetheless preserving that connection in grimly epic proportions.

It is significant that Nick (vaguely) learns about Esmeralda's rape and murder only after she has been "transfigured." He learns at a distance, from his son, via, in turn, the Internet that a "young girl was the victim of a terrible crime," that her body was found "amid dense debris," that witnesses report the "miracle" of her image on the orange juice billboard (808). He remains vague about the physical details, removed from them. Instead, the apparition is cause for the narrative to shift quickly to Nick's introspection about things he feels are "the real miracle[s]": (1) the Internet, "where everybody is everywhere at once, and [his son] is there among them, unseen"; (2) the fact that his father simply disappeared: "the earth opened up and he stepped inside"; (3) and the "redemptive" garbage we recycle, which "come[s] back to us, alight with a kind of brave aging" (808–9). Esmeralda's rape and death thus become the occasion to reflect on the "redemptive qualit[y]" of the flows and recirculations of late capitalism, the miraculous fact that the compromised masculine self has been rendered invisible but has not been obliterated (809). Nick's father is the link, his mythic, underground presence somehow guaranteeing the value unstably preserved in these circulations—a value no longer sustained through industrial military production.

Esmeralda, on the other hand, who cannot speak, and certainly not in an affected gangster voice, is thus in death as in life subjected to a late-capitalist "logic of consumption" (M. Wallace 379): her material body is metamorphosed for the observer into a sign of the transformative potential of recycling. In this sense Esmeralda suggests a return of Eliot's and Pound's high modernist Philomela. Silenced ("dumb"), naturalized, and brutally raped by a figure disassociated from the narrative point of view, Philomela is shown at her moment of "change," a transformation of the material body "by the barbarous king / So rudely forced" to the more ethereal nightingale of "inviolable voice" ("A Game of Chess," Eliot, *Collected Poems,* 56). Esmeralda also is metamorphosed into the sign of transcendence; her victimization enabling the inhuman message of the billboard, as Philomela's suffering is transformed into birdsong. The message is no longer, however, one of submission per se, whether defined in human, religious, political, or economic terms. She is not, as are the Thames sisters and the Chorus of *Murder in the Cathedral,* a receptacle for a static higher power. No larger organizing schema seems on the horizon, hovering over the wasteland in an opaque promise of redemption. Rather, Esmeralda's apparition, significantly interwoven with an advertisement, is a testimony to the unseen flows of the late twentieth century and the extent to which other-worldly value seems to be generated through these very recirculations. The raped and subsequently "reborn" (Parrish 721) woman in this way ratifies the seemingly self-organizing power of the waste of late capitalism even as it paradoxically preserves the haunting effectivity of masculine violence/power/agency. The power of the lost (but not quite lost) father is a kind of buzz in the background.

Comaroff and Comaroff argue that there has been within the last few years an extraordinary intensification of interest in the occult throughout the world, a development they attribute to the increasingly dematerialized and deterritorialized nature of global investment capitalism. The recent obsession with the occult suggests, they argue, "the allure of accruing wealth from nothing," an allure clearly central to the "casino capitalism" of a global economy (313). DeLillo's work has for some time turned toward a certain opaque mysticism, in ways that clearly do suggest postnational, consumer capitalism (one thinks in particular of *The Names, Mao II*, and *White Noise*). Before *Underworld*, however, these occult suggestions are tempered with irony and distance. The German nun in *White Noise* is a case in point: "dumb head," she calls Jack Gladney, "If we did not pretend to believe these things [the devil, angels, heaven, hell], the world would collapse" (318). Sister Edgar's epiphany before the Minute Maid billboard is strikingly different; the ironic valence here is very low, surprisingly so given the extent to which she is elsewhere a parody of the classically styled "mean Catholic nun." Sister Grace's doubts do not outweigh the "reality" of Edgar's vision: "[Sister Edgar] sees Esmeralda's face take shape under the rainbow of bounteous juice and above the little suburban lake and there is a sense of someone living in the image, an animating spirit—less than a tender second of life, less than half a second and the spot is dark again" (822). DeLillo here illustrates the mechanics of the fetishized commodity and its relationship to the alienated consumer. As Wallace, following Baudrillard, argues of fetishism in the novel generally, "commodity fetishism is not only the reification of an object, not simply the effacement of its production, but also the effacement of the object itself in favor of its signifier, its image" (373). As the "real" object orange juice is lost to the clichéd representation of the "bounteous" plenitude of American suburbia, which signifier is eclipsed in turn by Esmeralda's effigy, so is Esmeralda herself sacrificed to the salvific, ephemeral image. Thus, although Mark Osteen is to some extent right to argue that the scene undermines the workings of commodity fetishism by suggesting "that the same forces and conditions that create bad faith and rampant waste may also germinate effective counterfaiths" (257), it is perhaps more accurate to say that the apparition replaces one fetishized object (orange juice) with another (the raped and murdered girl).

And what the image of the raped and murdered girl offers the alienated consumer—as does the recycling plant to which Nick takes his granddaughter—is a "reverence for waste, for the redemptive qualities of the things we use and discard" (809). Waste is the very stuff of transcendence and awe—it is not what must be "repressed," as Arthur Saltzman argues, in order to achieve "ecstasy" ("Awful Symmetries" 305). In the clutches of such ecstasy, Sister Edgar strips off her gloves to come into contact with the human detritus of capitalism—the crowded bodies that she has up until this point thought of with distaste—if not horror—as the debased embodiment of sin and mortality: "She feels something break upon her. An angelus of clearest joy. . . . Everything feels near at hand, breaking upon her, sadness and loss and glory and an old mother's bleak pity and a force at some deep level of lament that makes her feel inseparable from the shakers and mourners, the awestruck who stand in tidal traffic—she is nameless for a moment, lost to the details of personal history, a disembodied fact in liquid form, pouring into the crowd" (822–23). The billboard delivers more than has been intended by the corporate technological will—the promise of suburban safety, health, and well-being through product consumption. It has fallen into the volatile stream of the underworld, where things die and are reborn (babies are held up to the juice, to be "bathe[d. . . .] in baptismal balsam and oil" [821]) and where the airtight boundaries of self and place are put into question. Sister Edgar herself is "transubstantiated," as Osteen puts it, "into the 'living juice,' the blood of a new covenant that promises universal connection and even redemption" (258). Edgar's "transubstantiation" echoes that of Esmeralda herself, so that subject and object become one: both women live out the novel's nightmarish fears of permeability in the face of random, self-organizing force. Thus, as she has been for centuries, the violently penetrated woman is still the ultimate signifier of broken boundaries, whether defined in ecstatic or fearsome terms.

Clare Hansen makes the persuasive case that Gilles Deleuze and Felix Guattari figure the little girl generally in terms of the "dispersed libidinal energies ('molecular energies')" she deploys to destabilize those energies "which strive to aggregate into totalities ('molar' energies)": "Molar energies attempt to form and stabilize identities through divisions of classes, sexes and races, whereas molecular energies, in the words of Elizabeth Grosz, 'traverse, create a path, destabilize, enable energy seepage within and through these molar unities'" (qtd. in Hanson 187–88). The beatific image of Esmeralda reconstitutes Sister Edgar herself as a body less cleanly divided, and it is in echo of the rape/murder victim's "haecceity"—permeability and restless dispersion—that Sister Edgar should enter cyberspace when she dies (Deleuze and Guattari, *One Thousand Plateaus,* 276). Organizing as it does the fiscal mechanics of the world economy, the Internet is at once a vast well of accumulated waste and the non-site where postnational capital quietly circulates, "virtual money and commodities . . . exchanged instantly via an unregulated world network of computers" (Comaroff and Comaroff 320). In the Internet, Sister Edgar "is open—exposed to every connection you can make on the world wide web" (824)—open also to the fifty-eight-megaton Soviet bomb, "the largest yield in history," the detonation of which is "preserved in the computer that helped to build it" (826). If the rhetoric clearly denotes Baudrillard's "switching center," it also suggests female saint; Edgar, like the humanity she now represents, is left "vague, drained, docile, soft in [her] inner discourse" from the shock of the explosion (826). The femininity of the latter association is denied in the narrative, despite the fact that when her gloves are still on, Sister feels "masculinized, . . . condomed ten times over" (241); now stripped of those gloves as well as "pull [ed . . .] apart," Edgar is shown her essential unity with her "brother," J. Edgar Hoover, her union with all: "Sister and Brother. A fantasy in cyberspace and a way of seeing the other side and a settling of differences that have less to do with gender than with difference itself, all argument, all conflict programmed out" (826). Her final and ecstatic entry into "the lunar milk of the data stream" (826)—embraced by her fellow man, penetrated by the largest bomb in history—allows DeLillo to recapture the ending of Eliot's *Waste Land*, which, for all its obscurity, nonetheless offers "shantih," the peace which passeth all understanding (Eliot, *Collected Poems*, 69). If the novel ends on that same word "Peace,"[1] however, *Underworld*'s thunder does not suggest what Eliot's does: the positive impact of surrender to a higher power; its "Peace" will be derived from the active dissolution of boundaries and distinctions: "Fasten, fit closely, bind together" (827). The new god of the market requires less an acknowledgment of one's material emptiness and a faith in pure (if distant) value than an ecstatic leap into "the ephemeral and discontinuous," the "great decentred network of desire of which individuals seem the mere fleeting effects" (Eagleton 132).

For all the explicit surrender of the mythos of epic-scale production, consumerism, and accumulation, however, the vision that redeems the new wasteland is dependent on familiar images of violent force and penetration, images that finally serve to cordon off a shadowy and motile space for a masculinity defined in terms of its penetrative power. The reader is on the surface of things allowed the moral high ground—the rapists are those not like us; they are outside our moral city, haunting the outskirts. The rapist is a scapegoat—a debased figure who is distanced from the reader and protagonist and onto whom the violence of classic masculinity can be projected. In the case of *Underworld*, his (outcast) presence powers the epiphany that redeems the wasteland. In a skewed sense, he is thus a travestied return of the muscled, blue-collar laborer under advanced capitalism, "producing" the ultimate consumer item, one that not only effaces its own violent production and material existence but that circulates within "the placeless, selfless sphere of electronic transcendence" (Tabbi 206). And Esmeralda is the ultimate throw-away commodity—she gains value in being thrown, literally, from a building and, figuratively, into the Internet; her rape is the underbelly of consumerist fetishism in an age of waste crisis.

Thus, to the extent that the sacrifice of Esmeralda satisfactorily invests the underground circulations of advanced capitalism with transcendent value, we are revealed as entangled, complicit in the blind workings of "waste management" and displaced labor. DeLillo makes our collusion clear in the recording of Esmeralda's rape and murder, both of which are narrated as if on the Internet, website http://blk.www/dd.com/miraculum (810). The words "*Keystroke 1*" and "*Searching*" sandwich the scene, and what they suggest is that the description has been deliberately accessed by the Internet user—by us. Agency and will are thus seemingly preserved— and highlighted—in the late-twentieth-century non-place that courts fantasies of boundlessness and invisibility, where "one thing leads to another, always another link leading you deeper into no thing and no place" (Stewart 18). Further, that voyeuristic agency identifies itself with the rapist's point of view. If, then, the prerogative to rape has been renounced, the desire to do so has been reterritorialized, allowed to seep down into the "soft organic murk," the underground stream "leading you deeper into no thing and no place" that is the circulatory system of *Underworld.* Here the father and "the killer [live] on," having accumulated "life-credit." It is in this way, Murray Siskind tells Jack Gladney in *White Noise,* that "violence is a form of rebirth" (290).

The Murray Siskind role is filled in part in *Underworld* by Lenny Bruce, whose "comedy" skits punctuate the novel and who seems able (up to a certain tragic point) to survive without mythologizing the flows of late capitalism. There are no buried riches for Lenny—no transcendent moments, no fellowship with the bomb, no nostalgia for the "dumb-muscled" violence of youth, no grief for a lost father (or for "all that old industrial muscle" [818]), no ecstasy in cyberspace. There are not, in fact, even punch lines, at least not in the bits that DeLillo narrates in full. What there is is a relentless movement toward the specifics of material existence, the possible details, in fact, of Esmeralda's life. Lenny's story of Esmeralda begins in the "illiterate sad-eyed virgin [who] lives in a whorehouse in a slum district of San Juan" and who blows "gorgeous smoke rings" from her vagina (630). Her "gift," Lenny continues, is by some interpreted "in a religious manner": "They think it's an omen, a sign from heaven that the world is about to end. God has selected a poor illiterate undernourished orphan girl to convey a profound message to the world" (630). A rich American widower buys her from the madame, brings her to his "hilltop mansion overlooking the Hudson River," and civilizes her into "a healthy young woman who speaks four languages and shows a talent for the oboe" (631). At this point of inevitable punch line, Lenny changes direction: "No, yes, wait. We've got it backwards"; the man regrets his actions, believes he has "destroyed a strange, crude, beautiful and eerie perversion";

and "he longs to see smoke rings come out of her puss, her nook" (631). Lenny changes directions again: "Wait, listen, no. The millionaire is a myth, isn't he? . . . We made him up. Let's tell the truth this time" (632). In spite of audience discontent, Lenny plunges on: "Let's make her human. She's real like us" (632). The "us," of course, denies the rendering of masculinity preserved in the earlier bits, the subject constructed in relation to the woman-object. The girl lives in the South Bronx "with her junkie mother" who "comes and goes"; the phone is disconnected, and the apartment is dispossessed; "the girl's hiding in the empty lots, down the maze of back alleys" (632–33). And this is where Lenny's story ends. He wants to give her a name, but "couldn't think of a name. Not a real name" (633). After retreating to mother-in-law jokes with punch lines DeLillo does not narrate, Lenny leaves the stage, "remorseful" (633).

Lenny's stunted story resists the version the larger novel relates. While the Esmeralda of "Das Kapital" moves quickly from the concrete to the mythic, thus finally enabling a classic—albeit kindly and sympathetic— pose of voyeuristic distance, the nameless girl of Lenny's self-dismantling story leaves the mythic for the (finally unknowable) concrete. In this sense Lenny almost achieves what Joseph Tabbi argues of DeLillo himself: a clear vision "of the embodied reality beneath the information grid" (207). The audience for Lenny's story—unlike the audience for Esmeralda's (reader, Internet user, crowd in front of the billboard)—is left dissatisfied, denied not only the closure of an ending (let alone the haunting chill of a ghost story) but a quick and voyeuristic dip into the rivulet of raw, phallic violence that flows silently through the plot.

The novel does not end with Lenny, however; the novel ends with the transformation of Esmeralda, and the affective quality of that ending is anything but dissatisfying. In the city known more than any other for its radical twentieth-century transformation from industrial to financial center, from steel to electronic communication, we are given a vision of the ephemeral that promises itself amidst the material excess and decay of that "old industrial muscle." The pathos Esmeralda generates is large scale and cathartic, and as such it contributes to the solidity and sympathetic quality of the non-raping men of the novel, even as it underwrites the continued underground existence of violent productivity perceived as masculine. In this sense, the novels of John Irving are similar to DeLillo's *Underworld*. Irving again and again reserves a central and heart-wrenching space for the redemptive young rape victim. In fact, in Irving the "integrity" of her rape (*Hotel New Hampshire*) is often directly related to the protagonist; to recoil in horror as a young man from the spectacle of a rape is to be on the path of a coming-of-age epiphany. To help the victim recover from her trauma is to reclaim masculinity from a fatherless past—or to forge an alliance with a father from whom one has been temporarily disconnected. A self-consciously feminist, postindustrial white masculinity is thus defined in sharp contrast to sexual violence, is actually dependent on the repeated and emphatic casting out of the desire to rape. As in DeLillo's novel, the rapist is thus preserved as he is scapegoated, and he remains to haunt the borders and underground of the text; his violence necessarily continues to operate, denounced and yet crucial for masculine (anti)definition. The rape victim herself is heavily fetishized, becomes a holy martyr in what would otherwise be a morally withered universe. She is the muse of grief, self-examination, and finally agency.

Like *Underworld,* Irving's novels are haunted by the (actually or figuratively) missing father. Garp's father is nothing more than an erect penis and a surname at the moment of Garp's conception and dies immediately after (*The World According to Garp*); Homer Wells's father has presumably abandoned his mother before his birth (*Cider House Rules*); Fred "Bogus" Trumper's father has disinherited him (*The Water-Method Man*); John Berry's father is dreamy and removed throughout most of *Hotel New Hampshire.* Generally, the son is left to navigate in a world that has already lost (or is in the process of losing) its gleam (only the fathers are or were idealists), in postwar establishments and locales that have passed their moments of success and glory. More precisely, the sons have been left with a vague sense of guilt for the masculinity of the father and without a blueprint for a new, morally acceptable masculinity. *The Water-Method Man* opens with (and is dominated by) a central image for this disconnection: Bogus Trumper's painfully "narrow, winding" urethra, which birth defect his father, a urologist, has been unable to diagnose (12). The deformed, inadequate penis of the son is not only unfixed but unrecognized by the father.

Evidence of the absent father's irresponsible productivity, on the other hand, survives in the scores of damaged orphans and in the wasted bodies of girls and women—the dying prostitutes, the victims of homemade abortions, the abandoned wives and girlfriends, the women who cut out their own tongues, the victims of rape. Vienna, for example, seems to embody the wasteland created by the World War II–era father: Vienna is a "dead bitch," a "cadaver," "a museum housing a dead city," where there are few young people because the only babies born between the Nazi and Soviet occupations were the result of rapes, and where many of Irving's young protagonists are initiated to prostitution (*Garp* 164–65, 122–23). The hospital/orphanage in *Cider House Rules* is similarly constructed—is reminiscent of the waste management business in *Underworld,* as Dr. Larch is the grim equivalent of Nick Shay. Denying himself the pleasure of (re)production (as Nick denies himself the pleasure of consumption),

Wilbur Larch devotes himself to the management of what are clearly represented as the hidden waste products of reproduction (and sexual consumerism) under patriarchy. Early in his career he performs a Caesarian (of a "stillborn child") on a prostitute whom he has himself visited and finds that her internal organs have disintegrated from ingestion of an illegal aborticide: "when he tried to sew up Mrs. Eames's uterus, his stitches simply pulled through the tissue, which he noticed was the texture of a soft cheese. . . . when he sponged the blood away, he perforated the intestine, which he had hardly touched, and when he lifted up the injured loop to close the hole, his fingers passed as easily through the intestine as through gelatin" (45–46). A nightmare of permeability and broken boundary, Mrs. Eames resists the portrayal of female body as matter (mater), blank material open to the form, order, and organization of the father.[2] She is rather matter that has literally dissolved, refusing (or incapable of taking) the imprint of the father (the biological father of the dead baby, the internal surgical reorganization of the male doctor). In economic terms she is equally lethal: her doubly suggestive role as consumer item (she is a prostitute) and as producer (she is pregnant) is cut short because of her inability to contain, let alone to hold order or value. She is simply the end of things—she enters the whirlpool beyond profit and loss—like the mysterious and oddly frightening waste ship in *Underworld.*

As Nick feels in part responsible for the waste that envelopes the late twentieth century, so too does Dr. Larch feel complicitous in the dissolution of Mrs. Eames, and his dreams of vulnerability reinforce the sense that a part of the horror of the image of Mrs. Eames disintegrating on the operating table is based in the extent to which she suggests the impotence of the masculine, idealist inscription: "The night she died, Larch had a nightmare—his penis fell off in his hands; he tried to sew it back on but it kept disintegrating; then his fingers gave way in a similar fashion. How like a surgeon! he thought. Fingers are valued above penises. How like Wilbur Larch!" (46). If Jean-Joseph Goux is correct to argue that genetic effectivity "has come to be signified by the indestructible, ever-renascent penis" (232), then reproductive failure bespeaks not only the destructibility of the penis but the bankruptcy of productive action—the hands also cannot build, reconstruct, or otherwise manufacture a product that can be sent out into circulation (again). Further, the disintegrating body Dr. Larch dreams suggests the antithesis of masculinity as it has been defined in the white, Western tradition. As Anthony Easthope puts it, "The most important meanings that can attach to the idea of the masculine body are unity and permanence. . . . Very clear in outline and firm in definition, the masculine image of the body appears to give a stronger sense of identity" (53). They are thus feelings of guilt, impotence, and horror that are inspired by the death of Mrs. Eames and her daughter and which propel Larch into a determinedly celibate life in the backwater of St. Cloud's hospital and orphanage. There Larch will extol the virtues of "work"—"aren't we put on this earth to work?" (188)—while, seemingly single-handedly, not only performing the only safe abortions in Maine but also fixing all of the bungled or incomplete abortions in the same state. Thus, while the waste matter of *Underworld* seems almost self-organizing, the waste management business in Irving's work is more taxing.

The destructive creation enables the return of the work ethic in a post-productive era; it similarly reinvests the potency of the father, but in ways that sidestep the explicitly patriarchal systems of white Western tradition. If production has shifted to waste management, then the role of white father/heterosexual husband within the nuclear family has been similarly displaced to a variety of forms of recycling. Dr. Larch, for example, is "father" to the orphans he delivers. He recycles what has been discarded by the biological parents. Even here, the fatherhood is vaguely homoerotic and incestuous, ever so slightly resistant to the paternal script, as his kiss (on the lips) of adolescent Homer Wells suggests: "He couldn't even think, he was so agitated from kissing Homer Wells. If Homer Wells had received his first fatherly[3] kisses, Dr. Larch had given the first kisses he had *ever* given—fatherly or otherwise—since the day in the Portland boarding-house when he caught the clap from Mrs. Eames" (136). The "fatherhood" of Dr. Larch is skewed in ways typical of Irving's novels; Alison Booth points out that "The best-laid plans for chastity, exogamy, and the transfer of property through patriarchal, heterosexual generation oft go awry" in Irving's work (288–89). With the old productive/accumulating father of high industrial capitalism removed from the scene, the son who would be father is released from the old paternal laws against incest, homosexuality, and monogamy. Non-participant in systems of exchange (including the exogamy which "makes women the objects of exchange by male subjects" [Goux 217]), fatherhood (like sex) becomes a matter of unbounded and generally non-(re)productive association, submersion in Eagleton's "great decentred network of desire" (132) in which the prime directive is, as it finally is in *Underworld*, to "fasten, fit closely, bind together" (827). Thus John Berry (*Hotel New Hampshire*) has an incestuous relationship with his sister, marries his sister's lesbian lover, and adopts his sister's child; Homer Wells (*Cider House Rules*) sleeps with his best friend's wife, pretends his own son is his best friend's, and lives for years in a three-way marriage.

This reterritorialization of masculinity and familial relationship is marked by anxiety in Irving's work—an anxiety, however, that is inevitably resolved by novel's end. Garp is made particularly articulate concerning this generalized unease—Irving has him wrestle self-consciously and emotionally with the problematic status of (white, middle-class) masculinity after (white, middle-class) feminism. Invariably Garp struggles with what he feels is contemporary feminism's association of masculinity in general with the propensity to rape (contemporary: the novel was published in 1976). His long-standing rage at the Ellen Jamesians, for example, a crucial theme in the novel since it leads to his death, is based in what he feels to be the injustice of his being held culpable: in answer to his mother's claim that "rape is every woman's problem," Garp replies, "It's every man's problem, too, mom. The next time there's a rape, suppose I cut my *prick* off and hang it around my neck" (192). Sarcasm aside, the offer of the penis *to the mother* in a gesture of sacrificial castration in solidarity with women suggests that the new order of masculinity will take away what was only threatened under the law of the old father. Like the detached penis and fingers of Dr. Larch's dream, the new castration suggests not only feminization but disintegration of the sort embodied in the "soft organic murk" of Mrs. Eames and the underground flows of late capitalism (waste accumulation included). Garp's ambivalence about disassociating himself from the rapist is thus based in anxiety about just what it might mean not to be a rapist: "Perhaps rape's offensiveness to Garp was that it was an act that disgusted him with himself—with his own very male instincts, which were otherwise so unassailable. He never felt like raping anyone; but rape, Garp thought, made men feel guilt by association" (209). He both is and is not anything like a rapist. To the extent that there is in fact an association, it is by virtue of "very male instincts," immutable evidence of a natural state of masculinity residing deep below surface constructions. As in *Underworld*, then, the "real" masculinity is the violent one, buried deep in the past or deep in the psyche, but not allowed expression in the narrative now of the sympathetic protagonist's actions—because another aspect of "real" masculinity, presumably, would be the repression of precisely that underground volatility (For Nick Shay, violence "drain[s] out" [801], "go[es] under" with the missing father [809]).

And as in *Underworld*, one's eye is not allowed to rest on the repressed violence and possible misogyny of the hero. In both novels, these qualities are displaced onto a rapist scapegoat, a figure constructed to be completely without readerly appeal. Irving, however, goes further than DeLillo, who removes Nick from the rape itself. Irving resolves Garp's anxieties not only by displacing the violence of "his own very male instincts" but by making him not a rapist but a hunter of rapists, the two figures haunting the same underworld. Thus it is Garp, not the police officers, who discovers the identity of the rapist of the ten-year-old girl in the park and delivers him to justice (although we later learn that the rapist has been released; the danger of the violent underworld will never be eliminated). Significantly, Garp hunts for the rapist like an animal, relying on "instinct" and his sense of smell: he accosts an "elderly gentleman" and forces him to submit to Garp's sniffing his genitals for "the smell of sex" (200–201); later, he recognizes the real rapist by the smell of aftershave.

The intensity of Garp's search through the park and attempts to comfort the girl is marked, and it shows up again later in the figure of Arden Bensenhaver, a character in Garp's novel, *The World According to Bensenhaver.* Irving's inclusion of so much of Garp's novel is odd—the plot does not necessarily speak to the plot of *The World According to Garp,* except in terms of the representation of rape, and in that sense the inclusion reinforces several aspects of the larger novel: the horrific quality of the experience; the utterly depraved—other—nature of men who rape; the inestimable value of a good man's sympathy toward rape victims; the almost ethereal strength and innocence of the rape victim. The rapist in the story is put well beyond the pale; his animal life and animal death serve as an easy focus for moral outrage and disgust. Inspector Arden Bensenhaver, on the other hand, "who knew a good deal about rape" (418), is a man of uncommon sympathy for the rape victim: "It was Arden Bensenhaver's experience that husbands and other people did not always take a rape in the right way" (440). There is little sense, however, that those "other people" can be taught: Bensenhaver himself is the lone and alienated protector, "a lurker at the last edge of light—a retired enforcer, barely alive on the rim of darkness" (445). The first chapter of *Bensenhaver* thus enacts very sharply what *Underworld* and Irving's rape novels work out at great length: the splitting off of sexual violence from the sympathetic, sad male character while still retaining that violence as a "natural" core of animal man.

The rape victim of Garp's novel is named, significantly enough, Hope, and she is "recognized" by others after her rape in a way that is reminiscent of Esmeralda's apparition:

> A car came along, but Hope was unaware of it. . . . The bloody, praying woman, naked and caked with grit, took no notice of him driving past her. The driver had a vision of an angel on a trip back from Hell. . . .
> "Help!" he cried. The vision of the woman had so terrified him that he feared there might be more like her around. (432)

A vision of transcendence in a post-religious world, the rape victim in both novels serves as an image of saintly beauty and "hope" precisely at the moment when she is metamorphosed into the emblem of permeability and fluid boundaries (Hope herself is bathed in the rapist's blood and bowels). That Esmeralda is actually thrown away, her soon-to-be-dead body visually becoming refuse, is matched by Hope's being raped, finally, by a dead man: even after having his throat cut, his kidney impaled, and another knife wound to his back, "his penis, still moving, still attached himself to Hope" (429). It is thus unsurprising that the passing motorist presumes that Hope is an angel just arrived from Hell, as opposed to Heaven, the customary habitat for "angels"; like Esmeralda, Hope is a sign of grace to the extent that she redeems the underworld of non-productive waste and violence. (It is worth noting that, in the same non-productive sense that fatherhood and sex are often incestuous in Irving, the rapist in Garp's novel has in the past only had intercourse with farm animals, whom he has killed afterward just as he intends to murder Hope).

Debra Shostak has examined the role of repetition in Irving's fiction, paying particular attention to the embedded stories written by the characters themselves. She argues that plotted repetition contributes substantially to the uncanny streak that runs through Irving's work, and it highlights Irving's concern with faith and the sacred. Certainly it is true that Garp's return to the idea of rape lends the larger novel a transcendent, sacred aura that emanates precisely from that nucleus of the raped female body. In *Hotel New Hampshire,* similarly, the iterations of Franny's rape—Frank's sexual abuse does not "repeat" in the same way and does not achieve the same central status—culminate in a recognition of the "holy" (441). After a lifetime of regret for not being man enough to fight off Franny's rapists, John Berry at last achieves the "fairy-tale hotel" of which his father has always dreamed—but that hotel is in actuality a "rape crisis center" (450). There rape survivors come to recover—to be, in a sense, recycled. Significantly, and bearing out Susan Jeffords's claim that rape can (in popular film) serve as "an occasion for the reform and reproduction of masculinity" (112), the caretaking role in the "fairy-tale hotel" has fallen to the returned father, at least in cases of great despair ("When someone's really fucked up" [442]): Wyn Berry, literally and figuratively blind, explicitly out-of-touch with his children and their needs throughout the bulk of the novel, now waves his murderous baseball bat over the psychically wounded as if it is a "magic wand," "as if he were a holy man blessing some other holy person" (441). This, says Susie—John's wife and ex-lover of his sister Franny, rape survivor and director of "the real rape crisis center in our unreal hotel"—"is how you should treat a rape victim . . . ; they are holy" (442, 441). The father is thus rehabilitated as "the best counselor" of raped women (441), accruing cultural capital through presiding over the salvation of the damaged and cast aside. One is reminded of Nick Shay at the end of *Underworld,* when he takes his granddaughter with him to the waste recycling plant, to show her, from the vantage point of a catwalk, the "redemptive qualities of the things we use and discard. Look how they come back to us, alight with a brave kind of aging" (809).

In fact this is the classic happy ending of an Irving novel: the male protagonist has at last come of age, and in so doing he has redirected masculine characterizations to include caretaking responsibility for children and women—particularly for those who have been produced and damaged by what is presented as the tatters of an old form of patriarchy. John Berry will adopt the child of his movie-star sister Franny, whose rape he has at last helped to avenge: "you look after everybody," Franny said, sweetly. . . . "it's kind of like your *role*. You're a perfect father." "Or a mother, man," Junior added (443). John Berry's desire to "take care" of a baby (the word "adopt" is not actually used) is the final and mature outgrowth of his lifetime obsession with Franny's rape—that original violence thus has the eventual effect of shifting the traditionally feminine attribute of domestic nurturing to the sphere of masculine authority and power. Garp is also a stay-at-home dad, a role that complements (repeats, following Shostak) his concern with rape and his desire to protect the victims of rape; he goes so far as to informally adopt Ellen James, the young woman whose rape and mutilation have initiated the organization of the Ellen Jamesians. Similarly, after the shock of discovering that Rose Rose's baby is the result of incestuous rape—evidence of a break in the new domestic contract—Homer Wells assumes responsibility for providing abortions and deliveries for the women who come in desperation to St. Cloud's. Thus Rose Rose's rape is the impetus for and validation of "the reform and reproduction of masculinity" (Jeffords 112); it is her permeable and helplessly excessive body that compels Homer to heed at last the words of Dr. Larch, his "father": "Women are trapped. Women are victims. . . . HOW CAN YOU FEEL FREE TO CHOOSE NOT TO HELP PEOPLE WHO ARE NOT FREE TO GET OTHER HELP?" (518). As Alison Booth points out, it thus "turns out that abortion, and even rape and father-daughter incest, are about a man's [. . .—a white, straight man's—. . .] right to choose" (289). Homer's final status as a (good, white, straight) man with the power to choose a destiny is wholly dependent on the establishment of a human detritus—"trapped," "victim[ized]," "not free"—as vehicle for portraying the power and emotional sensitivity of the new, non-productive father. This accumulation of faceless, permeable flesh is defined as distanced from volition, even from consciousness (the helplessly uncontrollable excesses of these bodies are dealt with surgically when the nervous systems are anesthetized); it provides a "gelatin[ous]" contrast to the sharp outlines of masculine prerogative.

Irving's rape stories within rape stories, similarly, provide therapeutic work for his male protagonists. Garp writes *The World According to Bensenhaver* when recovering from the faithlessness of his wife and death of his son. By the same token, it is the translation of the Low Old Norse epic "Akthelt and Gunnel" that enables Bogus Trumper to come of age and return to the baby his girlfriend has tricked him into fathering and the son being raised by his ex-wife and best friend. Before taking this step into what is clearly portrayed as a positive renovation of classic white masculinity, Bogus has been unable to complete the violent epic, has in fact actually begun to cheat in the translation. At the point, however, when his life becomes particularly directionless and painful—painful enough at a physical level to undergo the surgery to have his urethra straightened and widened—Bogus makes the difficult decision to translate the violent epic accurately, narrating truthfully the faithlessness and childishness of the traditional male hero and the rape of the heroine. In this new period of commitment to textual accuracy, Bogus takes particular pains on the subject of rape. In the case of Sprog, "Whatever he did, he didn't do it fast enough. The text reports that Gunnel was 'nearly humbled by him.' Nearly" (274). Hrothrund, on the other hand, is a "father-murderer, wife-raper" bent on "sport"; Bogus takes care to provide an academic note: "In Old Low Norse, *sport* means rape" (353, 351). Gunnel is in fact raped by him, repeatedly, until she kills him, stuffing eels in his severed head. (Her maidservants are also raped, and killed—points only mentioned in passing.) When her husband later kills the child born of the rape of Hrothrund, she kills him as well, also stuffing eels in his severed head and presenting it to the Council of Elders. The only poetic license Bogus allows himself in the translation is to allow Gunnel to castrate her rapists: "It fit, after all. It suited the story, it certainly suited Gunnel, and most of all, it suited Bogus" (354).

The "bogus" man's induction into a reformed version of classic masculinity is thus dependent on a clear translation of an ancient (albeit presumably fictional) rape. What is crucial is the preservation of the integrity of the original rape text; the only elaboration allowed is one that does not detract from the rape itself but rather heightens the sexual violence while contributing a moral valence to the event: the new man is one who is the violent defender of raped, brutalized women—the author, in this case and in Garp, who places the castrating knife in the victim's hands. Significantly, Bogus Trumper's reclamation of Gunnel's rape from the obscurity of Old Low Norse and the animalistic men who sexually abuse women is accompanied by his being awarded knighthood, by virtue of his "Phallic Phortitude" in enduring the urethrectomy, in "The Brotherhood of the Golden Prick" (318). The new masochistic "knighthood" is thus associated not with the defense or rupture of the virgin's purity as in older forms of patriarchal mythology but with defense of the integrity of the rape itself.

In *The Hotel New Hampshire*, Susie tells John that every rape has its own "integrity" and that he has "robbed [Franny's] rape of *its* integrity by running off to find the hero instead of staying on the scene and *dealing* with it yourself" (241).

In *The World According to Garp*, the hero does not run off, and the "integrity" of the rape is preserved. Garp dies protecting—literally—the integrity of Ellen James, her status as "the real Ellen James" (511), "the real thing" (538), in a world of pretenders; "'Ellen James is *not* a symbol,' Garp wrote" (553). Garp's hatred of the Ellen Jamesians, on the other hand, those "sour imitators" who finally kill him, is based first in their retreat to symbols in the face of "real" violation and second in the self-inflictedness of their wounds, which self-generation denies the very vulnerability to others (to men) that defines "*The* Ellen James": "She struck him as one of those doomed children he had read about: the ones who have no antibodies—they have no natural immunities to disease. If they don't live their lives in plastic bags, they die of their first common cold. Here was Ellen James of Illinois, out of her sack" (192, 538, 507, 508–9). "*The* Ellen James" is thus a kind of walking miracle—the quintessence of vulnerability and yet alive, "real," she embodies the late-twentieth-century subject of consumer capitalism. At the same time, the pathos she generates carves out a different kind of space for the man who would take her side—who would defend not only her but the "integrity" of her penetrability. The story her raped body tells is that male violence and effectivity are intact; that the man who would protect her is not a rapist. Like Esmeralda, she offers "Hope" and validation through her vulnerability, but only to the extent that it is betrayed. Garp's status as a man of the new era and as a writer—a new kind of worker, one who arranges and circulates information while "producing" very little—is ratified only when Ellen James tells him that *The World According to Bensenhaver* is "The best rape story I have ever read" (508).

It is interesting to note that in her physical appearance Ellen James suggests the underworld of decay and waste from which Esmeralda emerges: "Oddly at the fringe of their group, but seeming to have no connection with them, was a wraithlike girl, or barely grown-up child; she was a dirty blond-headed girl with piercing eyes the color of coffee-stained saucers—like a drug-user's eyes, or someone long involved in hard tears" (502). Like Esmeralda, "wraithlike" Ellen James is otherworldly, set apart from the social order, and yet that idealization is dependent on markers of corruption. Ellen is by nature "dirty blond," her eyes the color of stains. She seems thus to have everything to do with the kind of seepage that dominates *Underworld*, born with the look of something open to the generally unseen flows of dark waste. She looks like a drug user, like someone accustomed to ingesting dangerous, possibly infected substances in a space out-side the order of law (Esmeralda, daughter of a crack addict, eats from garbage cans). This look of permeability is further reinforced through the association with moisture—old coffee and hard tears. Like the abject itself as Julia Kristeva describes it in *Powers of Horror,* the raped Ellen/Esmeralda is the abolishment of boundary and difference; her body "confus[es] inside and outside" (160). Her/their abjection demands and ratifies the existence of a "third party, the doctor"—more powerfully yet, the "writer"—who will "[provide] the lay counterpart of religious abominations, excisions, and purifications" (160–61). Writer and adoptive father, Garp presides over the sacrificial purification, casting out demons of feminism and rape alike, and in so doing formulating a new masculine contract. He is also, of course, a writing teacher—Ellen has come to him because she wants him to teach her. Thus, he presides as well over the transformation of yet anoth-er Philomela; it is he who out of kindness will give words to the body muti-lated and rendered voiceless by a cruel, other, man. Upon his death, then, which is clearly sacrificial, Garp stands to be remembered not for his pro-ductive writing life, which the narrative has carefully understated, but for the reworking of what had—through neither fault nor agency of his own—been broken.

What Garp also achieves, of course, as do Irving and DeLillo, is the nar-rative legitimacy of "men like me" (212). Self-consciously feminist and paternalistic at the same time, the postindustrial educated white man "like me" is everything the rapist is not. Having relinquished the agency of cap-italist desire—the desire to produce, the desire to consume—the masculine protagonist is defined also by his distance from sexual violence. That vio-lence—along with the agency it signifies—is displaced onto a rapist scape-goat, a figure constructed to be completely without readerly appeal. The rapist is thus preserved as he is scapegoated, and he remains to haunt the borders and underground of the text; his violence necessarily continues to operate, denounced and yet crucial for masculine (anti)definition. Yet because that violence is precisely so visibly *displaced,* it is also given as belonging somehow originally within a natural masculine core. It is thus unsurprising that this reterritorialization of masculinity is figured—often explicitly—as sacrificial self-castration, suggesting that the prerogative to rape is in fact just that, a natural right self-denied, immutable evidence of a natural state of masculinity residing deep below surface constructions. The "real" masculinity is the violent one, buried deep in the past, deep in the text, or deep in the psyche, but not allowed expression in the narrative now of the sympathetic protagonist's actions—because another aspect of "real" masculinity, presumably, would be the repression of precisely that underground volatility, where "natural" heterosexual violence joins the "soft organic murk" of the underground flows of late capitalism. Covering over this displacement is the glowing apparition of the holy rape victim. Heavily fetishized, the raped woman or girl becomes sacred, and her protection or worship the one gesture capable of recuperating masculine subjectivity. She is the one true thing, and the new man, like Garp's Bensenhaver, is the lone and alienated protector, "a lurker at the last edge of light—a retired enforcer, barely alive on the rim of darkness" (445). Alive nonetheless.

8

CONCLUSION

A DIFFERENT RAPE STORY?

It is of some significance that the "bad guys" in *The World According to Garp* are not only the rapists—the category includes the Ellen Jamesians as well. Pretenders to the role of victim, these are women who cut out their tongues to protest being "raped," when "what they meant was that they *felt* as if their tongues were gone. In a world of men, they felt as if they had been shut up forever" (539). Lacking the personal experience of rape, they make a mockery of the real Ellen James's enforced silence: they are about nothing so much as a surplus of representation, excesses beyond the unrepresentable phenomenon of Ellen's (and Hope's) suffering. In John Irving's defense, the tone in which the Ellen Jamesians are represented brings to mind the point made by Linda Alcoff and Laura Gray—in this case in reference to the media but still relevant here: that representations of rape survivors disempower the speech of real rape survivors (Mardorossian 743, n. 1). The Ellen Jamesians instill a sense of injustice—if not rage—in Garp (and one presumes in Irving) because their noisy affectations crowd out the reality of Ellen herself as survivor. Ellen, of course, is necessarily voiceless, but in one way of looking at it, that silence is a clear metaphor for the way she is silenced by the rape culture that has victimized her.

The issue of representing and/or theorizing rape is a vexed one, suggestive of several different problems. To what extent, for example, do representations of rape written/spoken by non-victims cloud the individual experience of the crime? Does the burgeoning discursive field growing around the topic of rape work ironically to exclude from the conversation actual survivors' retellings of the crimes they have experienced? To what extent would a "true," firsthand report of rape hold itself apart from that discursive field? What vacuum would allow for this isolation, and yet still keep open the possibility of communication? And why, for this particular crime, does the value of the story impinge as nervously and emotionally as it does on the status of a hypothetical absolute veracity? The simplest answer is the most obvious and the most compelling: women have been

181

and continue to be raped: "in 1996, a woman was raped every three min-
utes in this country; seventy-eight percent of them knew their attackers"
(from the Bureau of Justice National Victim Center, qtd. in Horvitz 1).
Moreover, prosecution of suspected rapists is notoriously ineffectual; the
justice system as we know it is seemingly hopelessly biased against accusations of rape and assumes immediately that accusations of rape are false:
"[A]rt and criticism share the well-documented bias of rape law, where
representations of rape after the event are almost always framed by a masculine perspective premised on men's fantasies about female sexuality and
their fears of false accusation, as well as their codified access to and possession of women's bodies" (Higgins and Silver 2).

The rape victim's word is thus positioned to work against the current
to maintain its own authority within a system built to discredit it. Given
that the stakes are so high, it makes a great deal of sense that many feminist scholars are nervous—at best—about any discussion of the *representation* of rape. In a section of *Signs* dedicated to recent feminist theory of
rape, Beverly Allen, for example, writes of the difficulty she experiences
when entering an academic conversation about rape when she is herself
deep in the reality of postwar Bosnia and Herzegovina, and she goes on
to discuss instead the value of the type of work that attempts simply to
record the narratives of the victims (a genre placed in clear opposition to
the theoretical work of those inside the academy). Allen's concerns are
echoed by Carine Mardorossian, who, even in the context of arguing for
more theoretical discussion, criticizes a discourse that crosses the line and
loses touch with the reality of rape: she critiques what she calls "postmodern" feminism for "analyz[ing] rape victims and the antirape movement
by looking at or implying hidden depths and inner meanings lodged
within an individualized configuration" (761).

These concerns are legitimate. Representations of rape, even when
explicitly condemnatory of the rapist and sympathetic toward the victim,
can nonetheless quite easily serve to reinforce the patriarchal status quo, as
I hope these chapters have shown. And we have all too long a history, as
again I hope these chapters have shown, of deploying "rape" as a textual
event or image to signify something other than rape, in the meantime (and
by so doing) preserving rape as a structuring component of Western culture. It is far more often the case than not, in fact, I would argue, that rape
stories do indeed direct the reader away from the materiality and gender
politics of the event and toward "hidden depths" and "inner meanings."
Nonetheless, to cordon off as acceptable only those rape stories grounded
in material physical violence, verifiable personal suffering, to some extent
perpetuates the traditional tendency to sanctify the silent victim: the more
horrific her abuse and the greater her voicelessness, the greater her heights,

or depths, of martyrdom. This is not to say that—in fact, in history, liter-ature, science, and art—rape victims have not been silenced.

What I am rather attempting to point out is that the continued isola-tion of rape and the rape victim in some extra-linguistic zone—the accept-ance of only that language which is beyond the shadow of a doubt *purely* and *truthfully* a representation of only the precise physical details of the victim's personal experience—preserves the binary of passive victim/active subject and reinforces the sense that rape is an inevitable fact. Pure silence/truth or lying representational excess—the relentlessness of the dualism evokes centuries of courtroom decisions. This *discursive* binary structure highlights the extent to which it is the function of the rape vic-tim within the symbolic contract of compulsory heterosexuality to be without agency and without voice (unless a protective, sympathetic space is carved for her)—even when or perhaps particularly when that fact is bewailed. Sharon Marcus argues that it is thus precisely through treating rape as a "*linguistic* fact" in turn that we can begin to understand the fact of rape as "subject to change" (388–89): it behooves us to regard "rape not as a fact to be accepted or opposed, tried or avenged, but as a process to be analyzed and undermined as it occurs. [. . . One way to achieve this is to] . . . ask how the violence of rape is enabled by narratives, complexes and institutions which derive their strength not from outright, immutable, unbeatable force but rather from their power to structure our lives as imposing cultural scripts" (389). The project of unveiling the discursive mechanisms of patriarchy is thus in my view well worth the risks it entails. If it is true that the rape narrative is one of the load-carrying beams of patriarchal culture, then it makes sense to evaluate how the structure might be differently constructed.

Janice Haaken makes the case that any theory of sexual violence is "mis-guided if the issues are cast monolithically as a debate between 'agency' and 'victimization'" (785). In the same vein, Donna Haraway attributes the full-scale adoption of that same binary structure by earlier waves of radical feminism to the work of Catharine MacKinnon (in what is perhaps an exaggerated assignment of blame):

> Ironically, MacKinnon's 'ontology' constructs a non-subject, a non-being. Another's desire, not the self's labour, is the origin of 'woman.' . . . Feminist practice is the construction of this form of consciousness; that is, the self-knowledge of a self-who-is-not. . . . MacKinnon's radical theory of experience is totalizing in the extreme; it does not so much marginalize as obliterate the authori-ty of any other women's political speech and action. It is a totaliza-tion producing what Western patriarchy itself never succeeded in

doing—feminists' consciousness of the non-existence of women,
except as products of men's desire. (159)

Haaken and Haraway thus both implicitly suggest that a retelling of rape
must necessarily find a way out of the binary structure sustained by patriarchy and adopted, at least according to Haraway, by some forms of feminism. That would mean a rejection not only of the totalizing distinction
between agent and victim but a deconstruction of the strict differentiation
between the discursive and the material. "Ultimately at stake" in this
effort, as Ellen Rooney puts it, is the ability to "read the scene of sexual
violence" for evidence of a feminine subject defined by more than the sole
abilities "to consent or refuse to consent" (92), to be necessarily and
"always either already raped or already rapable" (Marcus 386). This would
be a struggle, then, over the form of the rape story.

Over the last twenty or thirty years, a great number of writers have
risen to this challenge. In a variety of ways, they have self-consciously
experimented with narrative (and poetic, for that matter) form in order to
show rape in different lights, from different angles. Their narrative experimentation calls to mind Teresa de Lauretis's directive for theoretical feminism and feminist film practice: "to articulate the relations of the female
subject to representation, meaning, and vision, and in so doing to construct the terms of another frame of reference, another measure of desire"
(*Alice Doesn't* 68).

What follows is a brief overview of *some* of the attempted formulations
of "another frame of reference, another measure of desire" through the
reclamation and reconstruction of the rape story. The project has involved
work with linear plot and narrative time; character construction and narrative voice; readerly placement and point of view; internal narration and
external reportage. Themes include the status of the real, the nature of language, the constitution of subjectivity, the questionable inevitability of
female masochism, and the redefinition of masculinity to include physical, sexual vulnerability. In all cases, the central concern is to write the
"victim," whatever that might mean, and to consider through her (or him)
the (im)possible construction of "another measure of desire."

One of the most powerful efforts toward dismantling the traditional forms
of the rape story has been the reinsertion of the woman's voice into the
narrative. In literary criticism, this has meant a new form of conscious,
critical reading, one that deflects the transcendent aura the rape text generates. The aestheticized promise of the transcendent is replaced by mate-

rial, bodily experience, which returns to the text, in theory, some approximation of the psychological trauma undergone by women and repressed by history (Horvitz 2). This is not just a matter of "listening to the silences," as Lynn Higgins and Brenda Silver put it; rereading requires invention—a restoration of rape "to the literal, to the body: restoring, that is, the violence—the physical, sexual violation" (4). Rereading rape also entails, for Higgins and Silver, the identification and flattening of figurative language in an effort to return to the text the materiality of violence and sexuality. The reconstruction does not come easily, and when it is confronted in a finished piece of fiction, as Tanner has noted, the effect can be effectively discomforting. Reading conventions traditionally involve the exploitation of what Laura Tanner terms "the reader's bodiless status" in order to sanction and "invite a voyeuristic participation in the scene of violence" (x). As a matter of course, the reader is admitted to the titillating scene of violence only after leaving his or her body, as it were, outside the text. By the same token, the reader is shielded from the point of view of the victim, is left safely to objectify the body in pain.

Tanner identifies contemporary fiction that deliberately revises this narrative structure, generally written by women. These are texts which relentlessly "attach the reader to the victim's tortured body," relocating the traditional point of view and by so doing "subverting the scopophilic gaze of the reader by turning it inward to focus on the victim's pain" (x). The subject of reading is thus compelled to identify with the "victim of violation," who is in turn explicitly constructed as "the object rather than the subject of violence, a human being stripped of agency and mercilessly attached to a physical form that cannot be dissolved at will" (3). The texts Tanner studies that effect this reversal include most centrally novels written by women of color, namely Gloria Naylor's *The Women of Brewster Place* and Louise Erdrich's *Tracks*. In both cases, Tanner examines the narrative techniques used to "collapse the distance between disembodied reader" and a victim defined through narrative and historical tradition by her embodiment. The task is not easily accomplished, and the prose struggles against itself to "subvert" its own "distancing conventions" (10). Similarly, as Tanner points out of *The Women of Brewster Place,* the silence of the victim is also presented as a struggle, not a passive necessity. In fact, the scene is loud with the victim's "voice," even if externally she is silent; framed by a more traditional narrative structure and point of view, the silence would be available for interpretation—perhaps even for an occasion to muse and to wonder. Perhaps most strikingly, the victim's experience is not narrated as a coherent whole. Rather, the rape sequence is disjointed and portrays an explicit rift between the mind experiencing pain and the body that has been taken away from the mind's control; subjectivity is splintered. And as if in a final reference to and dismissal of the traditional rape narrative, the point of view shifts briefly, after the event, to an external view of the injured woman. Given this chronological placement, the voyeuristic point of view is much more difficult to take. Its insufficiency is clear.

Texts like *The Women of Brewster Place* and *Tracks* thus in several ways respond to Teresa de Lauretis's directive to "articulate the relations of the female subject to representation, meaning, and vision, and in so doing to construct the terms of another frame of reference, another measure of desire" (*Alice Doesn't* 68). Placing point of view with the rape victim changes the frame of reference at the most basic of narrative levels. Whether that revision constructs another, possibly non-reactive, measure of desire is another question. And in fact, it is precisely that directive to construct "another measure of desire" that remains the central problematic within rape stories written by women in the late twentieth and early twenty-first centuries, and there are many, many such texts. To relocate the point of view of a rape story to the victim is still to write a rape story, a model of the inconsequence of the victim's pain and the inevitably secondary nature of female desire and sexuality. In all of the different narrative forms with which contemporary feminist writers experiment, it is that secondary nature of female desire that constitutes the central conflict—or at least one of the central conflicts—of the rape story. A few texts posit qualified success, as does Alice Walker's *The Color Purple*. Most do not. And although that obstruction can seem insurmountable within the context of the narration of rape, writers nonetheless return to the genre, struggling to articulate a way out from under what can appear to be a rhetorical, cultural checkmate.

Christa Wolf's *Cassandra* takes up the issue of an "other measure of desire" through the narrative form of retrospective internal monologue. Here again the text places the reader firmly within the point of view of the rape victim. Unlike Naylor, Erdrich, or Walker, however, Wolf barely touches on the material, bodily experience of rape, as central as that event is within the short novel. Instead, she develops a narrative form that focuses our attention on the intellectual and emotional struggles of the main character, a process of growth defined in large part by negativity—by what Cassandra cannot see, articulate, or act upon as a result of being alienated from patriarchal culture. The finality of that alienation is formally highlighted by the narrative frame: the day of her execution. All of the internal struggles within the text, then, necessarily fall within the overarching reality of the death of the female subject. On this day of her execution, the Trojan prophetess Cassandra—doomed by Apollo to be scorned by her people—recalls her life and the stages of internal development that have led her to where she is—resolutely choosing death over escape with Aeneas.

What she has always wanted, the first-person narrator establishes very early on, has always been "[t]o speak with my voice"; this, she claims, is the "ultimate. I did not want anything more, anything different" (4). What the text establishes, however, is that the voice that emerges from her has nothing to do with some core or even individual identity—it is anything but her own. Enforcing an "ultimate estrangement from myself and from everyone," the voice is an alien "torment" that in a violent parody of childbirth "force[s] its way out of me, through me, dismembering me" (59). Later, in what is rather a reference to rape than childbirth, the voice "had to subdue me before I would breathe a word it suggested" (106). If the voice is not her or hers, however, nor does it express an abstract "truth"; that version of the Cassandra story—that she is doomed to see the future truthfully but never to be believed—is invented by "the enemy," the Greeks, for whom "there is no alternative but either truth or lies, right or wrong, victory or defeat, friend or enemy, life or death" (106). The voice rather embodies the "smiling vital force" beyond and oblivious to human reason and language, representative of "other realities . . . seeping into our solid-bodied world" (106).

What the voice enables Cassandra to see, unlike those around her, is the intrinsic meaninglessness of "truth" or "right," a revelation that Cassandra herself struggles against. The voice and its "other realities" threaten the patriarchal "reality" upon which understanding depends. For Cassandra, for example, there is no "tragedy," a form that assumes a certain order in the universe, an order that coincides with words and with art and which induces a cathartic sense of closure. Similarly, she discovers that there is no Helen of Troy over whom the war is being waged, that "Helen" is the fantasy that makes culture reasonable and legitimizes (violent) action: "In the Helen we invented, we were defending everything that we no longer had. And the more it faded, the more real we had to say it was" (85). As this example suggests, the "solid-bodied world" that provides the only coherence available is thus one that functions in the service of patriarchy and violence; it holds her and her body in contempt. Achilles stands as the representative of the "naked, hideous, male gratification" at the core of "reality." He is a killer, and he is a rapist, even of the dead: "Achilles the Greek hero desecrates" the dead Amazon, Penthesilia. Yet Aeneas, whom Cassandra loves, is also a hero, and a hero by the standards of the same general culture that names Achilles a hero; it is Aeneas who saves a living memory of Troy's greatness, founding as he does so an even greater, more patriarchal, more violent civilization. But what Cassandra asserts from the beginning—which in chronological time she discovered only gradually— is that she "cannot love a hero" (138). In spite of and because of the fact that "Aeneas was the reality," a part of the patriarchal order that defines all knowable language and order, she feels she cannot escape with him (75). Instead, she chooses her own death.

It is significant that Cassandra herself is raped in the "grave of heroes," and it is significant that the event is narrated on the second to the last page of the text. In spite of her growing revelation about the unnaturalness of "reality," as she terms it, she finds that she is nonetheless consigned to it. There are no words, she notes earlier in the text, for those "other realities" that are spoken through her; "[w]e have no name for" them (106). They remain alien to her. Even during the relatively happy period of her life, when she lives amongst the community of women, she finds that they don't "know any script to write in," and so the reprieve is only a brief one (133). The framed novel begins and ends on the same note: there is "[n]othing left to describe the world but the language of the past. The language of the present has shriveled to the words that describe this dismal fortress. The language of the future has only one sentence left for me: Today I will be killed" (14). The voice Apollo grants her—by spitting in her mouth when she refuses his sexual advances—dooms her to a knowledge of the meaninglessness and cruel artificiality of the patriarchal order but with no ability to articulate, much less formulate, the "other realities" that might provide an alternative life. Her rape in the grave of heroes by Ajax the Lesser is an anticlimactic punctuation mark, taking up less than two sentences and narrated without emotion or physical description.

In the four essays that Wolf includes in the text *Cassandra,* she writes about a desire for an "inconspicious" word (270) and a narrative form that focuses attention on "subjectivity" and away from the "sealed 'objectivity'" of the Western tradition (287). She celebrates as exemplary the female character "who simply cannot get a grip on her life, cannot give it a form; who simply cannot manage to make her experience into a presentable story, cannot produce it out of herself as an artistic product" (301). The ideal narrative, then, is one that has pretensions neither to accurate representation of an unproblematic external reality nor to expression of a stable extra-linguistic subjectivity or subjective experience. By contrast, Wolf critiques the traditional epic form, "born of the struggles for Patriarchy, . . . *by its structure* an instrument by which to elaborate and fortify the patriarchy" (296). The relentlessness of the linear plot, "the struggle and victory of the heroes, or their doom," is "The blood-red thread [of] narrative" (296). Wolf's description of plot calls to mind Teresa de Lauretis's revision of Mulvey's phrase, "sadism demands a story": "Story demands sadism, depends on making something happen, forcing a change in another person, a battle of will and strength, victory/defeat, all occurring in a linear time with a beginning and an end" (132–33). This is the pattern that Wolf works against, largely through revision and relocation of the climactic rape scene. As a result, *Cassandra* lacks the traditional "feel" of a novel: the inevitable progression of linear plot is undermined. The rape comes out of nowhere, from an otherwise unnoteworthy antagonist, caps the nonchronological series of memories, and only in retrospect informs the earlier text. Partly as a result, what would more traditionally be constructed as the metaphoric power of the scene is undermined. Eileen Julien makes the argument that, in the African novels she studies, rape surfaces not as metaphor but as metonymy: "Rape is represented . . . not as an isolated, gratuitous instance of violence that can be read *metaphorically*. . . . It is portrayed rather, as the French term *viol* makes clear, *metonymically*, as a *quintessential* act of violence in a context of rampant abuse, both political and sexual" (161). In *Cassandra,* similarly, the rape is the final and "quintessential" act in a narrative world within which there is no exit—no way to articulate the "other realities" that might supplant the oppression and violence of the patriarchal order. Ironically, then, in form the novel undermines the "blood-red thread" and the transcendent metaphors of patriarchal narrative; in content it stages the death of female subjectivity.

Kathy Acker works more aggressively yet to rid rape of its metaphoric valence. For Acker the effort is relentless, and the fact that she returns to sexual violence with such frequency has made her writing suspect—if not offensive—to many. For Acker, as for Wolf, rape functions metonymically within the text as a "*quintessential* act of violence in a context of rampant abuse, both political and sexual." The rapes woven through her narratives are, as is Cassandra's, anticlimactic—just culminating examples of the constant stream of brutal events that constitute life under patriarchal capitalism. They are narrated in terms blank, coarse, and extreme, as in this example from *Great Expectations,* chosen more-or-less at random:

> The soldiers wake up stand up again tuck in their canvas shirttails suck in cheeks stained by tears dried by the steam from hot train rails rub their sex against the tires, the trucks go down into a dry ford mow down a few rose-bushes, the sap mixes with disemboweled teenagers' blood on their knives' metal, the soldiers' nailed boots cut down uproot nursery plants, a section of RIMA (the other army) climb onto their trucks' runningboards throw themselves on their females pull out violet rags bloody tampaxes which afterwards the females stick back in their cunts: the soldier's chest as he's raping the female crushes the baby stuck in her tits. (8)

Unlike the rape sequences discussed in earlier chapters, however, which similarly locate point of view outside the rape victim, this distance is hardly conducive to titillated voyeurism (referencing one's tampon, in fact, is offered in rape prevention workshops as an effective emotional deterrent, at least for acquaintance rape)—nor does it encourage pathos. Transcendent metaphor, as well, has no place in this scene. More the rule than the exception, instances of sexual violence in Acker's work are constructed as typically harsh features of the world of, in this case, soldiers, interchangeable armies, crushed babies, and murdered children. In fact, Acker's plots are in large part structured by the metonymic chain of brutal events the protagonist endures. This chain, for Acker, replaces the traditional features that constitute narrative.

Serving to link this distinctive narrative chain is the female protagonist. Victim of rape, abuse, torture, incest, cruelty, slavery, disease, and the medical community, her subjectivity is formulated in and around the inevitable fact of gender violence. "Daddy taught me to live in pain, to know there's nothing else," narrates Abhor, protagonist of *Empire of the Senseless,* through male character Thivai; "I trusted him for this complexity" (10). The matter-of-fact quality of this sort of pronouncement, spoken by a child victim of incest and rape, resembles the flatness with which Acker narrates rape scenes. This blank narrative style of what I will call flat affect, together with the female characters' resigned acceptance of their abuse—if not masochistic desire *for* it—suggest that Acker's protagonists are inescapably complicit in the gender ideology that oppresses them. Abuse, pain, sex, and love become tangled, inextricably, as in this example from *Blood and Guts in High School,* in which Janey likens sex to abortion: "The orange walls were thick enough to stifle the screams pouring out of the operating room. Having an abortion was obviously just like getting fucked. If we closed our eyes and spread our legs, we'd be taken care of. They stripped us of our clothes. Gave us white sheets to cover our nakedness. Led us back to the pale green room. I love it when men take care of me" (32–33). Katherine Ginn finds in this scene and others like it evidence of one of Acker's "most striking and consistent features": "a seemingly total lack of optimism about the potential for popular liberal political movements, particularly radical feminism, to alleviate social ills" (51). Feminist resistance (through abortion rights, for example) is as grounded in the ideology of capitalism as is the incest and rape that occasion its need, in this case.

The helpless complicity of Acker's female protagonists is always in her work presented as a function of a textual as well as a sexual and gendered order. Thus, the "problem of feminine subjectivity" in Acker, as Karen Brennan puts it, is "a textual, as well as a sexual, one, implicated as it is in the sexual/textual dilemma that positions women as objects of discourse and desire" and men as the subjects (246). Acker's female characters are born into a world and language in which, with Medusa, they confront a final brick wall that disallows female "subjectivity" as such: "I'm your desire's object, dog, because I can't be the subject" (*Don Quixote*, 28). Since Acker's women are thus constituted by a discursive field that in form and content "fully inform[s] the speaking subject even as she speaks," one might well ask, with Martina Sciolino, "how can one write a revolution to find a space for her own desires when she is already written by patriarchy?" (439). As Don Quixote discovers on her quest to become a knight, she is inhabited by the language of patriarchy, one that constitutes her and yet which nonetheless does not belong to her; she cannot be the subject of this language: "BEING BORN INTO AND PART OF A MALE WORLD, SHE HAD NO SPEECH OF HER OWN. ALL SHE COULD DO WAS READ MALE TEXTS WHICH WEREN'T HERS" (58). Hence the attempts of her female protagonists somehow to write a new story are confronted by what Brennan calls "the circularity of cultural discourse," which makes "real transformation impossible" (267).

In one of the narrative moments typical of Acker when point of view seems to merge with the voice of the author, the narrator of *Empire of the Senseless* clearly articulates the dilemma: "Ten years ago it seemed possible to destroy language through language: to destroy language which normalizes and controls by cutting that language. Nonsense would attack the empire-making (empirical) empire of language, the prisons of meaning. But this nonsense, since it depended on sense, simply pointed back to the normalizing institutions" (134). As in Wolf's novel, in spite of any suspicion that "solid-bodied reality" is a function of patriarchal discourse, one is nonetheless trapped within it, lacking the words to formulate the "other realities" that seem to offer themselves. Vincent King makes the case that Dorothy Allison's *Bastard Out of Carolina* also follows this general pattern. Incestuously abused throughout the first eight chapters of the novel, beginning in chapter 9 Bone is overtaken by a desire to survive; a part of that project involves rewriting the rape story of her life. In this effort, however, she is compelled to repeat "the names and stories that make her vulnerable to violence," thus indelibly reprinting the rape script—along with her passive, victimized role in it—within her emerging subjectivity—this in spite of her understanding that her own stories are in conflict with "the names and stories thrust upon her by others" (124).

In the quotation above from *Empire of the Senseless*, Acker's narrator concludes that any attempt to destroy language "simply point[s] back to the normalizing institutions." The "empire-making" language and reason to which her texts refer, in other words, are grounded in a force either larger than or complicit with patriarchy. "Reason is always," Acker writes, earlier in *Empire*, "in the service of the political and economic masters" (12). I make the case earlier (chapter 6) that Acker revises the work of male authors to reveal that the gender violence folded within heroic narrative is a fantasy of man as a subject-effect, locked in, dreaming his rape dreams in what is a profoundly grave misrecognition of the ideology of late capitalism and his own oppressed role within it. If Acker identifies masculinity as a secondary function of capitalism, however, I would add, she goes further to establish femininity as not only secondary—an effect of power relations larger than herself—but painfully, constantly, and in fact dysfunctionally conscious of that fact, mainly because of the extent to which patriarchal capitalism is inscribed on her body through sexual violence. As Colleen Kennedy puts it, Acker "recognizes that 'woman' is a kind of commodity" (177). A product used and exchanged by man, woman is the living (Acker often writes "dead") fetish whereby he through violence disavows his own lack within the proliferating operations of late capitalism. "How can such objects of use and transaction claim the right to speak and to participate in exchange in general?" Irigaray questions: "Commodities, as we all know, do not take themselves to market on their own" (*This Sex* 85).

Speaking, however, is something that Acker's texts do in fact attempt, in spite of the saturation of language and reason, and in spite of the paralyzing recognition of the status of the female self within the rape logic of patriarchal capitalism. In *Empire of the Senseless,* in a brief passage of explicitly romantic declaration, Acker pits the power of literature against the deadening "reason" of the state "which always homogenizes and reduces": "Reason is always in the service of the political and economic masters. It is here that literature strikes, at this base, where the concepts and actings of order impose themselves. Literature is that which denounces and slashes apart the repressing machine at the level of the signified. [. . . The German Romantics] . . . tore the subject away from her subjugation to her self, the proper; dislocated you the puppet; cut the threads of meaning; spit at all mirrors which control" (12). The aggressive action of "literature" is described in metaphors of doubling, if not reflection, and the separation of doubled pairs. It would seem, in short, that "literature" drives a rift between the face of power and the human face that receives and incorporates it, in so doing threatening the political and economic "base" of reason. Some significance lies in the fact that Acker herself is perhaps best known—or most criticized—for her own literary doublings, her "plagiarism" of such works as *Great Expectations, Huckleberry Finn, Sanctuary,* and *Neuromancer,* to name just a few, and so obviously one might question how these repetitions might function to disrupt a structure she already perceives as doubled.

At the end of *Blood and Guts in High School,* before what appears to be Janey's sacrificial death, the narrative introduces the topic of plagiarism:

"End of abstract haze. Now the specific details can begin in the terrible plagiarism of The Screens. The writing is terrible plagiarism because all culture stinks and there's no reason to make new culture-stink" (137).
Following "abstract haze" is the concrete of the "terrible plagiarism," a repetition whose function or at least limitation it is, presumably, to represent
the "stink" of a culture given to legitimizing abstraction. After abstraction,
perhaps, comes parody. In chapter 6 of this book, I examine Acker's "plagiarism" of William Gibson's *Neuromancer*, making the case that what the
recreation draws our attention to is both the grittiness and the artificiality
of the sexual violence that disappears smoothly (abstractly?) into Gibson's
own slick prose. *In Memoriam to Identity*, as Sabine Sielke points out,
Acker similarly parodies Faulkner's *Sanctuary*, "disengages Temple's [rape]
story from its Southern context" and "spells out Faulkner's subtleties"
(141). These parodies denaturalize what is revealed to be ideological. Ellen
Friedman makes the case that "the male texts" doubled in Acker's work
"represent the limits of language and culture within which the female
quester attempts to acquire identity" (243). Lacking a new language—
lacking, in fact, any faith that a new language is possible—Acker is left, as
is Cassandra, with the old. But a repetition, as Marx shows, is never exact.
If the original delimits the boundaries of culture and language, a repetition—and certainly a parody—must in one direction or another diverge
from those boundaries. The "stink" must stink differently.

Colleen Kennedy makes the case that parody is active in Acker's texts
even when the source is nonspecific. In particular, she argues that Acker
deliberately parodies the genre of pornography throughout her work and
that she does so in an effort "to prevent the patriarchy from establishing
pornography as something other from itself" (181). Patriarchy, presumably, can stare into the still life of pornography without realizing that it
gazes into a mirror; Kennedy argues that Acker's texts make this reflection
visible. The argument is persuasive: the representations of sexual violence
and sadism are so extreme—narrated with typically flat affect—that it is
difficult *not* to read them as deliberate parodies. Arthur Redding, similarly, identifies a certain theatricality in Acker's rape victims—their
masochism seems overplayed (301). Again, one might argue, given this
premise, that Acker highlights the desperation and masochism of her
female characters as a corrective to the female masochism naturalized within the mainstream texts of patriarchy.[1]

For all its scathingly parodic power, however, Acker's writing, like
Wolf's, stops short of attempting to define de Lauretis's "other measure of
desire," and certainly eschews committing to any potentially essentialist
conception of a "NEW LANGUAGE" (*Blood and Guts* 96). As Kennedy
puts it, "Acker does not believe, naively, that women as women control

something called 'women's writing,'" and she resists the temptation to
articulate an alternate form of "sense"—"A LANGUAGE THAT MEANS
SOMETHING TO ME" (177; *Blood and Guts* 96). In *Blood and Guts in
High School*, in a narrative move reminiscent of *Cassandra*, the protagonist—like female subjectivity itself—is killed off just at the point the text
seems to move toward revelation.

The voice of revelation, however, continues without her, creating the
illusion of a voice after death—a voice that is thus not "real" (the pages are
not numbered in this section) and yet clearly *is* there, in some liminal zone
outside the sexual violence of the rest of the novel, in a space designed to
evoke an archetypal creation story:

> A light came into the world.
> Dazzling white light that
> makes lightness dazzling burn
> ing happiness. Peace. . . .
> [. . . .]
> . . . Shall we stop being dead
> people? Shall we find our way
> out of all expectations?

Brennan makes the case that this section, "Acker's last word, . . . functions
. . . to alleviate the darkness of the inevitable death of the female subject.
Within this pictorial, highly pastiched space, this voice, which has been
figuratively silenced, speaks eloquently" (266). In a move reminiscent of
The Waste Land (and in fact, Acker's work seems often to "plagiarize" *The
Waste Land*), the authority of voice is/is not established in this obliquely
suggestive ending; the rain both does and does not come. But the mere
suggestion of its presence—even if explicitly denied—is enough to carry
away from the novel. The tone overrides, to some extent, that of the rest
of the novel. This final tonal shift—ungrounded yet compelling—is typical of Acker's endings. Don Quixote, for example, "drunk, awoke to the
world which lay before me" (207). Abhor, after listening to the graphic
story of a rapist member of a motorcycle gang, decides that "I didn't want
to be part of a motorcycle gang" and muses: "I stood there, there in the
sunlight, and thought that I didn't as yet know what I wanted. I now fully
knew what I didn't want and what and whom I hated. That was something. And then I thought that, one day, maybe, there'd be a human society in a world which is beautiful, a society which wasn't just disgust"
(*Empire* 227).

It is this fantastical space of uplift into which Acker ventures—tentatively, and most distinctively in the after-death ending of *Blood and Guts*

in High School—that in paradoxical ways some feminist writers have claimed as the context for retelling the rape story. Acker's texts—like Wolf's, and like those of the writers who explore the embodiment of the rape victim—emphasize the trap of the "real," even if (perhaps particularly if) the "real" is explicitly defined as the material world experienced through a subjectivity constituted in and through the ideology of patriarchal capitalism. Writers like Lois Gould, Ana Castillo, Angela Carter, and most recently Alice Sebold juxtapose the enforced corporal and mental suffering of the rape victim with a narrative space of fantasy, magic realism, or surrealism. Sebold's *The Lovely Bones,* for example, begins where *Cassandra* and *Blood and Guts in High School* end, with the death of the female subject: "My name was Salmon, like the fish; first name, Susie. I was fourteen when I was murdered on December 6, 1973. In newspaper photos of missing girls from the seventies, most looked like me: white girls with mousy brown hair" (5). Placing administration speak (first name, Susie) side by side with that impossible past tense ("my name was"), the text initiates what will become a disarming, heart-wrenching narrative, told from the first person point of view of the murdered child in heaven, alienated from the life of her family but close to it, watching it. The larger gap, of course, lies between the relentlessly close, first-person description of the rape itself, which falls early on but is referenced often enough to create a solid, dark layer that runs the length of the book, and the safe removal of the narrative now, beyond death.

Brennan argues that the final section of *Blood and Guts in High School* "functions . . . to alleviate the darkness of the inevitable death of the female subject" (266). Certainly the after-death narrative of Susie Salmon alleviates the darkness of what begins, in this case, as the brutal rape and death of the girl protagonist. Here, quite literally, the "voice, which has been figuratively silenced, speaks eloquently" (266). Silenced by the red cap shoved in her mouth during her rape, and silenced by her death (presumably, in fact, her throat is cut), in heaven Susie's voice is articulate, sympathetic, almost adult. Yet this voice, predicated on death, is also the voice that expresses the gradual acceptance of alienation and absence of self: "These were the lovely bones that had grown around my absence: the connections—sometimes tenuous, sometimes made at great cost, but often magnificent—that happened after I was gone. . . . The events that my death wrought were merely the bones of a body that would become whole at some unpredictable time in the future. The price of what I came to see as this miraculous body had been my life" (320). What Susie is responding to in this particular passage is the way her family and friends have at last healed from her death and its aftereffects. More than the story of a family's recovery, however, this is the voice of a female subject articulating the

worth of her own absence. Moreover, the passage above locates the internal climax of the novel—the moment of epiphany—and is written so
smoothly that the reader is positioned to receive this development as a
positive, if bittersweet, resolution. Thus, this text goes where Wolf's and
Acker's will not—to a new voice and new reality beyond the death of
female subjectivity under patriarchy. Yet where it ends up, in circular fashion, is with the value for the social order of female sacrifice.

Linda Nicholson asks what postmodern approach to language might
best suit the needs of feminism. "The answer," she argues, "is a discourse
that recognizes itself as historically situated, as motivated by values and,
thus, political interests, and as a human practice without transcendent
justification" (80–81). Sebold's novel is a beautifully written, fabulous
emotional reprieve from the close rape narrative, yet in a sense one might
suspect that it finally nullifies the female subject in its gambit for the
transcendent. Ana Castillo's *So Far From God* generates the same unease.
Again, the novel stages a compelling escape from an unbearably brutal
rape—the magic realism of the text allows Caridad a miraculous recovery, a new, transcendentally focused life, and a magical metamorphosis in
death. To what extent is Castillo vulnerable, then, like Sebold, to the
types of suspicions that Angela Carter confronted throughout her
career—that her surreal exaggerations of the status quo, together with her
fantastically staged narrative escape routes, constructed a vision of "feminism" that was at best ambiguous? Carter herself was articulate in her
own defense. "The point" of her narrative as well as her feminism, she
asserted in a 1988 interview, was "the here and now, what we should do
now" (in Katsavos).

What the problem of the "here and now" was for Carter, most centrally, was the inescapable and naturalized presence of patriarchal reason and
definition. Like Cassandra, Carter saw all around her an old language
unfit for the present, certainly unfit for the female subject in the present,
for whom the reasonable order, once noticed, became impossible not to
feel excluded from: "Something that women know all about is how very
difficult it is to enter an old game" (in Katsavos). Unlike Cassandra, however, for whom the "language of the future" can only express the idea that
"[t]oday I will be killed," Carter eventually turns to the surreal as the
means to "storm the ideological castle" (*The Infernal Desire Machines of
Doctor Hoffman* 33). The order of patriarchy, for Carter, is embodied in
the Minister of Determination in her novel *The Infernal Desire Machines
of Doctor Hoffman.* Wed to the preservation of socially ordered reality in
the face of Doctor Hoffman's "asymmetrical" illusions, the Minister is
committed to freezing the mobility of language: "He decided he could
only keep a strict control of his actualities by adjusting their names to

agree with them perfectly. So, you understand, that no shadow would fall between the word and the thing described. For the Minister hypothesized [that Doctor Hoffman] worked in that shadowy land between the thinkable and the thing thought of" (194). In the Minister's world "desires do not exist" unless named by the state (207). Doctor Hoffman's world, on the other hand, is semiotically productive: "reason cannot produce the poetry disorder does" (206). The material world is explicitly secondary to "liberated" desire (33): "For us, the world exists only as a medium in which we execute our desires. Physically, the world itself, the actual world—the real world, if you like—is formed of malleable clay; its metaphysical structure is just as malleable" (35). In the nebulous world of liberated desire, however, sexual violence is oddly central, a fact difficult to resolve in the face of Doctor Hoffman's explicit rejection of the Minister's patriarchal world.

Carter did not actually discover surrealism until midway through her career. In her earlier, gothic work, however, she was already at work "trying to find out what certain configurations of imagery in our society, in our culture, really stand for, what they mean, underneath the kind of semireligious coating that makes people not particularly want to interfere with them" (in Katsavos). In pursuit of this goal, Carter works self-consciously with myth, defined "in the sense that Roland Barthes uses it in *Mythologies*—ideas, images, stories that we tend to take on trust without thinking what they really mean. . . ." (in Katsavos). As in her later, surreal work, then, Carter undertakes early on "to storm the ideological castle." She also turns to sexual violence to articulate that confrontation. In *The Magic Toyshop,* for example, a chilling narrative of three orphans under the control of a diabolic uncle, a toy maker, the climactic scene involves the protagonist's being forced to play Leda in a puppet show of "Leda and the Swan." The swan itself is a "grotesque parody," "nothing like the wild, phallic bird of her imaginings," and she herself is unexpectedly rendered nameless ("Uncle Philip hissed: 'Get started, what's yer name!'") (165). One of patriarchy's most alluring mythological stories—the rape of Leda—is rendered visibly depraved in this grotesque repetition (a repetition reminiscent of Acker's parody). At the same time, and partly as a consequence, the protagonist's own insubstantial place in the known order is lost. The point of the scene, Carter argues, is that "it turns out that the swan is an artificial construct, a puppet, and, somebody, a man, is putting strings on the puppet" (in Katsavos). The rapist is not a god or beautiful bird but the repulsive puppet of a cruel, fat man; the victim is a scared child. This revelation of the artificiality and patriarchy-serving nature of gender violence, however, is bought at the cost of what reads as a rape scene, with the terrified child protagonist finally lapsing into unconsciousness.

In paradoxical ways, sexual violence remains the price of entry into the liberated desire of Doctor Hoffman's world as well. In her essay "The Alchemy of the Word," Carter implies that the sexual violence of her novels is not intrinsic to the surreal. In fact, in this essay Carter associates the surreal with beauty and liberty, with the potential to reason anew: "Surrealist beauty . . . exists as an excitation of the nerves. The experience of the beautiful is, like the experience of desire, an abandonment to vertigo, yet the beautiful does not exist as such. What do exist are images or objects that are enigmatic, marvelously erotic—or juxtapositions of objects, or people, or ideas, that arbitrarily extend our notion of the connections it is possible to make. In a way, the beautiful is put to the service of liberty" (12). In *The Infernal Desire Machines of Doctor Hoffman,* beauty is centralized within the "enigmatic," shape-shifting daughter of Doctor Hoffman. She first appears to Desiderio, the narrator, in dreams as a black swan in a golden collar, singing a death song of "savage, wordless lament" in a "thrilling, erotic contralto" (30). Soon after, she is the exotic male Ambassador, with "luxuriantly glossy hair so black it was purplish," a "blunt-lipped, sensual mouth," and around his dark eyes "thick bands of solid gold cosmetic" (32). Throughout the novel she will take on a variety of additional forms, all mysterious and alluring. Yet when the translucently beautiful, shape-shifting character of Albertina comes up against the reality of Desiderio, rape, blood, and/or death are invariably the result. In perverse exaggerations of patriarchal dominance, she is repeatedly raped in her attempts to reach him, as in the horrific example of her gang rape by the entire village of centaurs, which event leaves her "mired with blood" (179).

During the rape of Albertina by the centaurs, Desiderio hears "a voice in my mind" telling him "that I was somehow, all unknowing, the instigator of this horror" (180). In fact this would indeed seem to be the case. The violence within the novel seems tied to the structure of surreal novel framed by a narrator who privileges only "the real," in the sense Wolf intends—a narrator who finally murders Doctor Hoffman. Desiderio, actually, is himself raped in moments of confrontation with the surreal he cannot accept, and the "exhibits" that introduce him to and block him from Doctor Hoffman's world are sometimes graphic portraits of female sexual abuse, as in exhibit four, in which "the headless body of a mutilated woman lay in a pool of painted blood. . . . The right breast had partially segmented and hung open to reveal two surfaces of meat as bright and false as the plaster sirloins which hang in toy butcher's shops while her belly was covered with some kind of paint that always contrived to look wet and, from the paint, emerged the handle of an enormous knife which was kept always a-quiver by the action (probably) of a spring" (45–46).

These images of the decimated, brutalized female body recur to mark the boundary Desiderio cannot cross. The highlighted artificiality of the image suggests, however, that—as Albertina discloses to him near the end of the text—what he sees mirrors only what he is, what he is capable of desiring: "You have never yet made love to me because, all the time you have known me, I've been maintained in my various appearances only by the power of your desire" (204). The novel closes on his pointless murder of Albertina—which Desiderio commits after "str[iking] her in the face with the heavy flat of my hand" and "pummel[ing] her breasts until they were as blue as her eyelids"—followed by the fifty years of regret that follow (204, 216).

In spite of Albertina's brutal death, the final line of the novel claims that "unbidden, she comes" (220). Like Sebold (and to some extent like Acker, like Castillo), Carter brings her dead character back, ambiguously suggesting either the power of masculinist fantasy or that female subjectivity lives beyond its violent destruction, returns in different forms, unsilenced, finally, by the brutality that would insist on socially controlled actualities and names and by a world where "desires do not exist" unless named by the phallic state. Thus a profound uncertainty closes the text, an uncertainty that Carter increasingly associated throughout her career with the unstable and unknowable nature of subjectivity. Carter says of the questionable nature of Fevvers from *Nights at the Circus:* "Part of the point of the novel is that you are kept uncertain. . . . When she is talking about being a new woman and having invented herself, her foster mother keeps on saying it's not going to be as simple as that" (in Katsavos). So like Acker, Carter decisively rejects an essential woman's language; the ongoing project of inventing a self involves rather the difficult machinery of the fantastic—the machinery that so disappoints Disederio because it seems so concrete, so nonmagical. For Carter, surrealism works to represent the self in progress because it involves particularly "complex interrelations of reality and its representations" (in Katsavos). Carter's statement evokes Judith Butler, who has similarly associated the formation of subjectivity with experimental configurations of reality and representation. "What," Butler asks, "enables the exposure of the rift between the phantasmatic and the real whereby the real admits itself as phantasmatic? Does this offer the possibility for a repetition that is not fully constrained by the injunction to reconsolidate naturalized identities?" (*Gender Trouble* 146).

At the same time, Butler notes that "[t]here is only a taking up of the tools where they lie, where the very 'taking up' is enabled by the tool lying there" (*Gender Trouble* 145). Discursive experimentation depends upon the figures and forms already established, but in configurations that enable different kinds of repetitions. In Carter's *The Passion of New Eve,* the always unfinished nature of subjectivity is embodied in the fantastical transvestism of the novel, but again the assertion of the impermanence of identity and gender confronts the "tools," or forms, already established to represent the gendered self: specifically, the polar nature of gender and, again, the seeming inescapability of sexual violence. Thus, the abusive "Evelyn" is violently re-sexed to be a woman, who is then, consequently, raped. Cross-dressing Tristessa, "the perfect man's woman," "unbegotten woman who made no concessions to humanity," is both raped and murdered in horrific acknowledgment of the violence that accompanies the struggle to perform gender: "'I thought,' he said, 'I was immune to rape. I thought that I had become inviolable, like glass, and could only be broken. . . . I was seduced by the notion of a woman's being, which is negativity. Passivity, the absence of being. To be everything and nothing. To be a pane the sun shines through'" (137). Gender is performed on real bodies; the confrontation, for Carter, is articulated in rape. Yet here, too, as in *The Infernal Desire Machines of Doctor Hoffman,* in some ways the consequences of that violence are nonetheless, albeit fantastically, bypassed. "All my wounds will magically heal," Leilah/Lillith claims. "Rape only refreshes my virginity. I am ageless, I will outlive the rocks" (174).

The conclusion of *Rape Stories,* a 1989 documentary on rape and rape trauma, begins: "One day it occurred to me that I would feel a lot better if I got rid of the rapist" (Strosser). Soon after, the rapist is killed and shaved into little pieces to be distributed amongst rape survivors. He is not, however, entirely "got[ten] rid of." He is rather spread abroad, disseminated amongst a presumably vast number of women. So too will the rape story that defines him outlive him. The documentary thus attests to the potential drawback to the narrative practice of current feminism—resistance through repetition. Wendy Hesford expresses unease with this paradoxical configuration: "the language of rape and dominant structures of gendered subjectivity continue to speak through women's resistance" (194). If Butler is right that "[t]here is only a taking up of the tools where they lie," then it is also true that discursive experimentation depends upon established narrative forms and old models for the interrelationships of gender, identity, and sex. Nonetheless, no repetition is exact, the point that Butler finally depends upon. As Elizabeth Grosz asserts, we are all "caught up in modes of self-production; these modes may entwine us in various networks of power, but never do they render us merely passive and compliant" (144).

Change is, in fact, a precondition of history. Consider David Foster Wallace's haunting "interview" in the second "Brief Interviews with Hideous Men" in the short story collection of the same name. Written in answer to a faceless female questioner, the voice of the interviewee attempts to wrap yards of language around a rape story—paragraphs and paragraphs of rape myth around what one assumes is the actual rape of a woman the speaker has known. The story he hypothesizes around the body of the female victim grows offensively into the stirring tale of a survivor who has not and will not be undone by the event, who in fact grows existentially in relation to it: "Her idea of herself and what she can live through and survive is bigger now. Enlarged, larger, deeper. She's stronger than she ever deep-down thought, and now she knows it, she thinks she's strong in a totally different way . . . . [N]ow she knows more about the human condition and suffering and terror and degradation. I mean, all of us will admit suffering and horror are part of being alive and existing, or at least we all pay lip service to knowing it, the human condition. But now she really *knows* it" (118). In the face of this celebratory—revelatory—humanist rhetoric, bought at the cost of a woman's rape, the narrative gradually repositions itself. There is, as it turns out, no traditional story here. No transcendent revelations, in all honesty, are forthcoming. Hardly the tale of "Leda and the Swan" and the knowledge the victim might or might not have "put on" with the god's power, the story the interviewee finally reveals is that of a man who has been raped with a Jack Daniel's bottle. The rape myth the story begins with thus ends on the simple fact of the physical vulnerability of the male body. What would this kind of rape mean? the narrator asks. What would the violence have to do with subjectivity? "You don't automatically have a name," he argues: "it's not just something you have, you know" (124). The rape has called masculine identity into question. At the same time, and in ways profoundly connected, the rape is not about "ideas." He claims: "For you this is all ideas, you think we're talking about ideas" (120). Rape is rather a meaningless physical event, semiotically absent. "You don't know shit," the narrative concludes (124).

As in Thomas Pynchon's work, the commensurability of penis and phallus is thus called into grave question. Unlike Pynchon, Wallace refuses the now common gesture of returning to images of the raped woman to articulate (and displace) this anxiety; it is rather the blank meaninglessness of the penis to which he draws the reader's attention. In "Signifying Nothing," the male narrator is dominated by the suddenly regained "memory" of his father "waggling his dick in my face one time when I was a little kid" (*Brief Interviews with Hideous Men* 75). The "event" is as outside language and coherent meaning as it is "weird":

> Part of the total weirdness of the incident of my father waggling his dick at me down there was that, the whole time, he did not say anything (I would have remembered if he said anything), and there was nothing in the memory about what his face looked like, like what

his expression looked like. I do not remember if he even looked at me. All I remember was the dick. The dick, like, claimed all of my attention. He was just sort of waggling it in my face, without saying anything or making any type of comment, shaking it kind of like you do in the can. (*Brief Interviews*, 75–76)

Obviously wielded as a visible demonstration of paternal power, the penis is in this imagined or remembered event ridiculously ungrounded as such. The organ is flaccid ("He did not have a boner"), associated with excretion rather than sexuality or reproduction ("Like you do in the can"). Its apotheosis, furthermore, is in some senses anticlimactic—it is stripped not only of the aura of the phallus but of any semiotic association at all. That the waggled penis claims all the narrator's attention thus suggests more a revelation of symbolic bankruptcy and masculine vulnerability than otherwise. "To be exposed as 'soft' at the core," argues Susan Bordo, "is one of the worst things a man can suffer in this culture" (*The Male Body* 55).

The "weird" threat of the father's soft penis—the organ that now "signifies nothing"—is echoed throughout Wallace's work. In "Adult World 1," the young wife worries compulsively about "[t]he rawness and tenderness and spanked pink of the head of [her husband's] thingie" (*Brief Interviews* 161). Sick Puppy, the psychotic main character of "Girl with Curious Hair," reveals that after having been caught having sex with (in fact, raping) his sister, his father "burn[ed his] penis with his gold lighter from the United States Corp and stated that if I ever touched his little girl again he would burn my penis off with his gold lighter and I had to go to a Dr. and obtain ointment for my burned penis" (*Girl with Curious Hair* 72). Still abusive, Sick Puppy is nonetheless rendered incapable of coition, just as he is, presumably, alienated from the use of common language. Most often, the spectacle of the vulnerable penis is embedded within a rape story—scenes that in Wallace's work tend to overturn the dynamics of traditional versions of the narrative. In the final "Brief Interviews with Hideous Men," although in fact raped, the victim "transfigures" the clichéd stories of "brutal sex slayings" or "grisly discoveries of unidentified remains"; she is "able to hold the focus and penetrate him," thus "address[ing] the psychotic's core weakness, his grotesque *shyness* as it were," causing him finally to "puk[e] from terror" in the recognition that he is "a hole in the world" (*Brief Interviews* 310, 293–94, 302, 303, 309, 310).

In *Infinite Jest*, Wallace's postmodern epic, the images and actuality of rape turn masochistically inward in an apparent textual attack on masculinity itself. Poor Tony Krause's withdrawal is imaged in terms suggestive of rape, by the embodiment of time: "Time spread him and entered him roughly and had its way and left him again in the form of endless gushing liquid shit that he could not flush enough to keep up with" (303). This image of primal abjection is joined to a hallucination of giving birth (to his own death): "he heard someone yelling for someone to Give In, Err, with a hand on his lace belly as he bore down to PUSH and he saw the legs in the stirrups they held would keep spreading until they cracked him open and all the way inside-out on the ceiling and his last worry was that red-handed Poppa could see up his dress, what was hidden" (306). Given the feminized setting, "what was hidden" would seemingly be the lack of penis, which revelation to the father results in the splitting open, the shattering of human/masculine boundary. Significantly, it is in the most explicit moment of human (re)production that the death of masculinity is also articulated. The terror of what might (not) be hidden under the transves-tite's dress is echoed by Steeply's fear of sitting: "'Crawling around. The skirt, it makes one sensitive about simply plopping down wherever you wish. Possibility of things . . . crawling up.' [H]e looked up at Marathe. He appeared sad. 'I'd never realize'" (530). Thus, in moments of production, recognition, and death, the male genitals become the central, problematic symbol of vulnerability.

What sometimes begins with the appearance of the postmodern recu-peration of the masculine prerogative to rape is also, in *Infinite Jest* as in *Interviews with Hideous Men,* reversed. The basic dynamics of the Western rape story—masculine raping agent, feminine rape victim—turn traitor-ously, masochistically, against the soft, vulnerable body of man himself. What begins as a male-on-male rape, on film, between a male prostitute ("sad beautiful boy" in "hunched, homosubmissive position") and aging actor Cosgrove Watt (whose "career consisted mostly of regional-market commercials on broadcast television") ends up the exposure of the "sadic-tive" Watt to HIV. The bloody violence of the scene, further, refuses an identification of who the final, and thus most potent, aggressor might be. The boy's repeatedly shouted "*Murderer! Murderer!*" is unclear in its refer-ence—there is no distinct human agent here; it is the virus itself, existing only to replicate its own proliferating code, which has claimed the final violent authority (944–46). Hal notes how the scene finally removes agency from the human actors: "almost a third of *Accomplice!*'s total length is devoted to the racked repetition of this word [*Murderer!*]—way, way longer than is needed for the audience to absorb the twist and all its pos-sible implications and meanings. . . . we end up feeling and thinking not about the characters but about the cartridge itself" (946). The film itself, like the "regional-market commercials" that define Watt, appropriates for itself the role of agent and functions self-reflexively. The phallus—*and* the penis—have been usurped by the larger system of the film industry.

Similarly, recovering alcoholic/drug addict Don Gately experiences his own illness and, presumably, death, as a rape. A committed AA member, Gately struggles actively and constantly throughout the novel to turn his will over to a higher power—a god in whom he does not believe and yet who seems in fact to be relieving him of the burden of his disease. His wounded body—figuratively and actually—has been throughout the long narrative the clear secondary function of the monetarily valuable exchange of addictive products, and his recovery has been predicated on the seemingly masochistic relinquishment of his own traditionally masculine prerogative. This commitment he retains to the bitter end, past the point where he experiences "[h]is throat fe[eling] somehow raped," and past the point where he succumbs to the "roaring" and "unwilled force" of the incomprehensible streams of words that penetrate his consciousness with "ghastly intrusive force": "the sensation is not only creepy but somehow violating, a sort of lexical rape. Gately begins to consider this hopefully nonrecurring dream . . . unpleasant" (809, 832). The feminine or feminized has no part to bear in this imagined "rape." The power dynamics boil down to a man seeking to relinquish what self-will he has and an inhuman, incomprehensible field of code. The word "sadism," Gately reflects, must be pronounced "saddism." (981). The novel closes, inconclusively but poignantly, when he awakes (or dies) "flat on his back on the beach in the freezing sand, and it was raining out of a low sky, and the tide was way out" (981).

The concluding, inconclusive sadness of *Infinite Jest* bodies forth a subjectivity founded in the refusal of will and the nonerotic acceptance of pain as a vehicle for the instantiation of a new model of the self. Such a stance works against the compulsory hedonism of late, market capitalism, which requires as a general good the constant demand for greater pleasure, finer articulations of identity. This conclusion is thus necessarily not a comfortable one to read, working as it does against ingrown habits of gender, power, and lived capitalism. I would make the case, however, that, like the other texts discussed in this chapter, it raises positive questions about the remaking of self and about an undiscovered political model. There are other implications as well. For most of these authors, the death drive is of provocative central importance in the establishment of a (masculine) subjectivity devoid of consumer, productive, or use value. Alice Jardine, in a sense, is thus proven correct in her surmise that the disappearance from narrative of the "woman-in-effect" signals the problem of "survival" itself (25). The subject—defined generically as white and masculine—is indeed, as it turns out, rendered unthinkable when "there is no more 'earth' to press down/repress, to work, to represent, but also and always to desire (for one's own)"; the "erection of the subject" is, in fact, "disconcerted [, it loses] its elevation and penetration" (Irigaray, *Speculum,* 133). Don Gately's death(?) silently insists on the question, what now?

NOTES

Notes to Chapter 1

1. See Sharon Stockton, "The 'broken rib of mankind.'"
2. See Sharon Stockton, "Making Men."
3. Whether or not I use the terms "white," "European/American," or "Western," then, these words are always associated with my use of "masculinity."

Notes to Chapter 2

1. See Lawrence Venuti's "The Ideology of the Individual in Anglo-American Criticism: The Example of Coleridge and Eliot." Venuti makes the case that this tension is generally present in capitalist ideology.

2. Lawrence Venuti argues that Eliot's "impersonal" theory of poetry turns back on itself in similar ways; it "quite paradoxically assumes that the poet is a free, unified consciousness who directs its cognitive acts and textual production" (175).

3. In *Speculum of the Other Woman,* Luce Irigaray discusses generally distrust of and yet dependency on the woman's symbolic potential in the context of the Platonic dialogues, showing that this ambiguity is at the heart of Western idealism: "The receptacle upon which the father inscribes his will, and casts the seed of his truth, is not designated *as such* in the present of speech. . . . She is always a clean slate ready for the father's impressions, which she forgets as they are made. Unstable, inconsistent, fickle, unfaithful, she seems ready to receive all beings into herself. Keeping no trace of them. Without memory. She herself is without figure or face or proper form, for otherwise '(she) would take the impression badly because (she) would intrude (her) own shape'" (*Speculum* 307).

4. For more on male sterility in Eliot, see Burton Raffel's *T. S. Eliot* and Robert Langbaum's "New Modes of Characterization in *The Waste Land.*"

5. An even more crucial excision Eliot performed on the draft of *The Waste Land* shows a deeper association of the speaker with the violated body—and reveals the extent to which rape was eroticized in Eliot's thinking. The drafts of "The Death of Saint Narcissus" narrate the saint "wish[ing] he had been a young girl / Caught in the woods by a drunken old man" in order to "taste of her own whiteness / The horror of her own smoothness" (*The Waste Land: A Facsimile* A93). This desire realizes itself in the ecstasy of his death: "Because his flesh was in love with the penetrant arrows / . . . He surrendered himself and embraced them / And his whiteness and redness satisfied him" (93). In "A Study in the Suicide of Selfhood," Paul Murphy examines the tension in the poem between "mastery over self and others" (37).

Christine Froula argues convincingly that what *The Waste Land* is ultimately about is the constant repression of such homoerotic and/or woman identified images.

6. In "Exploring the Aesthetics of Rape," Felicia Mitchell traces the Leda myth through the work of many modern and contemporary writers, particularly women.

Nancy Hargrove provides a useful close reading of Yeats's version, showing how the poem constantly counterpoises the material (usually female) and abstract (usually male).

7. In the *The Waste Land,* "I made no outcry" (51).

8. In the *The Waste Land,* the next line reads, "He had / I still feel the pressure of dirty hand" (53).

9. Eliot's portrayal of Beatrice in Middleton and Rowley's *The Changeling* is another example of the woman who is not only depraved but recognizes that depravity and spiritually submerges herself in her own "deflowering": "She becomes moral only by becoming damned. . . . But what constitutes the essence of the tragedy is something which has not been sufficiently remarked; it is the *habituation* of Beatrice to her sin; it becomes no longer merely sin but custom. . . . The tragedy of Beatrice is not that she has lost Alsemero . . . it is that she has won De Flores" (Eliot, *Selected Prose,* 191). Of this image of the consciously violated woman who has become habituated to her sin, Tony Pinkney argues that it is defined most explicitly in Sweeney's lines, "Any man has to, needs to, wants to / once in a lifetime, do a girl in" (18).

10. Nancy K. Gish makes the argument that all female speech in *The Waste Land* is carefully "incorporated into the ultimately single perspective of the poem's narrator" (41).

11. In another way of looking at it, as Christina Hauck points out, the abortion referred to in this scene also suggests that something is amiss in the machinery of production.

12. Robert Langbaum sees this woman as another victim of violation "in some special modern sense": "The violation would seem to lie in his inability to communicate with her" (105).

13. Jacqueline Rose has done a fascinating study of Eliot's estimation of Gertrude as insufficient cause. She argues that as "the aesthetic inadequacy of the play is caused by the figure of a woman, [so] the image of a woman most aptly embodies the consequences of that failure. Femininity thus becomes the stake, not only of the internal, but also of the critical, drama generated by the play" (35).

14. See Patricia Klindienst Joplin's "The Voice of the Shuttle Is Ours" for a full discussion of the Philomela myth.

15. Laura Severin traces the story of Philomela through Eliot's *The Cocktail Party.* This Philomel, according to Severin, is connected to another rape victim: this time, Shakespeare's Lavinia from *Titus Andronicus.*

16. Another connection to Philomel has been unearthed by H. A. Mason, who makes the case that the Lithuanian (German) woman of the opening of *The Waste Land* is based on a character in H. G. Wells's *The New Machiavelli.* Here is what this girl had gone through before seeking refuge in London: "She was a Lett from near Libau in Courland, and she was telling me—just as one tells something too strange for comment or emotion—how her father had been shot and her sister outraged and murdered before her eyes" (Mason 72).

17. Bush points out that "Eliot has altered the meaning of the Sanskrit term, *Damyata,* from 'self-control' to 'control'" (158).

18. Eloise Knapp Hay draws a parallel between the democratized masses represented by chorus in *Murder in the Cathedral* and the Kowalskis in *A Streetcar Named Desire;*

in both cases, the rootless inherit the earth (115). The difference, however, is that in Eliot the rootless masses are the one's figuratively raped and thus brought back under the wing of social and/or economic hierarchy; in Tennessee Williams, it is the democratized public, represented by Stanley Kowalski, which does the raping, thus evidencing its brutality and irrepressibility.

19. In "Eliot's Horrific Moment," Ronald Schuchard argues that Renaissance writers express generally for Eliot the "the horrific way to the beatific," which he attempted in his own writing and which I argue is promised in the recurring image of the raped female body: Eliot "believed of Shakespeare and all of his masters of horror that their artistic imaginations worked over the thin ice of profound spiritual awareness and terror" (195).

20. Another myth that is relevant here is that of Cassandra. Elsie Leach has done a remarkable job of tracing the similarities between *Murder in the Cathedral* and *Agamemnon* by Aeschylus, yet she concludes that Eliot's play "has in its action no characters comparable to Clytemnestra and Cassandra" (14). It seems to me that, to the contrary, Cassandra—raped by the God as well as by Agamemnon, given the gift of (incomprehensible) prophecy in order to tell (if incomprehensibly) the true fate of Troy—is clearly paralleled by the chorus of *Murder in the Cathedral.*

21. See Jo Ann Hoeppner Moran's article on Forster's revisions: "E. M. Forster's *A Passage to India:* What Really Happened in the Caves."

Notes to Chapter 3

1. Laura Frost argues, similarly, that the sexual deviance associated with fascism "can be traced to cultural preoccupations that were well in place even before the historical rise of fascism" (16).

2. See Walter Adamson's *Avant-Garde Florence* for a detailed examination of Italian fascist appropriation and secularization of the rhetoric of religion.

3. See Victoria de Grazia's *How Fascism Ruled Women* for a detailed analysis of the conscription of female bodies and labor by the Italian Corporate State. For more on the actual and imagistic use of the female body under German fascism, see Linda Mizejewski's *Divine Decadence.*

4. See John W. Robbins's *Answer to Ayn Rand* for a careful and extended discussion of Rand's stance on anarchy versus individualist achievement and right.

5. Mimi Gladstein comments opaquely of this scene that "a readership with a raised consciousness about the nature of rape might find this symbolism unpalatable" (23).

6. Douglas, interestingly enough, was an engineer, as Redman points out. Redman's *Ezra Pound and Italian Fascism* is crucial for an understanding of Pound's vision of economics.

7. In Canto VI, Pound quotes from a long passage that reports the outrage of the French king over the rape (and impregnation) of eight-year-old princess Alix (actually Adelaide) by Henry II (Terrell 25).

8. For a full exploration of the connections between Malatesta and Mussolini, see Robert Casillo, "Fascists of the Final Hour" and Peter d'Epiro, *A Touch of Rhetoric.*

9. In a useful biographical essay, A. D. Moody similarly shows that Pound's enthusiasm for Malatesta paralleled his own 1922 vision of a new journal and patronage scheme that he and T. S. Eliot would co-found—*Bel Esprit*—thereby drawing together all the greatest and most dynamic talent of their time. This plan was never realized.

10. See also A. D. Moody, "*Bel Esprit.*"

11. The reference to Procne and Philomela appears in Canto IV as well.

12. Christine Froula argues, to the contrary, that the references to Dafne are not about death but about the "transcendence of temporality: narrative becomes scene and temporal movement becomes spatial design" (*To Write Paradise* 29). Similarly, Froula's larger argument works to show that Pound was in fact reaching for a mimetic art and a form that would suggest the permanent and transcendent.

13. See Robert von Hallberg's "Ezra Pound in Paris": "Pound's Malatesta Cantos do not, I think, suggest that he was particularly enthusiastic about the antipsychological efforts of Marinetti and Tzara" (63).

Notes to Chapter 4

1. For a discussion of castration anxiety and fetishism in *For Whom the Bell Tolls,* see Carl Eby's "Rabbit Stew and Blowing Dorothy's Bridges: Love, Aggression, and Fetishism in *For Whom the Bell Tolls.*

2. In fact, one might go so far as to assert with Lynn A. Higgins and Brenda R. Silver that "rape and rapability are central to the very construction of gender identity and that our subjectivity and sense of ourselves as sexual beings are inextricably enmeshed in representations" (3). The various essays collected in Higgins and Silver's *Rape and Representation* begin with this premise and go on to examine the ways in which rape is nonetheless generally elided from representation, becoming a textual absence that is the source of endless anxiety.

3. See Sharon Stockton, "Aesthetics, Politics, and the Staging of the World," for more on Lewis's "enemy" stance and its rhetorical alliance with fascism.

4. Notwithstanding the possibility that Mellors "uses his power caringly," the first instance of intercourse between him and Constance Chatterley is, in fact, rape. I cannot agree with Kathleen Wall that Mellors's "caring" and his association with myth legitimate and rewrite the incident as an "initiation"—although this is clearly what Lawrence himself would claim (145). Wall is not alone in her apologia for the rape scene in *Lady Chatterley's Lover;* Swift argues that, when not looked at "superficially," the novel is about "the democracy of touch" (165), and many other critics have claimed that the sacredness of the event excuses its violence against women, including Michael Black, Mark Spilka, Mark Schorer, and nearly every contributor (all of whom are male) to Jeffrey Meyers's *The Legacy of D. H. Lawrence.* All of these apologies for Lawrence overlook not only the violence explicit in Lawrence's representations of sexual relationships but in Western constructions of gender and identity generally.

5. Judith Puchner Breen has seen the connection, likening one of Lawrence's male characters to "the demonic Pluto who rose out of darkness to claim Persephone for his bride" (65).

6. Much can be, and has been, said about these "loins" and Lawrence's latent homosexuality; I will avoid tracing this as it would take me too far afield.

7. This is not a rape scene, of course—this female body is docile and softly open to man's inscription. Her body willingly speaks his "meaning" from this point on—just as Ursula's character development throughout the novel consists in her gradual acceptance and articulation of Birkin's philosophies. And yet, as the passage above makes clear, it is his dark and electric "force" that is expressed in and through her, and her

submission to him is echoed in images of violent domination throughout the novel. One might, for example, examine the moon imagery in the novel for evidence of sexualized violence against femaleness, imaged almost always as white and/or electric light.

Notes to Chapter 5

1. And "rape" is in fact precisely the right word to use—the word that Nabokov has both Lolita and Humbert use, and yet which most critics avoid. See Elizabeth Patnoe for a discussion of the gendered critical response to the novel.

2. See Elizabeth Power for a discussion of the ways that Nabokov's (lack of) control over the screenplay for Kubrick's film version of the novel echo Humbert's filmic Lolita.

3. Dana Brand opposes Humbert's (higher) tendency to aestheticize Lolita to his consumerist tendency to commodify her. I would argue that, on the contrary, the two are not only interconnected but mutually reinforcing.

4. A slippery point of view in Nabokov, subject as it is to unstable transformations to moments of fetishism or contrition, this is nonetheless the perspective adopted, to the exclusion of all others, by an astounding number of critics. Most notoriously, Lionel Trilling made this case in 1958: "In recent fiction no lover has thought of his beloved with so much tenderness, no woman has been so charmingly evoked, in such grace and delicacy, as Lolita" (19).

In ways more limited yet, critics have gone beyond the notion that Humbert and Lolita are equal partners in love to the idea that it is Humbert who is the victim of a girl who deserved what she got. Consider, for example, the conclusion reached by Thomas Molnar in 1987: "The central question the reader ought to ask of himself is whether he feels pity for the girl. Our ethical ideal would require that we look at Lolita as a sacrificial lamb, that we become in imagination, her knight-protector. Yet this is impossible for two reasons. One is very simple: before yielding to Humbert, the girl has had a nasty little affair with a nasty little thirteen-year-old. . . . Besides, she is a spoiled sub-teenager with a foul mouth, a self-offered target for lechers" (11–13).

See Elizabeth Patnoe and Linda Kauffman, both of whom discuss these particular traditions of (misogynist) misreading in compelling detail. The current trend is to find these earlier readings "radically, troublingly wrong" (Levine 40).

A similar misinterpretation can be argued to have been put forward by Adrian Lynn and Stephen Schiff in their 1998 film adaptation of the novel. De Reus and Womack argue, "Through their deliberate obfuscation of Humbert's culpability as a child molester in the film, Lynn and Schiff transform Lolita from the precocious pre-adolescent of Nabokov's novel into an over-sexualized temptress" (58). Along the same lines, Susan Bordo makes the damning case that "[t]he idea of Hum and Lo mutually pleasuring each other (*The Joy of Sex*, perhaps, on the bookshelf behind them) is utterly at odds with Nabokov's depiction of the relationship, which never lets us forget that Lolita is a child, and that it is Humbert's fantasy-nymphetology . . . that endows her with sexual power" ("True Obsessions" B7).

See Timothy McCracken for a discussion of fictional retellings of the Lolita story that return a voice and a subjectivity to the raped girl.

5. Alice Jardine has noted that Sigmund Freud compared the "self-sufficient woman"—with her "narcissistic auto-sufficiency and her indifference"—to cats (as well as to children, criminals, and humorists). See *Gynesis* 199–200.

Notes to Chapter 6

1. See E. L. McCallum, "Mapping the Real in Cyberfiction," for a compelling discussion of the significance of this "real" geography in cyberpunk: "Examining the representation of real spaces in cyberpunk fiction not only reveals the narratives' reliance on events in 'real' space but also shows how their assumptions about organizing space and distributing power are more colonialist than futurist" (349).

2. Claudia Springer makes the solid (but for me unconvincing) argument that while "hardwired women" like Molly "clearly embody a fetishized male fantasy, . . . they also represent feminist rebellion against a brutal patriarchal system" (725).

3. In "Feminism for the Incurably Informed," Anne Balsamo argues that Cadigan thus makes a space for feminine technological mastery.

4. In the context of a discussion of *Gravity's Rainbow*, John Hamill argues that in fact this "impulse towards metaphysical transcendence . . . is a crucial stage in the development of sadomasochistic desire and is not opposed to it" (53).

5. It is a matter of conjecture whether or not Pynchon was self-consciously reworking *Lolita* when writing this novel. Certainly he would have read the novel—Pynchon had taken a course with Nabokov at Cornell University.

Notes to Chapter 7

1. I disagree with Molly Wallace, who argues that this "Peace" is deliberately undercut, offered up by DeLillo as a "push-button word" (378).

2. "What man brings to creation is the *form* of the progeny; what woman brings is *matter;* so say all mythical discourses on creation. . . . Aristotle clearly states that matter desires form as the female desires the male. On the female side, there is no order, no principle of internal organization, no generative power" (Goux 213).

3. "Fatherly" is a modifier used repeatedly, defensively, in this scene.

Note to Chapter 8

1. Karen Brennan argues that Acker's work "relies on both pastiche and parody" as Jameson defines these terms "—parody to subvert pastiche and pastiche to engender parody—vacillating hysterically between the two modes . . . to present a fiction of feminine subjectivity" (251–52).

BIBLIOGRAPHY

Acker, Kathy. *Blood and Guts in High School*. New York: Grove, 1978.
———. *Don Quixote*. New York: Grove, 1986.
———. *Empire of the Senseless*. New York: Grove Weidenfeld, 1988.
———. *Great Expectations*. New York: Grove, 1982
Adamson, Walter L. *Avant-Garde Florence: From Modernism to Fascism*. Cambridge, MA: Harvard University Press, 1993.
Affron, Matthew, and Mark Antliff, eds. *Fascist Visions: Art and Ideology in France and Italy*. Princeton, NJ: Princeton University Press, 1997.
Agee, James. *A Death in the Family*. New York: Grosset and Dunlap, 1967.
Allen, Beverly. "'Toward a New Feminist Theory of Rape': A Response from the Field." *Signs: Journal of Women in Culture and Society* 27 (2002): 777–80.
Althusser, Louis. *For Marx*. Translated by Ben Brewster. London: New Left Books, 1977.
Antliff, Mark. "La Cite Française: Georges Valois, Le Corbusier, and Fascist Theories of Urbanism." In *Fascist Visions: Art and Ideology in France and Italy*, edited by Matthew Affron and Mark Antliff, 134–70. Princeton, NJ: Princeton University Press, 1997.
Badenhausen, Richard. "'When the poet speaks only for himself': The Chorus as 'first voice' in *Murder in the Cathedral*." *Yeats Eliot Review* 11 (1992): 78–84.
Baker, James T. *Ayn Rand*. Boston: Twayne Publishers, 1987.
Baker, Nicholson. *The Fermata*. New York: Random House, 1994.
Baldwin, James. *Nobody Knows My Name: More Notes of a Native Son*. New York: Dell, 1961.
Balsamo, Anne. "Feminism for the Incurably Informed." *South Atlantic Quarterly* 92 (1993): 681–712.
Barth, John. *Giles Goat-Boy*. New York: Doubleday, 1966, 1987.
———. *Lost in the Funhouse*. New York: Doubleday, 1988.
Barthelme, Donald. *The Dead Father*. New York: Penguin, 1986.
Baudrillard, Jean. *Forget Foucault*. New York: Semiotext(e), 1987.
———. *Seduction*. Translated by Brian Singer. New York: St. Martin's Press, 1990.
———. *The Illusion of the End*. Translated by Chris Turner. Stanford, CA: Stanford University Press, 1994.
———. *Simulacra and Simulation*. Translated by Shiela Faria Glaser. Ann Arbor: University of Michigan Press, 1994.
Beaud, Michel. *A History of Capitalism: 1500–2000*. Translated by Tom Dickman and Anny Lefebvre. New York: Monthly Review Press, 1983.
Bedient, Calvin. *"He do the police in different voices": The Waste Land and Its Protagonist*. Chicago: University of Chicago Press, 1986.
Benjamin, Walter. *Illuminations*. Edited by Hannah Arendt. Translated by Harry Zohn. New York: Harcourt, Brace & World, 1968.

Berezin, Mabel. *Making the Fascist Self: The Political Culture of Interwar Italy.* Ithaca, NY: Cornell University Press, 1997.

Berman, Russell A. *Modern Culture and Critical Theory: Art, Politics, and the Legacy of the Frankfurt School.* Madison: University of Wisconsin Press, 1989.

Bhabha, Homi. *The Location of Culture.* New York: Routledge, 2002.

Black, Michael. *The Literature of Fidelity.* New York: Barnes and Noble, 1975.

Blamires, Harry. *Word Unheard: A Guide Through T. S. Eliot's "Four Quartets."* New York: Methuen, 1969.

Booth, Alison. "Neo-Victorian Self-Help, or Cider House Rules." *American Literary History* 14 (2002): 284–310.

Bordo, Susan. *The Male Body: A New Look at Men in Public and in Private.* New York: Farrar, Straus and Giroux, 1999.

———. "True Obsessions: Being Unfaithful to *Lolita.*" *The Chronicle of Higher Education* 24 (July 1998): B7.

———. *Twilight Zones: The Hidden Life of Cultural Images from Plato to O. J.* Berkeley: University of California Press, 1997.

Bornstein, Daniel. "The Poet as Historian: Researching the Malatesta Cantos." *Paideuma: A Journal Devoted to Ezra Pound Scholarship.* 10 (1981): 283–91.

Bose, Purnima. "'End-Anxiety' in T. S. Eliot's *The Waste Land:* Narrative Closure and the End of Empire." *Yeats Eliot Review* 9 (1988): 157–60.

Brand, Dana. "The Interaction of Aestheticism and American Consumer Culture in Nabokov's *Lolita.*" *Modern Language Studies* 17, no. 2 (1987): 14–21.

Braziel, Jana Evans. "Trans-American Construction of Black Masculinity: Danny Laferriere, le Negre, and the Late Capitalist American Racial machine-desir-ante." *Calloo: A Journal of African-American and African Arts and Letters* 26 (2003): 867–900.

Breen, Judith Puchner. "D. H. Lawrence, World War I and the Battle Between the Sexes: A Reading of 'The Blind Man' and 'Tickets, Please.'" *Women's Studies.* 13 (1986): 63–74.

Brenkman, John. *Culture and Domination.* Ithaca, NY: Cornell University Press, 1987.

Brennan, Karen. "The Geography of Enunciation: Hysterical Pastiche in Kathy Acker's Fiction." *Boundary* 2, no. 21 (1994): 243–68.

Brooker, Jewel Spears. "Substitutes for Religion in the Early Poetry of T. S. Eliot." In *The Placing of T. S. Eliot,* edited by Jewel Spears Brooker. Columbia: University of Missouri Press, 1991.

Brooker, Jewel Spears, and Joseph Bentley. *Reading* The Waste Land: *Modernism and the Limits of Interpretation.* Amherst: University of Massachusetts Press, 1990.

Brownmiller, Susan. *Against Our Will: Men, Women, and Rape.* New York: Simon and Schuster, 1975.

Bush, Ronald. "T. S. Eliot: Singing the Emerson Blues." In *Emerson: Prospect and Retrospect,* edited by Joel Porte, 179–97. Cambridge, MA: Harvard University Press, 1982.

Butler, Judith. "Against Proper Objects." *differences: A Journal of Feminist Cultural Studies* 6, no. 2/3 (1994): 1–26.

———. *Gender Trouble: Feminism and the Subversion of Identity.* New York: Routledge, 1990.

Cadigan, Pat. *Synners.* New York: Bantam, 1991.

Campbell, Christopher. "Sweeney Among the Bootleggers: Echoes of Eliot in Faulkner's *Sanctuary*." *The Faulkner Journal* 13 (1997–98): 101–9.

Carlston, Erin G. *Thinking Fascism: Sapphic Modernism and Fascist Modernity.* Stanford, CA: Stanford University Press, 1998.

Carter, Angela. "The Alchemy of the Word," in *Shaking a Leg,* 506–11. New York: Penguin, 1998.

———. *The Infernal Desire Machines of Doctor Hoffman.* New York: Penguin, 1972.

———. *The Magic Toyshop.* New York: Penguin, 1967.

———. *The Passion of New Eve.* London: Virago, 1982.

Casillo, Robert. "Anti-Semitism, Castration, and Usury in Ezra Pound." *Criticism: A Quarterly for Literature and the Arts.* 25 (1983): 239–65.

———. "Fascists of the Final Hour: Pound's Italian Cantos." In *Fascism, Aesthetics, and Culture,* edited by Richard J. Golsan, 98–127. Hanover, NH: University Press of New England, 1992.

Chalk, Linda and John-Paul Checkett. "Sexual Assault Prevention Education for First-Year College Students." Presentation at Dickinson College, 2001.

Chambers, Judith. "The Freak in Ourselves: The Grotesque in Pynchon's *V.* and *Gravity's Rainbow.*" *The Journal of the Association for the Interdisciplinary Study of Arts* 1 (1996): 55–78.

Chapman, Wes. "Male Pro-Feminism and the Masculinist Gigantism of *Gravity's Rainbow.*" *Postmodern Culture* 6, no. 3 (1996). http://titan.iwu.edu/~wchapman/pynchon.html (also available on Project Muse (accessed February 23, 2005).

Childs, John Steven. *Modernist Form: Pound's Style in the Early Cantos.* London: Associated University Press, 1986.

Ci, Jiwei. "Disenchantment, Desublimation, and Demoralization: Some Cultural Conjunctions of Capitalism." *New Literary History* 30 (1999): 295–324.

Cleaver, Eldridge. *Soul on Ice.* New York: Deal, 1992 [1968].

Comaroff, Jean, and John L. Comaroff. "Millenial Capitalism: First Thoughts on a Second Coming." *Public Culture* 12 (2000): 291–343.

Connell, R. W. "The History of Masculinity." In *The Masculinity Studies Reader,* edited by Rachel Adams and David Savran, 245–61. Malden, MA: Blackwell, 2002.

Crawford, Fred D. *Mixing Memory and Desire: The Waste Land and British Novels.* University Park: The Pennsylvania State University Press, 1982.

Crupi, Charles W. "The Transformation of De Flores in *The Changeling.*" *Neophilologus* 68 (1984): 142-49.

Dasenbrock, Reed Way. *The Literary Vorticism of Ezra Pound and Wyndham Lewis: Towards the Condition of Painting.* Baltimore, MD: Johns Hopkins University Press, 1985.

Davenport, F. Garvin. "Machines and Sexual Ambience in James Agee's *A Death in the Family.*" In *Beyond the Two Cultures: Essays on Science, Technology, and Literature,* edited by Joseph W. Slade and Judith Yaross Lee, 227–39. Ames: Iowa State University Press, 1990.

Davis, Kay. *Fugue and Fresco: Structures in Pound's Cantos.* Orono: The National Poetry Foundation, University of Maine at Orono, 1984.

D'Epiro, Peter. *A Touch of Rhetoric: Ezra Pound's Malatesta Cantos.* Ann Arbor, MI: UMI Research Press, 1981.

de Grazia, Victoria. *How Fascism Ruled Women: Italy, 1922–1945*. Berkeley: University of California Press, 1992.

de Lauretis, Teresa. *Alice Doesn't: Feminism, Semiotics, Cinema*. Bloomington: Indiana University Press, 1984.

———. *Technologies of Gender: Essays on Theory, Film, and Fiction*. Bloomington: Indiana University Press, 1987.

De Reus, Lee Ann, and Kenneth Womack. "Misreading 'Little Limp Lo' and 'Humbert the Terrible': The Obfuscation of Child Abuse in Adrian Lyne's *Lolita*." *Post Script* 19 (2000): 58–66.

Deleuze, Gilles and Felix Guattari. *One Thousand Plateaus: Capitalism and Schizophrenia,* translated by Brian Massumi. Minneapolis: University of Minnesota Press, 1987.

———. *Anti-Oedipus: Capitalism and Schizophrenia*. Minneapolis: University of Minnesota Press, 2000.

DeLillo, Don. *Underworld*. New York: Scribner, 1997.

———. *White Noise*. New York: Penguin, 1984.

Doane, Mary Ann. "Commentary: Post-Utopian Difference." In *Coming to Terms: Feminism, Theory, Politics,* edited by Elizabeth Weed, 70–78. New York: Routledge, 1989.

———. "Film and the Masquerade: Theorizing the Female Spectator." In *Writing on the Body: Female Embodiment and Feminist Theory,* edited by Katie Conboy, Nadia Median, and Sarah Stanbury, 176–94. New York: Columbia University Press, 1997.

Donahoo, Bob. "Moving with the Mainstream: A View of Postmodern American Science Fiction." In *Critical Essays on American Postmodernism,* edited by Stanley Trachtenberg, 152–65. New York: G. K. Hall & Co., 1995.

Dougherty, Stephen. "The Biopolitics of the Killer Virus Novel." *Cultural Critique* 48 (2001): 1–29.

du Gay, Paul. "Markets and Meanings: Re-Imagining Organizational Life." In *The Expressive Organization: Linking Identity, Reputation, and the Corporate Brand,* edited by Majken Schultz, Mary Jo Hatch, and Mogens Holten Larsen, 66–76. Oxford: Oxford University Press, 2000.

Duyfhuizen, Bernard. "'A Suspension Forever at the Hinge of Doubt': The Reader-trap of Bianca in *Gravity's Rainbow*." *Postmodern Culture* 2, no. 1 (1991).http://muse.jhu.edu/journals/postmodern_culture/v002/2.1duyfhuizen.html (accessed February 23, 2005).

Eagleton, Terry. *The Illusions of Postmodernism*. New York: Oxford University Press, 1996.

Easthope, Anthony. *What a Man's Gotta Do: The Masculine Myth in Popular Culture*. Winchester: Unwin, 1990.

Eby, Carl. "Rabbit Stew and Blowing Dorothy's Bridges: Love, Aggression, and Fetishism in *For Whom the Bell Tolls*." *Twentieth Century Literature* 44 (1998): 204–18.

Eliot, T. S. *Collected Poems, 1909–1962*. New York: Harcourt, 1970.

———. *Collected Shorter Poems*. New York: Harcourt, 1952.

———. *Murder in the Cathedral*. New York: Harcourt Brace Jovanovich, 1935.

———. *Selected Essays, 1917–1932*. New York: Harcourt, 1950.

———. *Selected Prose of T. S. Eliot*, edited by Frank Kermode. New York: Harcourt Brace Jovanovich, 1975

———. "*Ulysses*, Order and Myth." *Dial* 75 (1923): 480–83.

———. *The Waste Land: A Facsimile and Transcript of the Original Drafts*. Edited by Valerie Eliot. New York: Harcourt Brace Jovanovich, 1971.

Faulkner, William. *Sanctuary*. New York: Book-of-the-Month-Club, 1997.

Flint, R. W. "Introduction." In *Marinetti: Selected Writings*, edited by R. W. Flint. Translated by R. W. Flint and Arthur A. Coppotelli. London: Secker and Warburg, 1972.

Forster, E. M. *A Passage to India*. New York: Harcourt Brace & Company, 1924.

Forter, Gregory. "Faulkner's Black Holes: Vision and Vomit in *Sanctuary*." *The Mississippi Quarterly* 49 (1996): 537–62.

Foster, John Burt, Jr. "Magic Realism in *The White Hotel*: Compensatory Vision and the Transformation of Classic Realism." *Southern Humanities Review* 20 (1986): 205–19.

———. "Reading Nabokov with Jameson: Modernism, Postmodernism, and the Intertextual Litmus Test." *Southern Humanities Review* 31 (1997): 201–13.

Foster, Thomas C. *Understanding John Fowles*. Columbia: University of South Carolina Press, 1994.

Fowles, John. *The French Lieutenant's Woman*. New York: Signet, 1969.

Friedman, Ellen G. "Where Are the Missing Contents? (Post)Modernism, Gender, and the Canon." In *Critical Essays on American Postmodernism*, edited by Stanley Trachtenberg, 133–51. New York: G. K. Hall & Co., 1995.

Frosch, Thomas R. "Parody and Authenticity in *Lolita*." In *Vladimir Nabokov*, edited by Harold Bloom, 127–42. New York: Chelsea, 1987.

Frost, Laura. *Sex Drives: Fantasies of Fascism in Literary Modernism*. Ithaca, NY: Cornell University Press, 2002.

Froula, Christine. "Eliot's Grail Quest, or, The Lover, the Police, and *The Waste Land*." *The Yale Review* 78 (1989): 235–53.

———. *To Write Paradise: Style and Error in Pound's Cantos*. New Haven, CT: Yale University Press, 1984.

Fulmer, James Burton. "'First person anonymous': Sartrean Ideas of Consciousness in Barth's *Lost in the Funhouse*." *Critique* 41 (2000): 335–47.

Gentile, Emilio. "The Myth of National Regeneration in Italy: From Modernist Avant-Garde to Fascism." In *Fascist Visions: Art and Ideology in France and Italy*, edited by Matthew Affron and Mark Antliff, 25–45. Princeton, NJ: Princeton University Press, 1997.

Gibson, William. *Neuromancer*. New York: Ace, 1984.

Gilbert, Sandra. "Costumes of the Mind: Transvestism as Metaphor in Modern Literature." In *Gender Studies: New Directions in Feminist Criticism*, edited by Judith Spector, 70–95. Bowling Green, OH: Bowling Green State University Press, 1986.

Gilroy, Paul. *The Black Atlantic: Modernity and Double Consciousness*. Cambridge, MA: Harvard University Press, 1993.

Ginn, Katherine. "Reproduction in the Slave Economies of Morrison and Acker." Unpublished Senior Honors Thesis, Dickinson College English Department, 2003.

Gish, Nancy K. "Eliot and Marianne Moore: Modernism and Difference." *Yeats Eliot Review* 11 (1991): 40–43.

Gladstein, Mimi Reisel. *The Ayn Rand Companion*. Westport, CT: Greenwood Press, 1984.

Goldman, Michael. "Fear in the Way: The Design of Eliot's Drama." In *Modern Critical Views: T. S. Eliot*, edited by Harold Bloom, 43–57. New York: Chelsea House, 1985.

Goodman, Lisa A., Mary P. Koss, and Anela Browne, eds. *No Safe Haven: Male Violence against Women at Home, at Work and in the Community*. American Psychological Association, 1994.

Goux, Jean-Joseph. *Symbolic Economies after Marx and Freud*. Translated by Jennifer Curtiss Gage. Ithaca, NY: Cornell University Press, 1990.

Green, Geoffrey. *Freud and Nabokov*. Lincoln: University of Nebraska Press, 1988.

Green, Jeremy. "Disaster Footage: Spectacles of Violence in DeLillo's Fiction." *Modern Fiction Studies* 45 (1999): 571–99.

Grosz, Elizabeth. *Volatile Bodies: Toward a Corporeal Feminism*. Bloomington: Indiana University Press, 1994.

Guttman, Sondra. "What Bigger Killed For: Rereading Violence Against Women in *Native Son*." *Texas Studies in Literature and Language* 43 (2001): 169–93.

———. "Who's Afraid of the Corncob Man? Masculinity, Race, and Labor in the Preface to Sanctuary." *The Faulkner Journal* 15 (1999–2000): 15–34.

Haaken, Janice. "'Toward a New Feminist Theory of Rape': The Seduction of Theory." *Signs: Journal of Women in Culture and Society* 27 (2002): 781–86.

Hall, Jacquelyn. "'The Mind that Burns in Each Body': Women, Rape, and Racial Violence." In *Powers of Desire: The Politics of Sexuality*, edited by Ann Snitow, Christine Stansell, and Sharon Thompson, 328–49. New York: Monthly Review Press, 1983.

Hamill, John. "Looking Back on Sodom: Sixties Sadomasochism in *Gravity's Rainbow*." *Critique* 41 (1999): 53–70.

Hanson, Clare. "Little Girls and Large Women: Representations of the Female Body in Elizabeth Bowen's later fiction." In *Body Matters: Feminism, Textuality, Corporeality*, edited by Avril Horner and Angela Keane, 185–98. Manchester: Manchester University Press, 2000.

Harvey, David. *The Condition of Postmodernity*. Malden, MA: Blackwell, 1990.

Haraway, Donna J. "A Cyborg Manifesto: Science, Technology, and Socialist-Feminism in the Late Twentieth Century." Chap. 8 in *Simians, Cyborgs, and Women: The Reinvention of Nature*. New York: Routledge, 1991.

Hargrove, Nancy D. "Esthetic Distance in Yeats's 'Leda and the Swan.'" *Arizona Quarterly* 39 (1983): 235–45.

Hauck, Christina. "Abortion and the Individual Talent." *ELH* 70 (2003): 223–66.

Haws, Dick. "The Elusive Numbers on False Rape." *Columbia Journalism Review* November/December (1997) http://archives.cjr.org/year/97/6/rape/asp.

Hay, Eloise Knapp. *T. S. Eliot's Negative Way*. Cambridge, MA: Harvard University Press, 1982.

Hayles, N. Katherine. "The Illusion of Autonomy and the Fact of Recursivity:

Virtual Ecologies, Entertainment, and *Infinite Jest.*" *New Literary History* 30 (1999): 675–97.

Helyer, Ruth. "Refuse heaped many stories high": DeLillo, Dirt, and Disorder." *Modern Fiction Studies* 45 (1999): 987–1006.

Hesford, Wendy S. "Reading Rape Stories: Material Rhetoric and the Trauma of Representation." *College English* 62 (1999): 192–221.

Hewitt, Andrew. *Fascist Modernism: Aesthetics, Politics, and the Avant-Garde.* Stanford, CA: Stanford University Press, 1993.

Higgins, Lynn A., and Brenda R. Silver. "Introduction: Rereading Rape." In *Rape and Representation,* edited by Lynn A. Higgins and Brenda R. Silver, 1–14. New York: Columbia University Press, 1991.

Hilferding, Rudolf. *Finance Capital.* Edited by T. Bottomore. London: Routledge & Kegan Paul, 1981.

Hite, Molly. *Ideas of Order in the Novels of Thomas Pynchon.* Columbus: The Ohio State University Press, 1983.

Horvitz, Deborah M. *Literary Trauma: Sadism, Memory, and Sexual Violence in American Women's Fiction.* Albany: State University of New York Press, 2000.

Hutcheon, Linda. "Subject in/of/to History and His Story." *Diacritics* 16 (1986): 78–91.

Ingersoll, Earl G. *Representations of Science and Technology in British Literature Since 1880.* New York: Peter Lang, 1992.

Ingham, John M. "Primal Scene and Misreading in Nabokov's *Lolita.*" *American Imago* 59 (2002): 27–52.

Irigaray, Luce. *Speculum of the Other Woman.* Translated by Gillian C. Gill. Ithaca, NY: Cornell University Press, 1985.

———. *This Sex Which Is Not One,* translated by Catherine Porter. Ithaca, NY: Cornell University Press, 1985.

Irmscher, Christoph. "Anthropological Roles: The Self and Its Others in T. S. Eliot, William Carlos Williams and Wendy Rose." *Soundings: An Interdisciplinary Journal* 75 (1992): 587–603.

Irving, John. *The Cider House Rules.* New York: Bantam, 1985.

———. *The Hotel New Hampshire.* New York: Simon & Schuster, 1981.

———. *The Water-Method Man.* New York: Simon & Schuster, 1972.

———. *The World According to Garp.* New York: Simon & Schuster, 1976.

Jameson, Fredric. *Fables of Aggression: Wyndham Lewis, the Modernist as Fascist.* Berkeley: University of California Press, 1979.

———. *Postmodernism, or, The Cultural Logic of Late Capitalism.* Durham, NC: Duke University Press, 1991.

Jardine, Alice A. *Gynesis: Configurations of Woman and Modernity.* Ithaca, NY: Cornell University Press, 1985.

Jeffords, Susan. "Performative Masculinities, or, 'After a Few Times You Won't Be Afraid of Rape at All.'" *Discourse: Theoretical Studies in Media and Culture* 13 (1991): 102–18.

Johnsen, William. "Textual/Sexual Politics in Yeats's 'Leda and the Swan.'" In *Yeats and Postmodernism,* edited by Leonard Orr, 80–89. Syracuse, NY: Syracuse University Press, 1991.

Johnson, Loretta. "T. S. Eliot's Bawdy Verse: Lulu, Bolo, and More Ties." *Journal of Modern Literature* 27 (2003): 14–25.

Joplin, Patricia Klindienst. "The Voice of the Shuttle Is Ours." In *Rape and Representation,* edited by Lynn A. Higgins and Brenda R. Silver, 35–66. New York: Columbia University Press, 1991.

Julien, Eileen. "Rape, Repression, and Narrative Form in *Le Devoir de violence* and *La Vie et demie*." In *Rape and Representation,* edited by Lynn A. Higgins and Brenda R. Silver, 160–81. New York: Columbia University Press, 1991.

Kane, Richard. "From Loins of Darkness to Loins of Pork: Body Imagery in Lawrence, Eliot, and Joyce." *Recovering Literature* 17 (1989–90): 5–18.

Katsavos, Anna. "An Interview with Angela Carter." Center for Book Culture.org. http://www.centerforbookculture.org/interviews/interview_carter.html (accessed July 16, 2003).

Kauffman, Linda. "Framing *Lolita:* Is There a Woman in the Text?" In *Figuring the Father: New Feminist Readings of Patriarchy,* edited by Patricia Yaeger and Beth Kowaleski-Wallace, 131–52. Carbondale: Southern Illinois University Press, 1989.

Kavadlo, Jesse. "Recycling Authority: Don DeLillo's Waste Management." *Critique* 42 (2001): 384–401.

Kennedy, Colleen. "Simulating Sex and Imagining Mothers." *American Literary History* 4 (1992): 165–85.

Kenner, Hugh. *The Poetry of Ezra Pound.* Lincoln: University of Nebraska Press, 1985.

———. *The Pound Era.* Berkeley: University of California Press, 1973.

Kimmel, Michael, and Michael Kauffman. "Weekend Warriors: The New Men's Movement." In *Theorizing Masculinities,* Edited by H. Brod and Michael Kauffman, 259–88. London: Sage, 1994.

King, Vincent. "Hopeful Grief: The Prospect of a Postmodernist Feminism in Allison's *Bastard Out of Carolina*." *The Southern Literary Journal* 33 (2000): 122–40.

Knight, Peter. "Everything Is Connected: *Underworld*'s Secret History of Paranoia." *Modern Fiction Studies* 45 (1999): 811–36.

Kristeva, Julia. *Powers of Horror: An Essay on Abjection.* Translated by Leon S. Roudiez. New York: Columbia University Press, 1982.

Kroker, Arthur. *The Possessed Individual: Technology and New French Theory.* New York: Palgrave Macmillan.

Kuberski, Philip. "Pound's Sacred Technology." *Paideuma: A Journal Devoted to Ezra Pound Scholarship* 18 (1989): 105–19.

Kunzru, Hari. "You Are Cyborg." *Wired* 5, no. 2 (1997). http://www.wired.com/wired/archive//5.02/ffharaway_pr.html (accessed March 21, 2001).

Lacan, Jacques. *Ecrits: A Selection.* Translated by Alan Sheridan. New York: Norton, 1977.

Langbaum, Robert. "New Modes of Characterization in *The Waste Land*." In *Eliot in His Time: Essays on the Occasion of the Fiftieth Anniversary of* The Waste Land, edited by A. Walton Litz. Princeton, NJ: Princeton University Press, 1973.

Lawrence, D. H. *Lady Chatterley's Lover.* New York: Penguin, 1994.

———. *Women in Love.* New York: Penguin, 1976.

Leach, Elsie. "*Agamemnon* as a Source of *Murder in the Cathedral*." *Yeats Eliot Review* 11 (1991): 14–18.

LeClair, Tom. *In the Loop: Don DeLillo and the Systems Novel.* Urbana: University of Illinois Press.

Lenin, Vladimir. *Imperialism, the Highest Stage of Capitalism* (1916). Lenin Internet Archive, 1999. http://www.marxists.org/archive/lenin/works/1916/imp-hsc/index.htm (accessed February 14, 2005).

Levine, Peter. "*Lolita* and Aristotle's Ethics." *Philosophy and Literature* 19 (1995): 32–47.

Lewis, Wyndham. *Tarr.* London: Chatto and Wyndus, 1928.

Lury, Celia. *Consumer Culture.* New Brunswick, NJ: Rutgers University Press, 1996.

MacInnes, John. "The Case of Anna G.: *The White Hotel* and Acts of Understanding." *Soundings* 77 (1994): 253–69.

MacKinnon, Catharine A. "Feminism, Marxism and the State: Toward Feminist Jurisprudence." *Signs: Journal of Women in Culture and Society* 8 (1983): 635–58.

Madsen, Deborah. "The Business of Living: *Gravity's Rainbow*, Evolution, and the Advancement of Capitalism." *Pynchon Notes* 40–41 (1997): 144–58.

Marcus, Sharon. "Fighting Bodies, Fighting Words: A Theory and Politics of Rape Prevention." In *Feminists Theorize the Political*, edited by Judith Butler and Joan W. Scott, 385–403. New York: Routledge, 1992.

Mardorossian, Carine M. "Toward a New Feminist Theory of Rape." *Signs: Journal of Women in Culture and Society* 27 (2002): 743–75.

Marinetti, Filippo Tommaso. *Selected Writings.* Edited by R. W. Flint. Translated by R. W. Flint and Arthur A. Coppotelli. London: Secker & Warburg, 1972.

Mason, H. A. "The Lithuanian Whore in *The Waste Land.*" *The Cambridge Quarterly* 18 (1989): 63–72.

Materer, Timothy. "W. B. Yeats, T. S. Eliot, and the Critique of Occultism in *Four Quartets.*" *Yeats Eliot Review* 10 (1989): 1–4.

Matthews, John. "The Elliptical Nature of *Sanctuary.*" *Novel* 17 (1984): 103–23.

McCallum, E. L. "Mapping the Real in Cyberfiction." *Poetics Today* 21 (2000): 349–77.

McCracken, Timothy. "Lolita Talks Back: Giving Voice to the Object." In *He Said, She Says: An RSVP to the Male Text*, edited by Mica Howe and Sarah Appleton Aguiar, 128–42. Madison, WI: Associated University Press, 2001.

McHale, Brian. *Constructing Postmodernism.* New York: Routledge, 1992.

Medoro, Dana. "The Sieve and the Rainbow Serpent: Bleeding *Gravity's Rainbow.*" *The Journal of Narrative Technique* 28 (1998): 186–213.

Mesher, David R. "Science and Technology in Modern British Fiction: The Two Cultures." *Arts and Sciences* 13 (1984): 73–82.

Meyers, Jeffrey, ed. *The Legacy of D. H. Lawrence.* New York: St. Martin's Press, 1987.

Michael, Magali Cornier. "'Who Is Sarah?': A Critique of *The French Lieutenant's Woman's* Feminism." *Critique* 28 (1987): 225–36.

Michaels, Walter Benn. *The Gold Standard and the Logic of Naturalism: American Literature at the Turn of the Century.* Berkeley: University of California Press, 1987.

Middleton, Thomas and William Rowley. *The Changeling*, edited by Matthew W. Black. College Park: University of Pennsylvania Press, 1966.

Millgate, Michael. "*Sanctuary* (1931)." In *William Faulkner: Critical Collection,* edited by Leland Cox, 222–39. Detroit: Gale Research Company, 1982.

Mitchell, Felicia. "Exploring the Aesthetics of Rape: Leda and the Swan in Selected Poems by Women." *Phoebe* 3 (1991): 64–72.

Mizejewski, Linda. *Divine Decadence: Fascism, Female Spectacle, and the Making of Sally Bowles.* Princeton, NJ: Princeton University Press, 1992.

Molnar, Thomas. *The Pagan Temptation.* Grand Rapids, MI: William B. Eerdmans, 1987.

Moody, A. D. "*Bel Esprit* and the Malatesta Cantos: A Post-*Waste Land* Conjunction of Pound and Eliot." In *Ezra Pound and Europe,* edited by Richard Taylor and Claus Melchior, 79–91. Amsterdam: Rodopi.

Moorti, Sujata. *Color of Rape: Gender and Race in Television's Public Spheres.* Albany: State University of New York Press, 2002.

Moran, Jo Ann Hoeppner. "E. M. Forster's *A Passage to India:* What Really Happened in the Caves." *Modern Fiction Studies* 34 (1988): 596–604.

Mosse, George L. "The Political Culture of Italian Futurism: A General Perspective." *Journal of Contemporary History* 25 (1990): 253–68; reprinted in *Confronting the Nation: Jewish and Western Nationalism,* 91–105. Hanover, NH: University Press of New England, 1993.

Mulvey, Laura. "Visual Pleasure and Narrative Cinema." In *The Norton Anthology of Theory and Criticism,* edited by Vincent B. Leitch et al., 2181–92. New York: Norton, 2001.

Murphy, Paul. "A Study in the Suicide of Selfhood: T. S. Eliot's 'The Death of Saint Narcissus.'" *Essays in Poetics* 17 (1992): 33–42.

Nabokov, Vladimir. *Despair.* New York: G. P. Putnam's Sons, 1965.

———. *The Annotated Lolita.* Edited by Alfred Appel, Jr. New York: McGraw-Hill, Inc, 1970.

Nassar, Eugene Paul. *The Cantos of Ezra Pound.* Baltimore, MD: Johns Hopkins University Press, 1975.

Nel, Philip. "Amazons in the Underworld: Gender, the Body, and Power in the Novels of Don DeLillo." *Critique* 42 (2001): 416–36.

Newton, Judith. "Masculinity Studies: The Longed For Profeminist Movement for Academic Men?" In *Masculinity Studies & Feminist Theory: New Directions,* edited by Judith Kegan Gardiner, 176–92. New York: Columbia University Press, 2002.

Nicholson, Linda. "Feminism and the Politics of Postmodernism." In *Feminism and Postmodernism,* edited by Margaret Ferguson and Jennifer Wicke, 69–85. Durham, NC: Duke University Press, 1994.

Nitsch, Jessica, and Monica Parry. "Yeats's View of Power in 'Leda and the Swan.'" *Notes on Contemporary Literature* 22 (1992): 9–11.

Nixon, Nicola. "Cyberpunk: Preparing the Ground for Revolution or Keeping the Boys Satisfied?" *Science-Fiction Studies* 19 (1992): 219–35.

North, Michael. "The Architecture of Memory: Pound and the Tempio Malatestiano." *American Literature: A Journal of Literary History, Criticism, and Bibliography* 55 (1983): 367–87.

———. "Eliot, Lukacs, and the Politics of Modernism." In *T. S. Eliot: The Modernist in History,* edited by Ronald Bush, 160–90. Cambridge: Cambridge University Press, 1991.

———. *The Political Aesthetic of Yeats, Eliot, and Pound*. Cambridge: Cambridge University Press, 1991.

Olsen, Lance. "A Janus-Text: Realism, Fantasy, and Nabokov's *Lolita*." *Modern Fiction Studies* 32 (1986): 115–26.

Osteen, Mark. *American Magic and Dread: Don DeLillo's Dialogue with Culture*. Philadelphia: University of Pennsylvania Press, 2000.

Parrish, Timothy. "From Hoover's FBI to Eisenstein's *Unterwelt:* DeLillo Directs the Postmodern Novel." *Modern Fiction Studies* 45 (1999): 696–723.

Patnoe, Elizabeth. "Lolita Misrepresented, Lolita Reclaimed: Disclosing the Doubles." *College Literature* 22 (1995): 81–104.

Patterson, Laura. "Ellipsis, Ritual, and 'Real Time': Rethinking the Rape Complex in Southern Novels." *The Mississippi Quarterly* 54 (2000/2001): 37–58.

Pinkney, Tony. *Women in the Poetry of T. S. Eliot*. London: Macmillan, 1984.

Pinkus, Karen. *Bodily Regimes: Italian Advertising under Fascism*. Minneapolis: University of Minnesota Press, 1995.

Porush, David. "Hacking the Brainstem: Postmodern Metaphysics and Stephenson's *Snow Crash*." *Configurations* 2 (1994): 537–71.

Pound, Ezra. *The Cantos of Ezra Pound*. New York: Harcourt Brace Jovanovich, 1950.

———. *Guide to Kulchur*. New York: New Directions, 1970.

Power, Elizabeth. "The Cinematic Art of Nympholepsy: Movie Star Culture as Loser Culture in Nabokov's *Lolita*." *Criticism* 41 (1999): 101–18.

Pynchon, Thomas. *Gravity's Rainbow*. New York: Penguin, 1973.

Rabate, Jean-Michel. *Language, Sexuality, and Ideology in Ezra Pound's Cantos*. London: Macmillan, 1986.

Raffel, Burton. *T. S. Eliot*. New York: Continuum, 1991.

Rainey, Lawrence. "The Malatesta Cantos and the Making of Ideology." *American Poetry* 6 (1989): 15–27.

Rand, Ayn. *The Fountainhead*. New York: Penguin, 1952.

———. "This Is John Galt Speaking." *For the New Intellectual*. New York: New American Library, 1961.

Redding, Arthur F. "Bruises, Roses: Masochism and the Writing of Kathy Acker." *Contemporary Literature* 35 (1994): 281–304.

Redman, Tim. *Ezra Pound and Italian Fascism*. Cambridge: Cambridge University Press, 1991.

Robbins, John W. *Answer to Ayn Rand*. Washington: Mount Vernon Publishing Company, 1974.

Roberson, Susan L. "T. S. Eliot's Symbolical Woman: From Temptress to Priestess." *The Midwest Quarterly* 27 (1986): 476–86.

Roberts, Diane. "Ravished Belles: Stories of Rape and Resistance in *Flags in the Dust* and *Sanctuary*." *The Faulkner Journal* 4 (1988–89): 21–35.

Rooney, Ellen. "'A Little More than Persuading': Tess and the Subject of Sexual Violence." In *Rape and Representation*, edited by Lynn A. Higgins and Brenda R. Silver, 87–114. New York: Columbia University Press, 1991.

Rorty, Richard. *Contingency, Irony, and Solidarity*. Cambridge: Cambridge University Press, 1989.

Rose, Jacqueline. "*Hamlet*—the Mona Lisa of Literature." *Critical Quarterly* 28 (1986): 35–52.

Ross, Marlon B. "Race, Rape, Castration: Feminist Theories of Sexual Violence and Masculine Strategies of Black Protest." In *Masculinity Studies & Feminist Theory: New Directions,* edited by Judith Kegan Gardiner, 305–43. New York: Columbia University Press, 2002.

Rothstein, Eric. "Lolita: Nymphet at Normal School." *Contemporary Literature* 41 (2000): 22–55.

Safer, Elaine B. "The Allusive Mode and Black Humor in Barth's *Giles Goat-Boy* and Pynchon's *Gravity's Rainbow.*" *Renascence* 32 (1980): 89–104.

Saltzman, Arthur. "Awful Symmetries in Don DeLillo's *Underworld.*" In *Critical Essays on Don DeLillo,* edited by Hugh Ruppersburg and Tim Engels, 302–16. New York: G. K. Hall & Co., 2000.

———. *Understanding Nicholson Baker.* Columbia: University of South Carolina Press, 1999.

Savran, David. *Taking It Like a Man: White Masculinity, Masochism, and Contemporary American Culture.* Princeton, NJ: Princeton University Press, 1998.

Schnapp, Jeffrey T. "Epic Demonstrations: Fascist Modernity and the 1932 Exhibition of the Fascist Revolution." In *Fascism, Aesthetics, and Culture,* edited by Richard J. Golsan, 1–37. Hanover, NH: University Press of New England, 1992.

Schorer, Mark. "On *Lady Chatterley's Lover.*" *Evergreen Review* 1 (1957): 149–78.

Schuchard, Ronald. "Eliot and the Horrific Moment." In *T. S. Eliot: Essays from the Southern Review,* edited by James Olney, 1045–56. Oxford: Clarendon Press, 1988.

Sciolino, Martina. "Kathy Acker and the Postmodern Subject of Feminism." *College English* 52 (1990): 437–45.

Sebold, Alice. *The Lovely Bones.* New York: Picador, 2003.

Segal, Naomi. "Sexual Politics and the Avant-Garde: From Apollinaire to Woolf." In *Visions and Blueprints: Avant-Garde Culture and Radical Politics in Early Twentieth-Century Europe,* edited by Edward Timms and Peter Collier, 235–49. New York: Manchester University Press, 1988.

Severin, Laura. "Cutting Philomela's Tongue: *The Cocktail Party's* Cure for a Disorderly World." *Modern Drama* 36 (1993): 396–408.

Sherry, Vincent. *Ezra Pound, Wyndham Lewis, and Radical Modernism.* New York: Oxford University Press, 1993.

Shostak, Debra. "Plot as Repetition: John Irving's Narrative Experiments." *Critique* 37 (1995): 51–70.

Sicari, Stephen. "Reading Pound's Politics: Ulysses As Fascist Hero." *Paideuma: A Journal Devoted to Ezra Pound Scholarship* 17 (1988): 145–68.

Sicker, Philip. "The Belladonna: Eliot's Female Archetype in *The Waste Land.*" *Twentieth Century-Literature* 30 (1984): 420–31.

Sieburth, Richard. "In Pound We Trust: The Economy of Poetry, the Poetry of Economics." *Critical Inquiry* 14 (1987): 142–72.

Sielke, Sabine. *Reading Rape: The Rhetoric of Sexual Violence in American Literature and Culture, 1790–1990.* Princeton, NJ: Princeton University Press, 2002.

Silver, Brenda. "Periphrasis, Power, and Rape in *A Passage to India.*" In *Rape and Representation,* edited by Lynn A. Higgins and Brenda R. Silver, 115–40. New York: Columbia University Press, 1991.

Silverman, Kaja. *Male Subjectivity at the Margins*. New York: Routledge, 1992.

———. "Masochism and Male Subjectivity." In *The Masculinity Studies Reader*, edited by Rachel Adams and David Savran, 21–40. Malden, MA: Blackwell, 2002.

Spackman, Barbara. *Fascist Virilities: Rhetoric, Ideology, and Social Fantasy in Italy*. Minneapolis: University of Minnesota Press, 1996.

Spilka, Mark. "On Lawrence's Hostility to Willful Women: The Chatterley Solution." In *Lawrence and Women*, edited by Anne Smith. London: Vision Press, 1978.

Sponsler, Claire. "Beyond the Ruins: The Geopolitics of Urban Decay and Cybernetic Play." *Science Fiction Studies* 20 (1993): 251–63.

Springer, Claudia. "Sex, Memories, and Angry Women." *South Atlantic Quarterly* 92 (1993): 713–33.

Steinman, Lisa. "'A Poet's Handbook of Science': Technology and Modern American Poetics." In *Beyond the Two Cultures: Essays on Science, Technology, and Literature*, edited by Joseph W. Slade and Judith Yaross Lee, 241–53. Ames: Iowa State University Press, 1990.

Stephenson, Neil. *Snow Crash*. New York: Bantam, 1992.

Sterling, Bruce. "Preface." In *Mirrorshades: The Cyberpunk Anthology*, edited by Bruce Sterling, ix–xvi. New York: Ace, 1988.

Sternhell, Zeev. *Neither Right nor Left: Fascist Ideology in France*. Translated by David Maisel. Berkeley: University of California Press, 1986.

Stewart, Kathleen. "Conspiracy Theory's Worlds." In *Paranoia Within Reason: A Casebook on Conspiracy as Explanation*, edited by George Marcus, 13–19. University of Chicago Press, 1999.

Stockton, Sharon. "The 'broken rib of mankind': The Sociopolitical Function of the Scapegoat in *The Changeling*." *Papers on Language and Literature* 26 (1990): 459–77.

———. "Aesthetics, Politics, and the Staging of the World: Wyndham Lewis and the Renaissance." *Twentieth Century Literature* 42 (1996): 494–515.

———. "Making Men: Visions of Social Mobility in *A Petite Pallace of Pettie His Pleasure*." In *Framing Elizabethan Fictions: Contemporary Approaches to Early Modern Narrative Prose*, edited by Constance Relihan, 55–72. Kent, OH: Kent State University Press, 1996.

Stone, Marla. "The State as Patron: Making Official Culture in Fascist Italy." In *Fascist Visions: Art and Ideology in France and Italy*, edited by Matthew Affron and Mark Antliff, 205–38. Princeton, NJ: Princeton University Press, 1997.

Strosser, Margie. *Rape Stories*. Directed by Margie Strosser. Video. Women Make Movies, 1989.

Surette, Leon. "Ezra Pound and British Radicalism." *English Studies in Canada* 9 (1983): 435–51.

Svarny, Eric. *"The Men of 1914": T. S. Eliot and Early Modernism*. Philadelphia: Open University Press, 1988.

Swift, Jennifer. "The Body and Transcendence of Two Wastelands: *Lady Chatterley's Lover* and *The Waste Land*." *Paunch* 63–64 (1990): 141–71.

Tabbi, Joseph. *Postmodern Sublime: Technology and American Writing from Mailer to Cyberpunk*. Ithaca, NY: Cornell University Press, 1995.

Tanner, Laura E. *Intimate Violence: Reading Rape and Torture in Twentieth-Century Fiction*. Bloomington: Indiana University Press, 1994.

Tate, Alison. "The Master-Narrative of Modernism: Discourses of Gender and Class in *The Waste Land.*" *Literature and History* 14 (1988): 160–71.

Terrell, Carroll F. *A Companion to the Cantos of Ezra Pound*. Berkeley: University of California Press, 1980.

Thomas, Calvin. "Reenfleshing the Bright Boys; Or, How Male Bodies Matter to Feminist Theory." In *Masculinity Studies & Feminist Theory: New Directions*, edited by Judith Kegan Gardiner, 60–89. New York: Columbia University Press, 2002.

Thomas, D. M. *The White Hotel*. New York: Viking, 1981.

Thomieres, Daniel. "Cherchez la femme: Who Really Was Annabel Leigh?" *Journal of Modern Literature* 23 (1999): 166–71.

Tichi, Cecelia. *Shifting Gears: Technology, Literature, Culture in Modernist America*. Chapel Hill: University of North Carolina Press, 1987.

Trilling, Lionel. "The Last Lover: Vladimir Nabokov's *Lolita.*" *Encounter* [London] 11 (1958): 9–19.

Trotter, David. "Modernism and Empire: Reading *The Waste Land.*" *Critical Quarterly* 28 (1986): 143–53.

Tweedie, James. "Lolita's Loose Ends: Nabokov and the Boundless Novel." *Twentieth Century Literature* 46 (2000): 150–70.

Urgo, Joseph R. "Temple Drake's Truthful Perjury: Rethinking Faulkner's *Sanctuary.*" *American Literature* 55 (1983): 435–44.

Uyl, Douglas J. Den, and Douglas B. Rasmussen. "Capitalism." In *The Philosophic Thought of Ayn Rand*, edited by Douglas J. Den Uyl and Douglas B. Rasmussen, 165–82. Urbana and Chicago: University of Illinois Press, 1984.

Venuti, Lawrence. "The Ideology of the Individual in Anglo-American Criticism: The Example of Coleridge and Eliot." *Boundary 2* 14 (1985): 161–93.

Vlasoplos, Anca. "Gender-Political Aesthetics and the Early and Later Yeats." *Yeats: An Annual of Critical and Textual Studies* 8 (1990): 113–125.

von Hallberg, Robert. "Ezra Pound in Paris." In *On Modern Poetry: Essays Presented to Donald Davie*, edited by Vereen Bell and Laurence Lerner, 53–66. Nashville, TN: Vanderbilt University Press, 1988.

Von Rosador, Kurt Tetzeli. "Christian Historical Drama: The Exemplariness of *Murder in the Cathedral.*" *Modern Drama* 29 (1986): 516–31.

Wagner, Vivian. "Gender, Technology, and Utopia in Faulkner's Airplane Tales." *Arizona Quarterly* 49 (1993): 79–97.

Wall, Kathleen. *The Callisto Myth from Ovid to Atwood: Initiation and Rape in Literature*. Kingston: McGill-Queen's University Press, 1988.

Wallace, David Foster. *Girl with Curious Hair*. New York: Norton, 1989.

———. *Infinite Jest*. New York: Little, Brown and Co., 1996.

———. *Brief Interviews with Hideous Men*. New York: Little, Brown and Co., 1999.

Wallace, Molly. "'Venerated Emblems': DeLillo's *Underworld* and the History-Commodity." *Critique* 42 (2001): 367–83.

Wees, William. *Vorticism and the English Avant-garde*. Toronto: University of Toronto Press, 1972.

Whiting, Frederick. "'The Strange Particularity of the Lover's Preference': Pedophilia, Pornography, and the Anatomy of Monstrosity in *Lolita*." *American Literature* 70 (1998): 833–62.

Wiznitzer, Eileen. "Legends of Lil: The Repressed Thematic Center of *The Waste Land*." *Women's Studies* 13 (1986): 87–102.

Wolf, Christa. *Cassandra: A Novel and Four Essays*. Translated by Jan Van Heurck. New York: Farrar, Straus, Giroux, 1984.

Wolf, James B. "Imperial Integration on Wheels: The Car, the British and the Cape-to-Cairo Route." In *Literature and Imperialism*, edited by Robert Giddings, 112–27. New York: St. Martin's Press, 1991.

Wood, Michael. *The Magician's Doubt: Nabokov and the Risks of Fiction*. Princeton, NJ: Princeton University Press, 1994.

Wright, Anne. *Literature of Crisis, 1910–22:* Howards End, Heartbreak House, Women in Love *and* The Waste Land. New York: St. Martin's Press, 1984.

Wright, Richard. *Native Son*. New York: Harper & Bros., 1940. Reprint, Harper & Row, 1966.

Wutz, Michael. "The Thermodynamics of Gender: Lawrence, Science and Sexism." *Mosaic* 28 (1995): 83–106.

Yeats, W. B. *Selected Poems and Three Plays*. Edited by M. L. Rosenthal. New York: Macmillan, 1986.

i ek, Slavoj. *Looking Awry: An Introduction to Jacques Lacan through Popular Culture*. Cambridge, MA: MIT Press, 1991.

———. *The Sublime Object of Ideology*. New York: Verso, 1989.

INDEX

234 INDEX

Safer, Elaine, 123
Saltzman, Arthur, 134, 165
Sanctuary (Faulkner), 73, 86–90, 192–93
Savran, David, 21, 132–33
Schnapp, Jeffrey, 49, 67
Schorer, Mark, 208n4
Schuchard, Ronald, 207n19
Sciolino, Martina, 191
Sebold, Alice, 195–96, 199. See also *The Lovely Bones*
seduction, 57, 94, 97, 101, 137
Seduction (Baudrillard), 94, 97, 137
Segal, Naomi, 47, 74
Selected Essays, 1917–1932 (Eliot), 35, 37
Selected Prose of T. S. Eliot, (Eliot), 206n9
Severin, Laura, 206n15
Sherry, Vincent, 59, 78–79
Shostak, Debra, 175–76
Sicari, Stephen, 59
Sicker, Philip, 29–30
Sieburth, Richard, 55–56
Sielke, Sabine, 16–17, 193
Silver, Brenda R., 2–3, 16, 24, 182, 185, 208n2
Silverman, Kaja, 4–6
Simulacra and Simulation (Baudrillard), 127, 159
Snow Crash (Stephenson), 126–28
Spackman, Barbara, 49, 53–54
Spilka, Mark, 208n4
Sponsler, Claire, 130
Springer, Claudia, 210n2
stability/instability, 1–2, 4–5, 9, 11, 18, 46, 49, 55, 60, 63, 68, 74, 77, 84, 86, 88, 92, 109, 114, 118, 130–31, 133, 154, 156, 164, 166, 188, 199. *See also* capitalism; masculinity
Steinman, Lisa, 48, 72
Stephenson, Neil, 126–28, 132, 147. See also *Snow Crash*
Sterling, Bruce, 125
Sternhell, Zeev, 48, 54
Stewart, Kathleen, 157, 168
Stone, Marla, 59

Strosser, Margie, 200
subject: anxiety that accompanies masculine, 2, 12, 21, 24, 73, 84, 96–97, 126, 133, 137, 145, 154; of capitalism, 12, 21, 24, 92, 100–102, 108, 122, 125, 132, 146, 150, 153, 178, 195; of Enlightenment, 16, 24, 121,135, 137, 142, 145, 148, 152, 158, 183; under fascism, 63; female, 23, 96, 122, 145, 184–86, 189–91, 194–96, 199; Freudian, 105; as function of language, 3; and gender formation, 4–7, 12, 94; historically shifting nature of masculine, 2–3, 7, 11, 13, 21–23, 72, 98, 109–10,120, 126, 130, 132, 136–40, 143–44, 149, 154, 156, 169, 172, 180, 204; Lacanian, 3–6; as master of discourse, 135; postmodern, 21, 112, 124, 127, 147, 149, 189; modernist, 26; racial and ethnic dependence of, 13, 16, 17; rhetorical construction of, 29, 37, 93, 107, 113, 144, 185, 188, 199, 201, 204. *See also* discourse; female; feminine/femininity; Freud, Sigmund; Lacan, Jacques; masculinity; psychoanalysis; woman
Surette, Leon, 56
surplus value, 8, 11, 45, 103. *See also* alienation; economics; money; Marx, Karl; wealth
Svarny, Eric, 35
Swift, Jennifer, 208n4
Synners (Cadigan), 131–32

Tabbi, Joseph, 136, 150, 167, 169
Tanner, Laura E., 10, 13, 16, 23, 86, 185
Tarr (Lewis), 20, 47, 74–80, 83, 85, 131
Tate, Allison, 33
technology, 19–22, 48–50, 71–90, 120–36, 142, 144–45, 152–54, 166. *See also* capitalism; industry; the machine

www.ingramcontent.com/pod-product-compliance
Lightning Source LLC
Chambersburg PA
CBHW030328030726
47499CB00003B/682